Kinds of Reasons

Kinds of Reasons

An Essay in the Philosophy of Action

Maria Alvarez

OXFORD
UNIVERSITY PRESS

OXFORD

UNIVERSITY PRESS

Great Clarendon Street, Oxford OX2 6DP

Oxford University Press is a department of the University of Oxford.
It furthers the University's objective of excellence in research, scholarship,
and education by publishing worldwide in

Oxford New York

Auckland Cape Town Dar es Salaam Hong Kong Karachi
Kuala Lumpur Madrid Melbourne Mexico City Nairobi
New Delhi Shanghai Taipei Toronto

With offices in

Argentina Austria Brazil Chile Czech Republic France Greece
Guatemala Hungary Italy Japan Poland Portugal Singapore
South Korea Switzerland Thailand Turkey Ukraine Vietnam

Oxford is a registered trade mark of Oxford University Press
in the UK and in certain other countries

Published in the United States
by Oxford University Press Inc., New York

British Library Cataloguing in Publication Data
Data available

Library of Congress Cataloging in Publication Data
Library of Congress Control Number 2009943755

Typeset by Laserwords Private Limited, Chennai, India
Printed in Great Britain
on acid-free paper by
MPG Books Group, Bodmin and King's Lynn, Norfolk

ISBN 978-0-19-955000-5

10 9 8 7 6 5 4 3 2 1

For my parents

Acknowledgements

Many people helped and supported me in various ways during the writing of this book. Audiences at the various philosophical gatherings where I presented parts of the book helped to improve it with their comments and suggestions. I should like to thank in particular Hanoch Ben-Yami, Ido Geiger, Hanjo Glock, Peter Hacker, Alex Neill, Dawn Phillips, and Joseph Raz. In addition, three anonymous referees for OUP provided very helpful comments, and Peter Momtchiloff was an exemplary editor. Special thanks to John Hyman for his astute criticisms, valuable suggestions, and constant encouragement; and to Aaron Ridley, whose indefatigable help at every step always came with grace and good humour. Family and friends, both too numerous to mention by name, have supported me throughout with unwavering faith and enthusiasm.

Sections of Chapters 1 and 2 were published as part of my paper 'How Many Kinds of Reasons?' which was published in *Philosophical Explorations*, 12 (2009), 181–93 (http://www.informaworld.com). Ideas from Chapter 4 were incorporated into my 'Reasons, Desires and Intentional Actions' published in C. Sandis (ed.), *New Essays in the Explanation of Action* (Palgrave Macmillan, 2009). Parts of Chapter 5 were included in my paper 'Reasons and the Ambiguity of "Belief"', *Philosophical Explorations*, 11 (2008), 53–65 (http://www.informaworld.com). I thank those concerned for letting me use the relevant material here. I should also like to thank the Arts and Humanities Research Council for funding part of the period of research leave during which I completed this book.

M.A.

University of Southampton

Contents

Introduction

Man is a great deep, Lord. You number his very hairs and they
are not lost in Your sight: but the hairs of his head are easier to
number than his affections and the movements of his heart.

St Augustine, *Confessions*, Book IV, chapter XIV

As individuals, we want to understand the men and women around
us, because we like, love, or loathe them, or find them interesting
or intriguing—or, often enough, merely for practical purposes of
one kind or another. And so we try to work out how the affections
and movements of their hearts—their emotions, desires, values, and
reasons—combine and are manifested in what they say and do, and in
what they fail to say and fail to do. But as philosophers, we also want to
understand human beings in general, and their faculties and capacities.
Thomas Reid put it well:

The man of the world conjectures, perhaps with great probability, how a
man will act in certain given circumstances; and this is all he wants to know.
To enter into a detail of the various principles which influence the actions
of men, to give them distinct names, to define them, and to ascertain their
different provinces, is the business of a philosopher, and not of a man of the
world; and, indeed, it is a matter attended with great difficulty from various
causes. (1969: 96)

This book is a contribution to the task that Reid describes. In
particular, it aims to improve our understanding of reasons in the
context of human action. Some of the questions it addresses are:
What are reasons? Are there different kinds of reasons? Are reasons beliefs and desires? If not, how are they related to beliefs and
desires? And what role do they play in motivating and explaining
actions?

These are familiar questions. Philosophers have struggled with them since the time of Socrates. But in contemporary anglophone philosophy, Donald Davidson's work from the 1960s and 1970s is seminal. In particular, Davidson's conception of reasons, or something close to it, became the orthodoxy and remains so to this day. Following Davidson, most philosophers today maintain that a person's reason for acting is a combination of a belief and a desire. Belief and desire, in turn, are thought of as mental states with contents that can be expressed propositionally: Tom believes *that apples are healthy*; Henry desires *that there are eggs for breakfast*. So reasons are states of belief and desire with propositional contents. Or so it is said.

In recent years, however, there has been growing dissatisfaction with this conception of reasons. The dissatisfaction is, I think, well founded and it calls for a wholesale rethinking of the nature of our reasons for acting. In this book I propose to provide an account of reasons that results from just such a rethink. My account draws on the work of several of my contemporaries. But the most important influence on my ideas is the tradition that stems from Aristotle, includes Aquinas, and finds its best recent exponent in Elizabeth Anscombe. In this book I have tried to develop some of the insights in her classic 1957 essay *Intention*, together with ideas of my own, to expose the confusions and mistakes that are to be found in the current orthodoxy, and to defend a very different way of thinking about reasons.

A few contemporary philosophers have defended conceptions of reasons similar to mine. This minority view has thus been established as a serious contender in what is really a new debate about the nature of our reasons for acting. However, the minority view is still widely regarded as implausible or confused, either because it is not sufficiently well understood, or because it is thought to face decisive objections. Here I offer a detailed and distinctive version of that view, a version that is capable, I think, of meeting these objections. Furthermore, I shall propose an account of the relation between reasons and desires, and of the role these play in practical reasoning and in the explanation of action.

Three Basic Claims

The book is informed by three basic claims, which I explain in detail in several chapters, and which underpin some of the major views and arguments I defend.

The first claim is that all reasons are facts—or what I take to be the same, truths or true propositions. Thus, talk of different kinds of reasons is not to be understood in terms of different ontological categories—for instance, facts and mental states—but rather in terms of different roles that reasons play in different contexts.

The second claim is that discussions about reasons for acting have been adversely affected by an act/object ambiguity inherent in the terms 'belief' and 'desire'. Thus 'my belief' can be used to refer to *or* *content*? my believing something (the act) or to what I believe (the object): for example, to *my believing* that today is Monday, or to *what I believe*, namely, that today is Monday. The same is true of 'my desire'. This ambiguity is crucial when addressing questions about whether beliefs or desires are reasons for acting.

The third claim is that, in understanding actions performed for a reason, we need to distinguish between *motivation* and *explanation*; that is, between the task of identifying and characterizing what motivates an agent, and what explains his action. For only thus is it possible to understand that the reason that explains an action need not be a reason that motivated the agent to act.

The Argument

In the first two chapters I explore reasons broadly, in order to focus later on reasons for acting. I claim that, in general, reasons have both explanatory and normative force. The latter means that a reason can favour ϕ-ing, that is, it can make ϕ-ing right or appropriate. In the case of believing, rightness or appropriateness concerns the truth; in the case of acting and wanting, it concerns the good, broadly conceived, that is, as related to a variety of values. Because reasons

have both normative and explanatory force, they can play several roles.
I distinguish three main roles: justifying, motivating, and explaining
And I argue that since one and the same reason can play all of these
roles in relation to a particular action, the differences between these
roles do not correspond to any ontological differences between reasons
of different kinds.

In Chapters 3 to 5, I explore the connection between reasons and motivation. In Chapter 3, I canvass several possibilities
about what motivates actions. After a brief discussion of motives,
I focus on the relation between motivation and desire, and argue
that an adequate understanding of this relation depends on the
distinction between bodily appetites and rational desires, which
stand in importantly different relations to reasons. I then turn to
the act/object ambiguity inherent in the term 'desire' mentioned
above.

In Chapter 4, I examine and reject the idea that desires are motivating reasons, whether we think of desire as what is desired, or as
desiring something. What is desired is a goal or a purpose for the
sake of which someone acts, which can also be the intention in
acting. So what is desired can motivate us to act—but it motivates
as a goal rather than as a reason. On the other hand, my desiring something does not motivate me to act—rather, my desiring
something is my being motivated. If this is right, then the question remains what our reasons for acting are, which I answer in
Chapter 5.

In that chapter, I examine the relation between beliefs and motivating reasons, and defend an unusual interpretation of the claim
that motivating reasons are beliefs. On this interpretation, motivating
reasons are true beliefs, that is, they are things that we believe and
that are true—and since, if the belief that p is true, it follows that it is
a fact that p, I conclude that the reasons that motivate us are facts. It
might be thought that this account cannot apply in cases where we are
motivated to act by a false belief. However, I argue that false beliefs
are not reasons. We can and do mistake them for reasons; hence they
can motivate us to act. But I argue that false beliefs, that is, apparent
facts, are only apparent reasons.

An important corollary of the claims about motivating reasons defended in these three chapters is that, contrary to what the orthodoxy holds, motivating reasons are not mental states, for they are neither 'believings' nor 'desirings'.

The final chapter is devoted to the explanation of action. Again, I argue that all explanatory reasons are facts. Various facts can be cited as explanatory reasons. A reason that explains may be a motivating reason (in the sense of that phrase explained above), or a psychological fact about the agent, such as the fact that he believed and wanted certain things, or the fact that he had certain motives, character traits, emotions, habits, and so on. When the reason why an agent acted is *also* a reason for which the agent acted, the explanation is what I call a '*reason* explanation proper'. When an agent acts for an apparent reason, the explanation that cites this apparent reason is a 'Humean explanation', which typically has the form 'he ϕ-d because he believed that p and wanted x'.

In addition, actions performed for a reason can be explained with purposive or intentional explanations. Purposive explanations of actions identify the agent's purpose, which is also normally his intention in acting. Explanations of this kind can be supplemented by reason explanations, in which case the reason that explains the action is a fact that makes the action appear good in the agent's eyes.

This final chapter thus offers a picture of the way in which reasons explain actions. When someone acts for a reason, he is motivated by something he wants to do or achieve (his purpose in acting) which he regards as either intrinsically or instrumentally good; and he is also motivated by reasons, that is, by facts that make his action appear good in his eyes. These reasons can be premises in the agent's implicit or explicit practical reasoning.

If the argument of this book is convincing, it will not make man less of 'a great deep' than Augustine said he is. As individuals we remain complex; and the task of understanding how our rational, epistemic, and volitional capacities and tendencies combine to produce precisely *us* will still answer fully only to the powers of a novelist, a poet, or a dramatist. But the strictly philosophical task—to understand what these various capacities are, and what role they play in producing and explaining people's character and behaviour—*this* task will have been advanced. In other words, we shall have a clearer map than before of the concepts that questions about reasons for acting, and about the explanation of action, employ, and hence a correspondingly better chance of offering convincing answers to those questions. That, at any rate, is my aim in the present book.

1

Reasons

Introduction

This book is mainly concerned with reasons in relation to human actions. Human beings have several rational capacities, among which is the capacity to act for reasons: we have the capacity to recognize certain things as reasons to act, and to act motivated and guided by those reasons. Because of this, moreover, many human actions can be explained by reference to the agent's reasons for acting.

In subsequent chapters I shall investigate in detail the ways in which reasons can be said to motivate and guide agents to act, and to explain their actions. I begin, though, by mapping out some of the relevant territory and by highlighting some features of reasons that will prove useful in attempting to navigate it. This territory is, as we shall see, quite complex. And with it comes the temptation to suppose that the machinery required to find one's way around it must be correspondingly complex. I mean to resist this temptation as far as I can.

There is, undeniably, a certain heterogeneity in the use of the term 'reasons' which corresponds to the various roles that reasons play and the contexts in which they play those roles. For instance, reasons motivate and guide us in our actions (and omissions), in the sense that we can act in the light of reasons. And reasons can be grounds for beliefs, desires, emotions, etc. Reasons are also used to evaluate, and sometimes to justify, our actions, beliefs, desires, and emotions. And, in addition, reasons are used in explanations: both in explanations of human actions, beliefs, desires, emotions, and so on; and in explanations of a wide range of phenomena involving all sorts of animate and inanimate substances. So reasons can play a variety of roles, viz. they can motivate, guide, justify, or explain. And they can play those roles in characteristically human contexts of agency, as well as in contexts that are not related to agency, or not directly so. Moreover, and this is an important point, reasons can be used to explain all sorts of occurrences, including a wide range of natural phenomena that do not involve human rationality.

This diversity might encourage the thought that the term 'reason' is ambiguous or has different senses in different contexts.[1] In my view, however, it is more plausible to assume, at least at the outset, that there is some continuity or common thread linking the use of the term 'reason' in these different contexts—an assumption that would remain tenable even if the roles that reasons can play in some contexts involving certain characteristically human abilities should turn out to have peculiar features not found elsewhere. For instance, at the very least, it seems that, whenever reasons are used in any of the ways outlined above, it is possible to construct an argument (whether deductive or inductive, whether theoretical or practical) that underpins that use. So I shall not regard the diversity of contexts in which the term 'reason' can be used as prima facie evidence of its ambiguity. Instead, one of the things that I shall be trying to do in this chapter is to highlight some of the commonalities that this diversity threatens to mask, an undertaking that any premature judgement of ambiguity would thwart in advance. So, I shall begin by exploring the concept of a reason generally.

I said above that the territory we are to explore is complex, and that is so partly because, given the various roles that reasons can play, there seem to be many ways of partitioning the territory in order to begin an investigation. Thus, in the literature about reasons, it is common to introduce the discussion by drawing a distinction between different senses of the term 'reason', or between different kinds of reason.[2] However, I prefer to start my investigation by exploring something that is, I think, more illuminating and helpful for my purposes. What I

[1] See e.g. Broome (2004: 34).

[2] Dancy (2000: ch. 1) includes an illuminating summary of the history of this distinction, as well as a survey of the variety of distinctions about reasons for action found in the literature. Dancy himself draws a distinction between 'normative reasons', which he characterizes as 'features that speak in favour of [an] action (or against it). They are good reasons for doing the action' (2000: 1); and 'motivating reasons': 'the considerations in the light of which the agent chose to do what he did' (2000: 6).

have in mind is not a distinction between senses of the word or kinds of reason but rather an important feature of reasons, namely, the fact that reasons can have normative force.

1.1. Reasons and Normativity

I take the word 'normative' to mean 'prescriptive' relative to some norm or value and, by implication, concerning correctness: what is right or wrong by reference to what is prescribed by the relevant norm, or what furthers the relevant value. I therefore take the idea that reasons can have normative force to involve the idea that reasons can be invoked to support claims about what it would be right (for someone) to do, believe, want, feel, etc.[3] This feature of reasons underlies a wide variety of roles that reasons can play, namely, to guide, motivate, evaluate, justify, etc.

I say that reasons *can* have normative force not because this is a feature that reasons can have or lack, or that some reasons have and others lack. Rather, they *can* have normative force in the sense that a particular reason can make it right to do, believe, want, or feel something.

In principle, any reason can have normative force: the normative force that a reason has depends on a variety of things: logical and natural relations, conventions, rules and regulations, etc. For instance, the fact that the UK has the convention of driving on the left-hand side of the road is a reason to drive on the left as opposed to the right-hand side of the road: it is the fact that there is such a convention that makes it right (in this case prudentially right) to drive on the left-hand side. And so on.

The fact that the normative force of reasons is being invoked is often marked in language by talk of 'a reason *for* φ-ing' (or 'a reason *to* φ'), where 'φ' stands for any appropriate infinitival phrase. So there are reasons for acting (e.g. for going on a holiday),[4] for believing

---

[3] Although I shall have more to say about this in what follows, I should remark that, here, 'ought' should not be construed as restricted to 'morally ought'.

[4] I use 'acting' loosely to mean any doing susceptible to being explained by reference to the agent's reasons, including both someone's acting and not acting, as well as related concepts such as deciding, intending, trying.

something (e.g. for believing that he is telling the truth),[5] for wanting something (e.g. for wanting to improve one's serve at tennis),[6] for feeling an emotion (e.g. for feeling anger or fear), and so on. There are also reasons for not ϕ-ing, that is, reasons for not doing or for not believing something, for not feeling something, etc. In short, there are reasons for the variety of things where we are, typically, responsive to reasons.[7]

The linguistic mark is not infallible: sometimes a reason may be referred to as 'the reason for something' when the reason's normative force is not being invoked. For example, the reason why the catastrophe happened, say, that there had been three years of drought, can be called 'the reason *for* the catastrophe', and yet there is no sense in which that reason—that there had been three years of drought—made it right that the catastrophe happened, so no sense in which its normative force is at issue here. This is because the reason for the catastrophe is not *the catastrophe's reason* for happening but simply the reason why it did. — It's cause, or why God did it ?

In recent years there has been a great deal of debate about issues related to the normative force of reasons.[8] It is not my aim here, and it is beyond the scope of this book, to make an original contribution to those debates. Rather, I shall limit my discussion to exploring briefly those issues that will contribute to a better understanding of how reasons motivate and explain actions.

As I just noted, when the normative force of reasons is in play, reasons are typically referred to as 'reasons for ϕ-ing' or 'reasons to ϕ'. A reason for ϕ-ing is a reason for someone to ϕ, that is, for someone to do those things that can be done for reasons: act, believe, want, feel an emotion, or whatever else can be done for a reason.

(marginal note: It seems foolish to pretend that our word 'reason' is not ambiguous)

---

[5] And here, as for the most part in this book, I use 'to believe' as a generic term for a range of epistemic verbs such as suppose, suspect, presume. There are reasons for supposing and suspecting as well as for believing. However, we do not talk about reasons for knowing something—which suggests that there are important differences between knowing and these other epistemic notions.

[6] Also, except where otherwise indicated, I use 'to want' as a generic term for a range of related psychological attitudes, and use it as a variant for 'to desire'.

[7] Raz (1997) suggests that the notion of the active is roughly coincidental with the range of things where we are responsive to reasons.

[8] For some of the central issues debated, and for the views of some of the central contributors see Raz (1975 and 1999a); Scanlon (1998); Korsgaard (1996 and 1997); Quinn (1993); and also Wallace et al. (2004).

One of the most debated issues in this context is that of the relation between reasons for ϕ-ing and the concept 'ought'. It is often said that if there is a reason for someone to ϕ, then it follows that that person *ought* (at least pro tanto—more on this below) to ϕ; though in some cases it seems more plausible to say that what follows is that the person *may* (pro tanto) ϕ.

And, in any case, there is little agreement or indeed clarity about what, if a reason implies an 'ought'-claim, this 'ought' amounts to, and a variety of turns of phrase of varying strength have been used to try to capture it: that reasons favour, recommend, warrant, demand, ϕ-ing, or even that they create an obligation to ϕ.[9]

Perhaps we do not need to choose between them, as it is possible that what 'ought to' amounts to varies from case to case, depending on the circumstances. Thus, if A ought to ϕ, the circumstances of each case will determine whether A's ϕ-ing is merely recommended, or whether it is also required, or mandatory. What seems clear, however, is that it must be wrong to hold, as some do, that if A ought to ϕ, then it follows that A is obliged to ϕ (and a fortiori that it follows that A is *morally* obliged to ϕ).[10] For the notion of obligation, as Anscombe argued in her paper 'Modern Moral Philosophy' (1958), is associated with the notions of duty and law, but the reasons there are for someone to ϕ, and hence the reasons why one ought to ϕ, do not all depend on duties and laws, and certainly not on moral duties and moral laws (see Anscombe 1958: esp. 28 ff.). So, if, all things considered, you have a legal reason to ϕ, you may be *obliged* to ϕ. For instance, if you ought, all things considered, to disclose all your earnings to the tax authorities because the law says you must, then

---

[9] The word 'ought', like the word 'reason', is also said to be ambiguous between a normative and a non-normative sense. For example, the claim that John ought to have arrived by now can be read in two different ways, only one of which is supposed to be normative. On the first reading, the claim is that the right thing for John to have done is to have arrived by now (normative); on the second reading, the claim is that, given the circumstances, it is reasonable to believe that John should have arrived by now. But there is another way to construe the different readings, on which both are normative: the first reading concerns the right thing for John *to do* (according to, let's assume, norms of etiquette, or to his duties); and the second the right thing for us *to believe* (according to the available evidence). And, unless the term 'normative' is restricted to what one ought to do, as opposed to what one ought to believe, feel, want, etc., both these readings are normative. (This difference is noted in Spanish by using *debe* for the first, and *debe de* for the second.)

[10] This seems to be Korsgaard's view (1996).

you are obliged to do so. On the other hand if, all things considered, friendship dictates that you ought to ϕ, then it seems implausible to say that you are, therefore, obliged to ϕ: if you ought to give a present to your friend because it is her birthday, it does not seem to follow that you are therefore obliged to give her a present.

A reason for ϕ-ing may sometimes be defeated by a reason for not ϕ-ing.[11] A reason for ϕ-ing that can be defeated is sometimes called a 'pro tanto reason' for ϕ-ing. A pro tanto reason for ϕ-ing that is undefeated may be called an 'all things considered' reason for ϕ-ing; and such a reason makes ϕ-ing right all things considered.

Not all reasons for ϕ-ing may be defeated or cancelled. For instance, if p implies q, then the fact that p is a reason for believing that q, and this is a reason that cannot be defeated. It is, in other words, a conclusive reason for believing that q.

A reason for ϕ-ing may be defeasible but undefeated in different ways. For instance, a reason for ϕ-ing may be undefeated because it is stronger than any reasons for not ϕ-ing that there may be. But sometimes there is a different explanation of why a defeasible reason for ϕ-ing is undefeated: the explanation may be that A has a reason to ϕ and a reason not to ϕ and those reasons are incommensurable with each other (see Raz 1998). For example, financial prudence may militate against taking a rather expensive holiday, while the uniqueness of the opportunity, say, to join a polar expedition, may argue in its favour. Here, it may be impossible to measure the relative strength of the relevant reasons so that neither is defeated by the other, and both the decision to take the holiday and the decision to forgo it will accord with reason. This would mean that doing either will be supported by reasons, and that, as Raz says (1997), in deciding to do one rather than the other we forge, and reveal, our characters as prudent or adventurous, etc.

As mentioned above, the normative character of reasons tends to be construed in terms of the concept 'ought', or 'may', in that if a person has a reason for ϕ-ing then it follows that that person *ought to* or *may*

---

[11] Raz has done much to clarify different kinds of reasons for ϕ-ing and their interrelations. See Raz (1975), and (1999a: esp. chs. 1–3), where he discusses 'cancelling' reasons, the notion of an 'exclusionary' reason, etc. My discussion here is much indebted to Raz's writings on this topic though, needless to say, I do not claim that my discussion is a faithful representation of his views.

(if only pro tanto) ϕ. This might mean that the reason favours ϕ-ing, or recommends, permits, warrants, or demands, etc. ϕ-ing. But the question arises why a reason for ϕ-ing favours, warrants, or demands ϕ-ing? I suggested that the answer to this question is that a reason for ϕ-ing makes ϕ-ing *right* or *appropriate* (sometimes merely pro tanto right or appropriate), and I develop this idea further in the following section.

1.1.1. *Normativity and rightness*

A reason for ϕ-ing is a reason that makes ϕ-ing right and, because of that, a reason for ϕ-ing is a reason that justifies ϕ-ing.[12] Perhaps it sounds more intuitive to say that a reason for ϕ-ing makes ϕ-ing rational, or reasonable, rather than right. However, to say that ϕ-ing is rational is simply to say that it accords with reason, and then the question arises: What is it for something someone does, believes, etc. to accord with reason? And a first step in answering this question is to say that for something to accord with reason is for it to be right or appropriate (though, of course, not necessarily *morally* right or appropriate) according to some criterion to be specified.

The criterion or respect in which a reason makes ϕ-ing right, and hence in which something may be right or justified, varies depending on what ϕ-ing is. In the case of believing, the rightness or appropriateness of ϕ-ing, the justification of ϕ-ing, concerns the concept of truth (though perhaps not only that, as there may be pragmatic considerations that also play a role here). In the case of acting and wanting, it concerns the concepts of what is valuable and of the good.[13] In the case of emotions, it seems that reasons simply make the feeling or the emotion appropriate in the sense of reasonable, not because the reason makes the emotion good or true but because it makes it, as it were, fitting or proportionate to the facts. I shall have little to say about the relation between reasons and emotions.

---

[12] One may think that it is *we* who justify someone's ϕ-ing, e.g., by citing the reasons there are for her to ϕ. But in fact we can do that only because the reasons we cite make ϕ-ing right, that is, they justify it. The point here is analogous to explanation: it is people who explain by citing reasons, but they can do so only because, and to the extent that, the reasons they cite explain that thing.

[13] Adapting something Anscombe says in *Intention*, we might say that 'good' is the object of acting and wanting, as 'truth is the object of judgment' (1957: 77). The concept of the good is at the core of Anscombe's discussion of reasons for action in *Intention*.

A reason for believing something, say, that q, makes believing that thing (that q) right or appropriate in virtue of its relation to the truth of the proposition expressed by 'q'. Thus, the fact that p is a reason for believing that q, if the fact that p implies, increases the probability of, strongly suggests, etc., that q (and hence the truth of the proposition expressed by 'q'). For instance, the fact that he made a call at 10 p.m. implies that he was then still alive, so the fact that he made that call is a reason to believe that he was still alive at 10 p.m. If 'p' implies 'q' (as in the example just given), then the fact that p is a conclusive reason for believing that q. But the fact that p may be a reason for believing that q without being a conclusive reason to believe it. For instance, if Ann is Bertrand's blood sister, this fact is a conclusive reason to believe that Ann and Bertrand share at least one parent (for 'Ann is Bertrand's blood sister' implies 'Ann and Bertrand share at least one parent'). But the fact that Ann is Bertrand's blood sister is not a conclusive but rather a pro tanto reason to believe that they know each other, for the fact that two people are blood siblings highly increases the probability of their knowing each other but it does not guarantee that they do.

If what is believed is believed for a conclusive reason then what is believed is true. But if what is believed is believed for a less than conclusive reason, then what is believed may be false, even though the person may be right to believe it—for instance, if he had reason to believe it, and had no reason not to believe it (as might be the case with the belief that Ann and Bertrand know each other in the example above).

When the reason to believe something and the reason not to believe it are of equal strength, then believing either may be right. In our example, if Ann and Bertrand never mentioned each other, that would be a reason to believe that they do *not* know each other. This reason may be undefeat*ed* by, but also undefeat*ing* of, the reason there is to believe that they *do* know each other (namely, that they are blood siblings). In that case, believing either that they know each other or that they don't would seem to be right. And, as with actions, a person may be revealed as, for instance, more or less credulous or suspicious depending on what he is inclined to believe in such circumstances.

Reasons for acting and wanting make acting and wanting right or appropriate in relation to what is good or valuable. And since, to use a medieval slogan, *bonum est multiplex* (Aquinas, *Summa Theologiae* 1a, q.82, a.2), ϕ-ing might be right in different respects.[14] For instance, ϕ-ing may be good morally, aesthetically, prudentially, hedonically, etc., since what makes ϕ-ing good may be a moral, aesthetic, prudential, hedonic, etc., reason. Given that they are not necessarily mutually exclusive, ϕ-ing may be right in more than one of these respects. Thus, taking exercise may be right both hedonically and prudentially. When this is so, then the action of ϕ-ing will be right in each of those respects, that is, for different reasons. So more than one thing, that is, more than one reason, can make ϕ-ing right.

But it should be noted that the fact that reasons make ϕ-ing right in some respect or other does not mean that ϕ-ing can never be right *tout court*, that is, without qualification. For suppose that the reason that makes ϕ-ing good is, say, a hedonic reason. Then, if that reason is undefeated, ϕ-ing will be right without qualification and not merely from the hedonic point of view, even though what makes ϕ-ing right may be that it is fun or otherwise pleasurable.

Consider, for instance, bungee-jumping. If bungee-jumping is a good thing to do (at least for some people) this is presumably because it is fun, thrilling, exhilarating, and so on—that is, it is good for what might be called a hedonic reason. On the other hand, given the risks involved, there seem to be prudential reasons against bungee-jumping. However, if the hedonic reasons in favour of bungee-jumping defeat the prudential reasons against it (again, at least, for some people), then bungee-jumping is good *tout court*, that is, not simply from a hedonic point of view but 'all things considered', even though the feature of bungee-jumping that makes it good is hedonic, rather than, say, aesthetic or moral. (And, of course, this does not mean that bungee-jumping is wrong from those perspectives; it may be that from those perspectives it is neither right nor wrong.) So long as the reason that there is for someone to ϕ is undefeated, then their ϕ-ing is right all things considered, regardless of the fact that what makes their ϕ-ing right will be a reason that picks out some particular form of the good, or a value of a particular kind, e.g. aesthetic, prudential, or moral value.

When a reason there is for someone to ϕ *is* defeated by a reason against it, then it would be correct to say that, for that person, ϕ-ing is good and hence right from that perspective but not all things

---

[14] See Anscombe (1957: 74 ff.); and von Wright (1963).

considered. So for example, if bungee-jumping would be fun for me but very dangerous because I have a heart condition, and the second reason defeats the first, then doing it would be right for me from the hedonic point of view but not right all things considered.

Some people believe that moral reasons for acting always defeat other reasons. But even if that is right, it would not follow that ϕ-ing could be right all things considered *only* if there is a moral reason for ϕ-ing. For even if moral reasons always defeat other reasons, in order for ϕ-ing to be right all things considered, it would be sufficient that there was no moral reason *against* ϕ-ing. So, in the case of bungee-jumping, if the hedonic reasons for doing it defeat all other reasons against it, then bungee-jumping would be right all things considered, even if there are no moral reasons for bungee-jumping, since there would be none against it.

One may wonder whether reasons always make ϕ-ing right (even if merely pro tanto right), or whether, at least sometimes, a reason makes ϕ-ing simply not wrong, or perhaps neither right nor wrong. For example, suppose that the only reason that there is for you to go swimming is simply that you'll enjoy it. And suppose that there is no reason against your going swimming. In that case, one may think that it seems too strong to say that your going swimming is *right* and suggest instead that the fact that you'll enjoy it makes it neither right nor wrong. But although this line of reasoning seems prima facie plausible, it is, I think, mistaken.

First, there are things that it is neither right nor wrong for someone to do because there are no reasons for or against doing those things, so no reasons that make it either right or wrong to do it. For instance, I may feel like doing a cartwheel, and there may be no reason for me to do it,[15] nor a reason not to do it. If so, my doing a cartwheel is neither right nor wrong—but not because the reason there is for me to do it makes it neither right nor wrong but because there is no reason for or against my doing it.

or be
may be
because reasons
what there are
fall below
a thresh-
hold of
considerability.

[15] For reasons that will become clear in Chapter 4, I don't think that the fact that I feel like doing something is, at least normally, a reason for doing it, although it can be a reason that explains why I do something.

Second, although something may be right or wrong aesthetically, legally, etc., the question whether ϕ-ing is right arises most often, or in its most pressing form, in relation to morality. Because of this, we are prone to hear the claim that a reason makes ϕ-ing *right* as saying that it makes it *morally* right. And if 'it is right' is taken to mean that, then it may be true that there are many things that we might have, all things considered, reason to do but which are *morally speaking* neither right nor wrong for us to do. For instance, if the fact that it will look good is an undefeated reason for me to paint my sitting room terracotta, then it is right, aesthetically speaking, to paint the sitting room in that colour. And if we assume that there are no moral reasons for or against it, then my painting my sitting room terracotta will be neither right nor wrong *morally* speaking. But, as we saw a few paragraphs above, this does not mean that painting my sitting room terracotta is, *tout court*, neither right nor wrong. Rather it is, *tout court*, right—even though the reason that makes it right is an aesthetic reason.

A reason for ϕ-ing makes ϕ-ing pro tanto right but, even when it is undefeated, it need not make ϕ-ing the only right thing to do, or the best thing to do: ϕ-ing might simply be one right thing among a number of possibilities which are also right. For instance, suppose that I enjoy tennis. In some circumstances, that may be an undefeated reason for me to play tennis. But it doesn't follow that if I do play tennis in those circumstances, playing tennis was the only or the best thing for me to do then—I might have chosen to go for a walk instead if I also enjoy that, and it may be that either would have been right, and that neither would have been more right than the other.

This brings up a distinctive feature of actions, namely that they are the subject of choice—and the latter is generally guided by reasons (or at least by apparent reasons, as an agent may deliberate and choose on the basis of false premises which express only apparent reasons).

What kind of choice is possible in action? There seem to be two kinds of choice. One concerns different means of achieving one's goal; and the other concerns choice between possible but (at the time) incompatible goals.

Often, there may be more than one acceptable way of satisfying one's desire, or achieving one's end, and then it is up to one which to choose.[16] Geach expresses this point as follows:

> In theoretical reasoning it cannot be equally justifiable to pass from A, B, C, . . . to a conclusion D and to an incompatible conclusion D'. But in practical deliberation D may be a fiat expressing one way of getting our ends, and D' may express another incompatible way: in that case it may be *up to us* whether from A, B, C, . . . we pass on to accepting D as a guide to action, or rather, to accepting D'.   (1976: 98)

An example of this might be a choice between walking to work and cycling. Someone may consider the following reasons: both walking and cycling are equally economical, they are good forms of exercise, cycling would be faster but walking more relaxing, etc. Here, the overall set of reasons makes either right and therefore it leaves room for choice. It is important to note here that doing either will be explained by the reasons there are to do that thing. So suppose that in those circumstances I choose to walk. My reasons for choosing that, and hence my reasons for walking, will be that walking is a practical, healthy, and economical way to get to work and, though slower than cycling, it is still more relaxing, etc. Had I, on the other hand, chosen to cycle, then my reasons for choosing that would be that cycling is a practical, healthy, and economical way to get to work and, though less relaxing, is quicker than walking, etc. Each choice can be explained by the reasons I had.

The second kind of choice is one between incompatible goals. In that case, we may choose which of the goals to satisfy. An example of this would be a choice between going shopping with a friend, which will be enjoyable and will enable me to get something I need, but will mean I shan't be able to get on with my work; or staying at home, in which case I can do some work but which will certainly be much less enjoyable. On the balance of reasons, both might be fine (reasonable, appropriate, etc.) and it is up to me which thing I choose to do. Again,

---

[16] This is vividly illustrated in a *Non Sequitur* cartoon where, over the caption 'Back to normal life for the undecided voter', we see a somewhat nonplussed man standing by a traffic light, staring at the illuminated 'Walk' sign, and saying to himself: 'But is walking the best way to get across the street? Running would be a lot faster, but am I really in that much of a hurry?'

whichever I chose, I shall be able to explain my choice by reference to my reasons and yet it need not be true that the reasons I had dictated one course of action rather than the other: they left room for choice.

If the above is correct, then I see no obstacle to concluding that if A has a reason to ϕ, that reason makes her ϕ-ing, at least pro tanto, right. And this is so whether ϕ-ing is believing, wanting, or acting. There is, however, an important difference between reasons for believing on the one hand, and reasons for wanting and acting, on the other, which I examine in the next section.

1.1.2. *The person-relative character of reasons for acting and wanting*

All reasons for ϕ-ing are reasons *for* someone to ϕ. But, while reasons for believing are not person-relative, some reasons for acting and wanting are.

If the fact that p is a reason for someone to believe that q, then it is a reason for *anyone* to believe this, no matter what his or her circumstances and goals are. Whereas if the fact that p is a reason for A to want x, or to perform an action, it does not follow that it is also a reason for B to want x or to perform the same action. For instance, if the fact that it is a starry night is a reason for believing that it'll be sunny tomorrow, then it is a reason for anyone to believe it, whatever goals or other beliefs that person might have. And if the fact that the President said so is a reason for doubting the truth of what he said, then this is a reason for everyone to doubt it.

Of course, A might *take* the fact that the President said it to be a reason to believe what he said, and B might *take* it to be a reason not to believe it, but they cannot both be right (though they could both be wrong if e.g. that the President has said so is neither a reason to believe it nor a reason not to believe it). For some people, given their circumstances, goals, etc., the fact that the President has said so may be a reason for, for instance, *acting* as if what he had said is true. But no goals or circumstances would make the fact that the President said something a reason for A to believe what the President said, but a reason for B not to believe it.

But is this right? For couldn't one object that, for instance, the fact that the gardener owned the knife that killed the victim is a reason for the policeman to believe that the gardener killed her, while it isn't a reason for the (actually innocent) gardener to believe that he himself had killed her.[17] Although the objection has some force it is, I think, unsuccessful. The fact that the gardener owned the murder weapon is a reason for everyone (albeit a defeasible one) to believe that he was the murderer, and that includes the gardener himself. However, the fact that the gardener did not do it is a conclusive reason to believe that he did not do it, and it is, therefore, a reason that defeats any other reason to believe that he did it. And the same goes for any fact that implies that the gardener could not have done it, for instance, that he was elsewhere at the time. And, since the gardener *knows* that he didn't do it, he cannot take the fact that the knife was his as a reason to believe that he did it. Nonetheless, that fact is a defeasible reason to believe that he did it even for him. For suppose that the gardener had amnesia and didn't know he hadn't done it. Then, he might also take the fact that it was his knife as a reason to believe he was the murderer. But as a matter of fact, the fact that he didn't do it is still a conclusive reason for him to believe that he didn't do it—only, in his amnesiac state, he (like the policeman) doesn't know about that reason.

Another sort of objection to the view that reasons for belief are not person-relative is the following. Suppose that the fact that your boss has heart disease is a reason for your boss to change his diet. Then, the fact that your boss has heart disease is a reason to believe that he ought to change his diet. But, someone might object, surely it is a reason only for those who are aware that heart disease is aggravated by an unhealthy diet, so anyone who is not aware of this connection has no reason to believe that your boss ought to change his diet. But the objection fails. As I shall argue below (Section 1.1.3), one may have a reason to do something without believing that one has that reason. So someone who is not aware of the connection between heart disease and an unhealthy diet won't *see* that he has a reason to believe that your boss ought to change his diet. But he does have that reason nonetheless: we can be wrong about the reasons we have.

There is a related objection which also appears to suggest that reasons for belief are person-relative and which is based on the idea that, at least sometimes, there is a link between what we have reason

---

[17] I owe this objection to an anonymous referee.

to believe and what we have reason to want. This objection goes as follows. Surely, in the example given, you have reason to believe that your boss ought to change his diet only if you have some interest in his being in good health. Suppose, however, that you stand to be promoted to your boss' job if he becomes seriously ill. Then it seems you have no reason to believe that he ought to change his diet—indeed it might seem you have reason to believe that he ought *not* to do so. Again, however, the objection fails. If the facts dictate that he has a reason to change his diet, then you have reason to believe that he ought to change his diet, even if you also have reason to *wish* or to *hope* that he won't—because what is good for me may not be good for you but what is true is true for everyone.[18]

Thus, while reasons for believing are not person-relative, reasons for acting and wanting are. For instance, the fact that these are iron tablets might be a reason for me to (want to) take them but not for you because I need iron but you don't; likewise, that she is ill may be a reason for me to (want to) visit her but not for you, because she's my friend but not yours; that one can go skiing in Switzerland will be a (pro tanto) reason for enthusiasts of that sport to (want to) travel to that country but not for those who don't enjoy skiing; and that a particular handbag is the latest fashion might be a reason for wanting it, or for buying it, for fashion victims but not for those who don't care about fashion. Or at least this seems so, for it seems implausible that the right explanation in these cases should be that we all have a reason to do those things (visit that ill person, go skiing, or buy that ultra-fashionable handbag) but that for most people, these reasons are defeated by other reasons against doing those things (e.g. that they are already busy visiting *their* friends, that they don't actually like skiing, that it is far too expensive, etc.). That is an implausible explanation of why some reasons seem to apply to some people and not to others; an explanation that we ought to accept only if we cannot find a better one—but I think a better one is at hand.

---

[18] I reject, therefore, a claim sometimes made that, for instance, the fact that your believing that p will save a million lives gives you a reason to believe that p. In my view, this conflates reasons for wanting or acting, which pertain to the good, and reasons for believing, which pertain to truth. In the example, the fact mentioned concerns the good (saving millions of lives) and it may therefore be a reason for *wanting* to believe that p, and perhaps for *trying* to believe it, but it is not a reason for believing that p.

What reasons a person has for acting and wanting things depend partly on who that person is and on her circumstances and values, because, in general, things are not good or right *tout court* but in some respect; and that respect may be more or less relevant to different people depending precisely on what their circumstances and values are. So, the variety of circumstances in which people find themselves (which makes it the case that what is good for one person may not be good or may even be harmful for another), and the variety and incommensurability of goods available to them, together with different preferences they may have towards those goods, create this person-relative feature of reasons for acting and wanting. So, for example, for someone who enjoys skiing, the fact that there is a bargain offer for a week's skiing is a reason to (want to) take advantage of it, whereas for someone who does not enjoy skiing, the offer is no reason at all. And so on. Given these differences something may be a reason for one person to act but not for another (see Raz 1998).

This person-relative character of reasons does not mean that reasons are subjective in the sense that whether there is a reason for someone to ϕ depends on whether the person *believes* that there is. Rather, it depends on what things are good for, or valued by, that person. However, although what reasons a person believes she has does not determine what reasons she has, it does determine what reasons she can act for, as we shall see in the following section.

1.1.3. *Having a reason and believing one has a reason*

What, then, is the relation between what a person believes concerning the reasons she has and the reasons she does have?

First, a terminological point. I take the claim that there is a reason for A to ϕ to be equivalent to the claim that A has a reason to ϕ. It is tempting to think that these expressions are not equivalent because one might construe the second, 'A has a reason to ϕ', to mean 'A believes (or knows) that she has a reason to ϕ' or 'A takes something to be a reason to ϕ' and thus conclude that, while there might be a reason for A to ϕ independently of what A believes or knows, A *has* a reason to ϕ if and only if she believes she has. But this is in fact not how these expressions are used, because we generally allow that A may be mistaken about whether she has a reason to do something:

she may believe that she doesn't when in fact she does, and vice versa. For instance, if A does not know that the book she's been looking for is in the second-hand bookshop, she might not believe that she has a reason to go to that shop, but in fact she has.[19]

Someone may not believe that the fact that p is a reason for her to ϕ if she does not believe that p, either because she believes that not-p or simply because she has no opinion either way. Thus, it might be that if A came to believe that the book is in the bookshop, she would see that that fact is a reason for her to go to that bookshop, but perhaps the thought that it might be there never occurs to her. Or perhaps it has occurred to her but she has formed the mistaken belief that it is not there—she may have been misinformed.

On the other hand, someone may not believe that the fact that p is a reason for him to ϕ because, even though he believes that p, he does not believe that the fact that p is a reason for him to ϕ. For example, B may be aware that he has cirrhosis of the liver, but not be aware of the connection between that and drink, and hence not realize that the fact that he has cirrhosis is a reason for him to stop drinking.[20] Or, a different kind of case, B may be aware that he has cirrhosis of the liver and be aware of the connection but he may not believe that he has a reason to stop drinking because he does not care about his health.[21]

So, in general—that is, for beliefs, actions, and wants—it seems that someone may have a reason to do, want, or believe something without being aware that he has such a reason, or indeed, without being aware of what that reason is. (These last claims are different: a

---

[19] Audi, for example, distinguishes between 'normative reasons', which are reasons that there are for someone to ϕ, and 'possessed reasons' which are normative reasons that one also believes one has (2001: 119). This corresponds to the point I am making here, though I think it might be more helpful to call the second 'recognized' reasons.

[20] Someone may be aware that p is a reason for him to ϕ and still not ϕ, or ϕ but not for that reason. So, B may know that he has cirrhosis of the liver and believe that that is a reason for him to stop drinking, but not stop because he can't bring himself to do it, or stop, but for financial reasons.

[21] I am leaving aside the much-debated question whether there are reasons for one to ϕ that are independent of one's desires, that is, of whether one's desires would be furthered in any way by acting according to those reasons: for instance, whether B has a reason to give up drinking independently of whether he cares about his health (or would care, were he to deliberate properly from his current desires). This is a topic that has been much debated since Hume, and more recently in response to the seemingly Humean position defended by Williams (1981 and 1995).

person may know or believe that he has a reason to ϕ but not know what that reason is.)

The converse also seems true. In order for someone to have a reason to ϕ, it is not *sufficient* that he believe that he has such a reason. Suppose I believe that it is raining, and believe also that the fact that it is raining is a reason for me to take my umbrella. But suppose that it is not raining. Then I have no reason to take my umbrella, even though I believe I have, or even though there is something I believe, that it is raining, that I also take to be a reason to take my umbrella.

Some people have argued that, although, in such circumstances, I have no *objective* reason to take my umbrella, I have a *subjective* reason to do so. And they argue this because, they say, if I believe that it is raining and believe that that is (an undefeated) reason to take my umbrella and yet I choose not to take an umbrella, I act irrationally. And to act irrationally, the thought goes, is to act against reason. But, the argument continues, in this case there is no *objective* reason for me to take my umbrella. So, if I acted irrationally, then my acting irrationally must consist in my acting against a *subjective* reason, that is, a reason that I believed I had, namely that it is raining.

It seems true that acting against what one believes one has reason to do, all things considered, is a form of irrationality. However, I am not convinced that the best way of accounting for this irrationality is in terms of 'subjective' reasons, for I think the suggestion that there are such things as 'subjective reasons' is at best misleading.[22] Leaving that aside, though, this way of putting things would not threaten the claim made above that taking oneself to have a reason to do something is not sufficient for having a reason, because 'subjective' reasons are a peculiar kind of reasons—and it is possible to claim that one of their peculiarities is that they are not genuine reasons but rather things one *believes* to be reasons. In other words, one can argue that calling them 'subjective' reasons is just a way of acknowledging that we are not dealing with genuine but only with what I shall call 'apparent' reasons, that is, reasons that one, mistakenly, thinks one has, just as one may believe one has a gold bracelet when in fact one has something that appears to be a gold bracelet but is not a genuine one and is only a gilded bracelet (more on this in Chapter 5).

[22] For a helpful discussion of these issues see Hooker and Streumer (2004: ch. 4).

It may be agreed that, in cases like the one just described, your believing that it is raining, and your believing that its being raining is a reason to take your umbrella, are not sufficient for you to have a reason to take your umbrella. Nonetheless, one may object to the view I am defending, in this case you *do* have a reason: not a reason to take the umbrella *tout court* but rather a reason to 'take-the-umbrella-if-you-believe-that-it-is-raining'. But this, if right, has no bearing on the point under discussion, namely that believing that one has a reason to ϕ is not sufficient for one to have a genuine reason to ϕ. It has no bearing because what the view just outlined shows is, at most, that you have a reason to 'take-the-umbrella-if-you-believe-that-it-is-raining', which is to say that, in order to avoid irrationality, you must either abandon your belief that it is raining, or take your umbrella. But this 'must' has wide scope (over the disjunction), and so we cannot conclude from this that you must (that is, have reason to) take the umbrella.[23] Besides, in order to avoid irrationality, one can either act according to what one believes, or abandon one's belief. But if one's belief is false, then one has a conclusive reason to abandon that belief, for the fact that it is not the case that, say, your husband is at home is a conclusive reason not to believe that your husband is at home. So when one has a false belief, it is not at all clear that one has a reason to do what would be consistent with the false belief and one's goals.

It seems, then, that just as for someone to have a reason to ϕ, that person need not know, or even believe, that she does, it is not enough for someone to have a reason to ϕ that that person believes that she does.

What is true, however, is that only someone who is aware of a reason, that is, aware of the fact that p, and aware that that fact is a reason for him to ϕ, can ϕ for the reason that p. Unless B is aware that he has cirrhosis of the liver, the fact that he does cannot be his reason for doing anything. And unless he is aware that the fact that he has cirrhosis of the liver is a reason for him to give up drink, he cannot give up drink for that reason. Acting for a reason requires awareness of particular facts.

---

[23] For a discussion of this issue, see Dancy (2000: 42–3 and 53–4), and Broome (2004: 30). Broome puts the point in terms of 'normative requirements' rather than reasons but that difference is not relevant here.

Perhaps all this is fairly obvious and uncontroversial. But it is important because the consideration that the fact that p cannot be the reason for which I ϕ *unless* I believe that p has led many to conclude that, therefore, the reason for which I ϕ is that I believe that p, or my believing that p. I discuss this issue in detail in Chapter 5 but shall anticipate here that I think that reasoning is mistaken: my believing that p is only very rarely the reason for which I ϕ—and this applies to reasons for acting and wanting as well as to reasons for believing. So, if I believe that he is arriving tomorrow because he said he would, my reason for believing that he is arriving tomorrow is that he said he would, and not that I believe he said that, or my believing that he said that. If I poke you in the eye because you have insulted me, my reason for poking you in the eye is that you have insulted me, and not that I believe that you have. And if I want to hug the first person I meet because I have just had some excellent news, my reason for wanting to hug them is that I have just had excellent news, and not that I believe that I have. And so on.

Let me summarize what has been said about reasons and normativity. The normativity of reasons, I have argued, concerns reasons in so far as they make ϕ-ing right for someone. Thus, a reason for someone to ϕ is a reason that, according to some criterion, makes ϕ-ing, at least pro tanto, right or appropriate. A reason for believing something makes believing that thing right because of its connection to the truth of that thing. A reason for acting (or wanting, or deciding, etc.) makes acting, etc., right because of its connection to the good, according to some criterion, that is, to some value that so acting has for that person. And the reason might make acting, or wanting that, right for one person but not for another; while reasons for believing are not, in this sense, person-relative. Reasons make actions and wants right in some respect, say prudentially, or legally, etc. But if a reason that makes acting right is undefeated, then the action is not just right from that perspective but all things considered.

For someone to have a reason for ϕ-ing it is neither necessary nor sufficient that she believe that she has. But for someone to ϕ for the reason that p, it is necessary for her to be aware of the fact that p.

At the beginning of this chapter I noted that reasons play a variety of roles: among other things, reasons can guide deliberation about how to act, and can thus motivate actions; they can be used to evaluate actions, whether prospective or already performed, and they can explain why someone acted. Some of those roles depend on the normativity of reasons while others do not. The following section explores this aspect of reasons.

1.2. Reasons and Roles

In this section I shall first outline some of the main roles that reasons play generally.

We have seen that, given their normative force, reasons sometimes play a guiding role in reasoning about whether someone (oneself or someone else) ought to ϕ, e.g. whether I ought to reject an offer, believe that I have been betrayed, aspire to become a pop singer, etc., and also about how to ϕ. Such deliberation does not require that the agent should ask herself, or someone else: 'What should I do?' or 'What ought I to believe?', etc. Rather, it is sufficient that the person weighs up, implicitly or explicitly, the relative merits of the reasons that there may for or against doing or believing something.

The normative force of reasons is also in play when evaluating someone's ϕ-ing, when assessing whether it is or was right for him to ϕ or to have ϕ-ed, e.g. to believe that he has been betrayed, or to have revealed a secret. In such contexts, we often seek to justify someone's ϕ-ing: to show that it is or was right for him to ϕ.

These remarks highlight two principal roles that reasons can play: they can motivate (sometimes through a process of deliberation, whether theoretical or practical), and they can justify our actions, beliefs, wants, etc.

Another very important role that reasons play is that of explaining. Reasons are used to explain all sorts of things: the occurrence (or non-occurrence) of an event; the obtaining (or non-obtaining) of a state of affairs; someone's or something's ϕ-ing (or not ϕ-ing); etc. In the remarks that follow, I shall focus on explanations of someone's ϕ-ing, where, as above, ϕ-ing may be acting, believing, wanting, feeling an emotion, etc., or refraining from any of these.

Because reasons can be answers to 'Why?'-questions, a reason that explains something is often called the 'reason why p', where 'p' is a variable for sentences that express propositions; and such answers typically constitute an explanation. This is a non-technical sense of 'explanation' and, in this sense, explanations are multifarious and highly context-sensitive.[24]

So there are reasons why things happen (why she lost so much blood), why things are as they are (why the economy is in recession), why someone ϕ-ed (why he visited his uncle), and so on. And, just as there are reasons for not ϕ-ing, there are also reasons why not p, that is, reasons why things do not happen, why they are not as they are not, why someone didn't do something, etc.

There are also reasons that explain *why* A *ought* to ϕ. For instance, if Sam ought to exercise because he's overweight, then the fact that he's overweight explains why Sam ought to exercise. And it is important to note that a reason that explains *why* A ought to ϕ does so precisely because it is a reason *for* A to ϕ: the fact that Sam is overweight explains why he ought to exercise precisely because the fact that he's overweight is a reason for him to exercise.[25] This shows that, sometimes, reasons play an explanatory role because of their normative force: they explain why someone ought to ϕ because they make it right for that person to ϕ.

Some points of clarification concerning the explanatory role of reasons are in order. First, in addition to answers to 'Why?'-questions, there are other kinds of explanation, for instance, explanations of how to ϕ (how to iron a shirt), of how x ϕ-s (how a steam engine works), etc. But to explain how to ϕ, or how x ϕ-s, is not to give a reason; and since my primary concern is with reasons in contexts of action, I leave those other kinds of explanation aside.

Second, when an explanation is given in answer to a 'Why?'-question, the explanans of such an explanation can be called '*the* reason why'. There is, however, something a little misleading in talking about

---

[24] A technical sense of the word has been associated with the view that all 'genuine' explanations have a determinate logical form. This view once was (and perhaps still is) popular among philosophers, especially philosophers of science. These philosophers argued that all explanations are arguments that ineliminably involve (empirical, universal, exceptionless) laws as one of their premises. See e.g. Hempel and Oppenheim (1948), and Hempel (1962). See also Davidson (1976).

[25] Broome says: 'The key to understanding the concept of a reason is to look at how facts of a particular type are explained. I mean facts of the form that P ought to ϕ, where "P" stands for the name of an agent and "to ϕ" for an infinitival phrase. I shall call them "ought facts" ' (2004: 31). But see Schroeder (2007: 34 ff.), for a different view.

the reason why. For a 'Why?'-question can have many answers, and *which* answer (that is, which reason) is explanatory and appropriate depends, among other things, on the context in which the question is asked, and in particular on the background of explicit or implicit assumptions against which the question is asked. These factors provide the constraints for what is called 'the pragmatics of explanation'. Thus, given different background conditions for a 'Why?'-question, different answers might be appropriate as 'the reason why'. For example, if you ask me why my tulips died this April, I could say that the reason is that it was an unusually cold spring—and leave it implicit that I failed to bring them in then. But I could also say that the reason why they died is that I didn't bring them in, on the assumption that you know that the weather was unusually cold and that, had I brought them in, they would have survived. And so on.

Finally, as I just said, answers to 'Why?'-questions are 'reasons why' and they are, therefore, reasons. This use of 'reason' to designate answers to 'Why?'-questions is a perfectly ordinary and legitimate use of the word. Thus if the explanation of why there was an explosion is that there was a rise in pressure, the rise in pressure was the reason why there was an explosion. Likewise, if the explanation of why Mary cannot (legally) marry is that she is a minor, that she is a minor is the reason why Mary cannot marry. And, if the explanation of why you broke the Ming vase is that you didn't like it, that you didn't like the vase is the reason why you broke it.

Some philosophers have claimed that there is an important difference between the first case, on the one hand, and the remaining two, on the other. In the last two cases, they would say, what explains is indeed a reason; but, in the first case, what explains is a *cause*. However, as Strawson notes in his paper 'Causation and Explanation', that conflates two levels of relationship: that of causation and that of explanation. As Strawson argues, we must distinguish between causation which, in his characteristically cautious manner, he says is a relation that 'we perhaps think of' as a 'natural relation'; and explanation, which is an intensional relation 'that holds between facts or truths' (1987: 109). And this means that we must distinguish between causes and reasons (and consequently between causes and causal explanations). Thus, if the rise in pressure caused the explosion, then the rise in pressure was the cause of the explosion. If so, though, *the fact* that there was a rise in pressure (causally) explains *the fact* that there was an explosion. That is to say, if the rise in pressure caused the explosion, it does not follow that *the fact that there was* a rise in pressure is a cause and not a reason—on the contrary, it follows that it is a reason, since it is precisely because the rise in pressure caused the explosion that we can explain the fact that there was an explosion by citing the fact that the temperature rose. And the second fact is therefore a reason that explains the first.

Of course, not all explanations are causal explanations. But the point that matters here is that 'reasons why' are genuine reasons, regardless of whether they explain a natural occurrence or someone's rational action, and regardless of whether the explanations in which they feature are causal or not.[26]

It is true that in explanations of natural phenomena, such as the explanation of why the explosion occurred, the reason that explains is not *also* the phenomenon's reason (e.g. the explosion's reason) *for* occurring. And it is true that in explanations of why someone ϕ-ed the reason why someone did something can also be *their* reason *for* doing it. For instance, in the third example three paragraphs above, the reason that explains why you broke the Ming vase, that you didn't like it, was also your reason for breaking it. But this doesn't show that the first 'reason why' is not a genuine reason: it only shows that it is a reason why something occurred that is not also that thing's reason for occurring.

Conclusion

As I said at the beginning, the aim of this chapter was to prepare the ground, and the conceptual tools, for an exploration of reasons in contexts of human action, of how reasons motivate us to act, and of the explanation of action.

We have examined the normativity of reasons: the fact that reasons have normative force in so far as they make ϕ-ing right. I have claimed

---

[26] An issue that exercised philosophers of action in the 1960s and since is precisely whether the reason for which an agent acts is a cause of his action, and the related question whether an explanation of action whose explanans is the agent's reason for acting is a causal explanation. I discuss action explanations in Chapter 6, although I shan't be addressing those questions about causation (but see the Conclusion to this book and Alvarez 2007).

that, in the case of believing, the rightness or appropriateness of ϕ-ing concerns the concept of truth. In the case of acting and wanting, it concerns the concepts of what is valuable and of the good, broadly conceived, and as related to a variety of values. Having explored the normative force of reasons, we explored the variety of roles that reasons can play. And we have seen that reasons can justify, they can motivate, and they can explain. In the following chapter I explore the implication this has for the classification of reasons and their ontology.

2

Reasons, Kinds, Ontology

Introduction

In the previous chapter, we examined the normativity of reasons and the various roles that reasons can play. In this chapter, I shall explore the implications this variety has for our understanding of reasons, and in particular for what might be called the 'ontology' of reasons: the conceptual category or categories to which reasons belong.

It is often assumed that the various roles played by reasons are played by different *kinds* of reason (indeed, as I noted in Chapter 1, some philosophers think that, on account of this fact, the word 'reason' is ambiguous). For example, a very widespread view is that there are essentially two different kinds of reasons: *justifying* (or 'normative') reasons, which are said to be reasons with normative force which play roles of guidance, evaluation, and justification; and *motivating* (or 'operative') reasons, which play the roles of motivating and explaining (and, on account of the latter, these are often also called 'explanatory reasons'). This view often goes hand in hand with the claim that reasons of different kinds belong to different ontological categories: to facts (or something similar) in the case of justifying reasons, and to mental states in the case of motivating reasons. Neither this view of reasons, nor the ontological claim, seems right to me.

First, the idea there are different kinds of reason, and that some of those kinds have special features on account of which they can play special roles (for instance justify) is mistaken. For one and the same reason can play a variety of roles—the same reason can justify in one context and explain in another, without becoming a different reason, or acquiring any special feature. And it is only on account of the role a reason plays in any particular context that it makes sense to think of is as 'justifying', or 'explanatory'. So the claim that there are different *kinds* of reason makes sense only if it is construed in terms of the different kinds of roles reasons can play.

Second, and relatedly, the idea that reasons of different kinds belong to different ontological categories is implausible, for it is implausible that the same reason should change ontological category depending on what role it happens to play in a particular context. Instead, I shall argue below, all reasons are facts or, what I take to be the same, truths, which are expressed propositionally, and which can be premises in reasoning, both theoretical and practical.[1]

Bearing in mind this qualification about what I mean by 'different kinds of reason', in Section 2.1 I shall offer a way of classifying reasons into different kinds. As will become clear, my classification of reasons into kinds is at odds with much of the literature on reasons in several respects: first, the kinds into which I suggest reasons should be classified; second, how I propose we should understand the claim that reasons are classified into different kinds; and, finally, the consequences I take this classification to have for the ontology of reasons. These are explored in Section 2.2, where I develop and defend the suggestion that all reasons are facts, understood as true propositions, and examine two routes that might lead one to deny this (in Sections 2.2.1 and 2.2.2 respectively).

2.1. How Many Kinds of Reasons?

The most common view on the classification of reasons to be found in the literature is that there are two basic kinds of reason: the reasons that there are for us to act ('justifying' or 'normative' reasons); and the reasons for which we act ('motivating' or 'explanatory' reasons). In my view this way of classifying reasons is in need of some refinement.

---

[1] Admittedly, this use of 'fact' as, to quote Strawson, 'what statements (when true) state', involves a touch of revisionism of the ordinary use of this word, which is perhaps more restricted—not that the ordinary use is neat and tidy. The Latin *factum* from which 'fact' derives, meant 'thing done'. But the English word 'fact', and at least some of its Romanic equivalent words—*hecho* (Spanish), *fatto* (Italian), etc.—have now a fairly wide range of related meanings: a deed, a feat, something that has occurred or is the case, something that is not fiction, something known to be true, etc.

First, there is a sense in which *any* reason, considered in the abstract, is justifying and explanatory, if by that is meant that a reason *can* have normative or explanatory force respectively because, as I explained in Section 1.1, any reason can have normative force and any reason can explain. In other words, any reason may be invoked to support claims about what someone ought to do, believe, say, feel, want, etc., just as any reason can be cited in an explanation. I don't of course mean that *any* reason can be used to support *any* 'ought'-claim, nor that *any* reason can explain *anything*, for example, that any reason can be cited to justify why Anne ought to move house, or to explain why male birds tend to be more brightly coloured than the female of the species. Rather, what I mean is that any reason, regarded in the abstract, can in principle support a relevant 'ought'-claim, or appear in a relevant explanation. There is nothing about any particular reason that, considered independently of a particular context, makes it better suited to play a justifying or an explanatory role respectively.

Second, as mentioned above, classification of reasons only makes sense in relation to the role(s) that a reason plays in any particular context. Or to put the same point differently, a reason is not a justifying, motivating, or explanatory reason, *tout court*, but rather relative to a role it plays in some particular case. For example, suppose that the nurse tells Jess that she ought to fast for the next twenty-four hours because she's having an operation in twenty-four hours' time. The nurse cites the fact that she is having an operation in twenty-four hours as a (justifying) reason for Jess to fast for the next twenty-four hours. Now suppose that Jess fasts as admonished on account of the fact that she'll have an operation at the end of that period. Here, the same reason that justifies her fasting, namely that she'll have an operation, is the reason that motivates her to fast. And suppose, finally, that when a friend invites Jess to meet her for dinner she explains that she's fasting because she has an operation the following day: now the same reason is used by Jess to explain why she's fasting.

Here we see that the same reason plays different roles: it is used by the nurse to tell Jess that she ought to fast (justifying role); it motivates Jess to fast; and it is used by Jess to explain her action to her friend; and we can think of it as justifying, motivating, or explanatory, etc., depending on the role played by that reason on which we choose to focus.

Finally, since the classification of reasons into different kinds is purely role-dependent, and since the role of motivating an agent to act and the role of explaining her action are different, there are no good grounds for thinking that we should regard motivating and explanatory reasons as being of the same kind. A reason is labelled as either 'motivating' or 'explanatory' on very different grounds. A reason is called a 'motivating reason' because it is something that motivates an agent, that is, it is what he took to make his ϕ-ing right and hence to speak in favour of his ϕ-ing, and which played a role in his deciding to ϕ.[2] On the other hand, a reason is called 'explanatory' because it explains why an agent ϕ-ed: it makes the agent's action intelligible.[3]

So a reason is a motivating or an explanatory reason on account of its playing quite different roles; a motivating reason is a reason in light of which an agent acts, and it can play the role of a premise in the agent's (implicit or explicit) reasoning about ϕ-ing, if there is such reasoning. An explanatory reason, by contrast, plays the role of (part of) the explanans in an explanation of the agent's ϕ-ing. Hence, the labels 'explanatory' and 'motivating', as applied to reasons, are not synonymous because each is applied to a reason on the grounds of its playing importantly different roles.

Moreover, given the difference between these roles, although it is true that sometimes one and the same reason can play both roles, it is not right to assume that, for any particular ϕ-ing, the two roles will always be played by the same reason. To be precise, a reason that plays a motivating role for a particular action can (arguably) always play an explanatory role for that action, but the converse does not hold.[4] So, the reason that motivated Mike to sell his car—that he needed cash—may also be the reason that explains why he did so. But, often, the reason that explains why someone ϕ-ed is not the reason that

---

[2] As with explanations, which reason is given prominence and presented as *the* agent's reason for ϕ-ing, or as *the* reason that motivated the agent to ϕ, is a matter of pragmatics: of what is required or appropriate in a given situation. Because of this, it seems right to regard all of the reasons that enter an agent's reasoning about whether to ϕ, even if they do so only implicitly, as reasons for which the agent ϕ-ed.

[3] Schueler (2003: 58) makes a similar point.

[4] I say 'arguably' because it has been claimed that if A is motivated by the fact that p, the corresponding explanatory reason is something like 'that *A believed* that p'. I examine this claim in Chapter 6.

motivated him to ϕ, i.e. the reason in the light of which he ϕ-ed. The reason that explains why Fred gave a lot of money to charities may be that he's a generous man; but that he's a generous man is not the reason that motivated Fred to give money to charities (it is not what he took to make his action of giving money right). And, a different kind of example, the reason that explains why Sarah bought a new mobile phone is that she thought hers had been stolen; but the reason that motivated her was not that *she thought* her phone had been stolen. And yet a different kind of case, the reason why Angie didn't go to the party may be that she forgot about it, but that she forgot is not a reason that motivated her not to go to the party. So in these cases, the reasons that explain why Fred, Sarah, and Angie ϕ-ed (gave money to charity, bought a new mobile phone, didn't go to the party respectively) are not the reasons that motivated them, and therefore they are not *motivating* reasons.[5]

In view of the above, I shall call a reason that there is for someone to do something a 'justifying reason'; a reason for which someone actually does something a 'motivating reason'; and a reason that explains why someone does something an 'explanatory reason'. Of course, as I have already said, one and the same reason can play all three roles: it can be the reason that there is for a person to ϕ, it can be the person's reason for ϕ-ing, and it can be the reason that explains her ϕ-ing (and indeed other things). For example, that there has been a drop in temperature can be a reason for me to bring my tulips in (justifying), it can be the reason for which Mrs B brought in her tulips (motivating), and it can also be the reason that explains why Mrs B brought in her tulips (explanatory) as well as the reason why, since I didn't bring them in, my tulips died (explanatory). So, in itself, the reason (that there has been a drop in temperature) is not any of these things (justifying, motivating, or explanatory) to the exclusion of the others. And this is also true of what are called moral reasons. Suppose that 'Lying is wrong' expresses a moral reason. Then, that lying is wrong is a reason for me not to tell a lie, and it may be the reason that motivates me to keep quiet, and also the reason that

[5] In Angie's case there was no motivating reason and she did not think there was. In Sarah's case the suggestion is that she thought there was a reason for her to act but there wasn't; while in Fred's case there was a reason but we have not been told what it was.

explains why people ought not to tell lies: again, the same reason plays different roles.

Thus, whether we call a reason 'justifying', 'motivating', or 'explanatory' depends on whether we invoke it to justify an action, whether it is a reason that motivates someone to act, or whether it is used to explain something. But this does not weaken the conceptual difference between the motivating and explanatory roles of reasons and hence between motivating and explanatory reasons.

So, contrary to what is widely held, there are no good grounds for grouping motivating and explanatory reasons together as if they were the same. Nonetheless, philosophers tend to assimilate motivating and explanatory reasons, and they do so on a variety of grounds, some of which I shall discuss in the remaining chapters. Here, I shall limit myself to one of those grounds, which concerns cases where one is motivated to ϕ by something that appears to one to be a reason for ϕ-ing but which in fact is not.

Mistakes in this respect can occur on (at least) two levels, corresponding to the fact that, when an agent takes something (for example, that the bus is late) to be a reason for her to ϕ (for example, to drive to work), she takes that thing both to be the case *and* to be a reason for her to ϕ, respectively. Consequently, an agent may be mistaken in taking that to be the case (because it isn't: the bus is not late); or she may be right in thinking that it is the case but wrong in thinking that that fact is a reason for her to ϕ (for example, because although the bus is late, driving will make her even later). Because of the possibility of mistakes of these kinds, a person may be motivated to ϕ by something that is either not a reason at all (because it is not the case), or by something that is a reason but not a reason *for her to ϕ*. For example, I may be motivated to demand money from someone by a false belief that he stole it from me: here I am motivated by something which is only an apparent reason, namely, the apparent fact that he stole it from me. Or I may be motivated to demand money by the fact that the person is parked illegally—but, if he is, that is a reason to motivate the parking authorities, not me, to fine him.

In these cases, we can explain the fact that the person acted as he did by saying that the reason why he acted so is that he mistakenly believed it to be the case that p, or that he mistakenly believed the fact that q to be a reason for him to ϕ. Since in some of these error cases what the agent takes to be a reason for ϕ-ing was not the case and yet his action can still be explained, it is tempting to think that whichever reason explains his action is also the reason that motivated him. And this in turn encourages the temptation to assimilate explanatory and motivating reasons. But the temptation ought to be resisted.

First, as I shall argue in Chapter 5, if someone is motivated to ϕ by the apparent fact that p (for example, by the apparent fact that James has stolen money from me) and this turns out not to be the case, then the apparent fact that p is merely an *apparent* reason and therefore not a genuine *reason*—in the same sense in which a mistaken solution to a problem is not a genuine solution, or in which fool's gold is not genuine gold. And since what motivated the agent is not a reason, it cannot be the reason that explains his action. Here what motivates, being something that is not the case, has no normative force; but, by the same token, neither does it have explanatory power. In such cases, the reason that explains why the agent acted is not what motivated him; rather it will be something such as that he (mistakenly) believed that p, which is indeed an explanatory reason. However, that explanatory reason is not the reason that motivated the agent, for the agent was not motivated by the consideration that he believed that p, but rather by the consideration that p, which he took to be true. Thus, the possibility of acting on a false belief does not justify the widespread tendency to assimilate motivating and explanatory reasons.

Second, when someone is motivated to ϕ for something that *is* a reason, but which is nonetheless not a good reason for him to ϕ, the reason for which he acted was a justifying reason, that is, it was a reason for someone to do something—nonetheless, it was not a justifying reason for *that person to do what he did*. So, suppose that Bill is motivated to kick his brother by the fact that his brother has borrowed his pencil case without asking. That his brother borrowed the pencil case is indeed a justifying reason but it is not a reason *for Bill to kick his brother* and hence it does not justify Bill's action. It is a reason for him to do something else: for example, for Bill to ask his brother not to do it again, or for someone else to do something else: for example, for his brother to apologize, etc. In this example, the reason that motivated Bill to kick his brother, that the latter had borrowed his pencil case, motivated Bill precisely because he took it to justify (from some perspective) his action of kicking his brother—although in fact it does not justify it.

Thus, when an agent acts for a reason, he takes that reason to justify his action: in his eyes, the action is made right or appropriate (though not necessarily morally so) by that reason. If the reason does not actually justify the action, we may still explain why the agent did it by saying that he thought it did—and here again the temptation might arise to think that the reason that explains is the reason that motivated, and so to conflate the two. But this would be mistaken.

Therefore, and to return to the classification of reasons, although the reason that motivates someone can be used to explain his action, there is still a conceptual difference between the role a reason plays in motivation, and the role it plays in explanation. And if we classify reasons according to the roles they play, there are, first, reasons that make ϕ-ing at least pro tanto right (i.e. what are called 'justifying' or 'normative' reasons); second, reasons that motivate someone to ϕ (which are called 'motivating reasons'); and third, reasons that explain why someone ϕ-s or ϕ-ed (i.e. explanatory reasons).[6] In the first two, the reason's playing that role depends on its capacity to have normative force (to be a reason for ϕ-ing) as discussed above. And although, as we saw, the same reason can play all three roles (justifying, motivating, and explanatory), the conceptual differences between them remain.

The claim that the differences between reasons are differences of role, rather than a difference in the reason's ontological character, flies in the face of the commonly held view that, while justifying reasons are perhaps facts, motivating and explanatory reasons must be mental states of the agent whose reasons they are. I shall next explore these issues concerning the ontology of reasons and the relation between that and the different roles that reasons can play.

---

[6] Audi distinguishes five types of reasons, three of which might seem to correspond to mine (2001: 119). However, there are very substantial differences between Audi's and my conception of reasons in general and also of what reasons of each of the relevant kinds are. For instance, Audi thinks that justifying reasons are propositions, though when 'possessed' by someone they are (or 'are expressed by') psychological states; explanatory reasons are, he says, facts, 'explaining' facts; and motivating reasons are 'explanatory, possessed' and have 'minimal prima facie justifying power' (2001: 119–20).

2.2. Ontology: Reasons, Facts, Truths

When we turn to the question of what ontological category (or categories) reasons belong in, the first striking point is that things of many different kinds are said to be reasons. For example, facts, propositions, goals, events, things, states of things (including states of minds), features or aspects of the world, considerations (moral, aesthetic, legal, etc.), states of affairs, absences, are all said to be reasons. So it seems that, despite the familiarity of the concept, reasons, whether inside philosophy or out of it, are not clearly assigned to any particular ontological category.

One way of approaching the question of the ontology of reasons is to examine the forms in which reasons are given. And it turns out that, just as many different things are said to be reasons, reasons are given in a variety of forms, although it is possible to group the various forms into three main kinds. First, there are reasons which are given in propositional form, either as what follows the 'that' in a 'that'-clause: 'The reason for the famine was that there was a drought', where the reason is 'there was a drought', or as what follows the 'because' in 'because'-statements: 'They fought because their grandfather's will was rather unclear', 'She fainted because the atmosphere was suffocating'. And second, reasons which are given by nominal expressions: 'The reason for the famine was the drought'. There is a third main form in which reasons are given, namely, using the infinitive form, such as 'Mao's reason for ordering the purge was to undermine potential rivals', 'Her reason for being helpful is to make herself indispensable', 'The cat jumped in order to reach the top shelf'.[7] These expressions denote purposes or goals, and I postpone discussion of whether these should be thought of as reasons to Chapter 4.[8]

When reasons are given as nominal expressions, the relevant expression may be a noun: 'The reason for the family feud was the inheritance'; or a gerundial nominal phrase: 'The reason for the party was her unexpectedly winning the tournament'. And these expressions may name an object (concrete or abstract), an event, an aspect or

[7] See Audi (1993: 15–16).
[8] In any case, I don't mean to imply that the list given above exhausts the possible ways of giving reasons; but they cover the ones that are of concern to us.

property of a thing or of an event, an action, an absence or lack, the non-occurrence of an event, etc.: 'The reason for the accident was a hole in the road', 'The reason for the cancellation of the lecture was her failure to turn up'. And so on.

A reason given by means of a nominal expression can be paraphrased, and sometimes specified more fully, by giving it in propositional form, either as the proposition following the expression 'the reason is that' or following the connective 'because', or similar. For instance, 'The reason for the accident was a puncture' (nominal expression) can be paraphrased as 'The reason for the accident was that we had a sudden puncture while driving at high speed', or 'We had an accident because we had a sudden puncture at high speed'. 'The reason for the family feud was the unfair will' (nominal expression) can be paraphrased as 'The reason for the family feud was that the will was unfair' or 'There was a family feud because the will was unfair'. (But, even when the paraphrase specifies the reason more fully, it seems always possible to paraphrase back into the nominal mode: 'The reason for the accident was an unexpected puncture at high speed', or 'The reason for the family feud was the unfairness in the division of the inheritance', etc.).

It is thus tempting to think that, since statements providing reasons can always be paraphrased into statements where reasons are expressed propositionally, we should conclude that that is the most perspicuous way of expressing reasons. And, on Strawson's view that facts are 'what statements (when true) state' (1950: 196), one may be inclined to go a step further and conclude that all reasons are true propositions and hence facts.[9]

However, the possibility of paraphrase is notoriously misleading in philosophy. For, if 'p' can be paraphrased by 'q', then 'q' can be paraphrased by 'p'. So, in any case where paraphrase is possible, we need some independent grounds for deciding which, if either, of the statements in question captures the more basic concept, or reveals a perhaps more fundamental feature of whatever is under discussion.

---

[9] This depends on the, in my view correct, assumption that both 'the reason is that—' and '—because—' are 'factive'; i.e. that they are true only if their constituent statements (i.e. the propositions they express) are true.

A better reason for arguing that the most perspicuous way of expressing reasons is propositionally is that reasons must be capable of being premises, i.e. things we reason, or draw conclusions, from, whether in theoretical or in practical reasoning. Otherwise, the connection between reasons and reasoning would be lost. If this is right, then reasons must be propositional in form. And then it seems that we can conclude that reasons are propositions, and hence facts.

The conclusion that reasons are facts may seem still unwarranted because, for all I've said in the previous paragraph, since it is possible to reason from false premises, reasons could be propositional in form and yet not be facts, or at any rate not all be facts: some reasons may be true premises and others may be false; or some reasons may be what is the case and others may be what is not the case. I shall discuss this point in more detail in Section 5.3.1; but the fact that one may reason from false premises, and indeed be motivated to act or believe things on the basis of false beliefs, does not show that, to paraphrase Strawson, what a statement, when false, states, may be a reason. All it shows is that such things can be mistaken for truths or facts, and hence for reasons.

Another type of worry with the claim that reasons are facts or true propositions concerns the precise relation between them: are all facts reasons? If not, what makes a fact into a reason? My view is that all facts are indeed reasons merely by virtue of being potential premises in (theoretical or practical) reasoning. It may be objected that it is at least odd to say that a fact that nobody has ever explicitly or implicitly reasoned from *is* a reason. But the oddness is only apparent. For surely, if it is a fact that carbon emissions contribute to global warming, then that fact can be a premise in an argument—for instance, an argument whose conclusion is that we ought to reduce our carbon emissions. Thus the fact about carbon emissions is a reason, as it can be a premise in reasoning; and it was a reason before anyone knew anything about carbon emissions since even then it could be a premise in reasoning—though to be sure, for the fact that carbon emissions contribute to global warming to *actually* be a premise in someone's reasoning, the person needs to be aware of the fact. (To say that facts that no one has ever thought about are reasons is analogous to saying that propositions that no one has ever believed are beliefs—but there is nothing untoward in talking about a belief that nobody has ever held.)[10]

Other perceived (difficulties) with the view that I am proposing involve the idea that propositions, and hence reasons, are more finely individuated than facts. But this view depends on the assumption that, say, the fact that Hesperus is a planet is the same fact as the fact that Phosphorus is a planet, while the corresponding propositions are different. Or that the proposition expressed by 'I'm meeting *Jim* on Tuesday' and that expressed by 'I'm meeting Jim on *Tuesday*' are different, whereas there is only one fact here: only one fact is needed to make both true, so to speak. (But) these are assumptions that someone who endorses the conception of facts I am advocating will simply reject. For instance, it could be argued that the proposition that 'I'm meeting *Jim* on Tuesday' can be used to express is true if it is a fact that, on Tuesday, I am meeting Jim and not someone else; while that which 'I'm meeting Jim on *Tuesday*' can be used to express is true if it is a fact that I am meeting Jim on Tuesday and not on some other day. And I see no reason to accept that these are the same fact.

One might feel reluctant to accept the view that reasons are facts if one has an austere or restrictive conception of facts. Some philosophers, for instance, feel that a sober ontology cannot contain negative facts.[11] Others have questioned whether there are moral or aesthetic facts. And again, facts are sometimes contrasted with values—or statements of fact with statements of value—and with logical, conceptual, or mathematical truths. And statements of facts are also contrasted with statements of possibility.

On the other hand, it is clear that, for instance, that something is vulgar, that I enjoy it very much, that it would be selfish, that it may rain, that nothing can be red and green all over, that he hasn't arrived, that I don't have any money, that there isn't enough oxygen, that

---

[10] A different question is whether facts are timeless or whether they come into existence. → This is a matter of stipulation This is not something I need decide here for my claim is simply that, *if* something is a fact, then it is a reason; or to put the point differently, if it is a fact that carbon emissions contribute to global warming, then that fact is a reason.

[11] Thus Russell wrote: 'there is implanted in the human breast an almost unquenchable desire to find some way of avoiding the admission that negative facts are as ultimate as those that are positive' (1956: 287).

it's a very unkind thing to do, that he is unlikely to help, can all be reasons for ϕ-ing (or not ϕ-ing) and reasons why someone ϕ-ed. And yet, these statements express negative truths, value judgements, moral views, conceptual truths, possibilities, etc.—which, according to the kind of austere conception of facts mentioned, implies that they could not be classified as facts.

I take it that there is no problem with the thought that things such as 'I enjoy it very much' or 'nothing can be red and green all over' can be reasons; and I take it that there is no problem with the thought that 'there isn't enough oxygen' or 'that is very unkind' can be reasons. Similarly, and despite the issues mentioned above, I take it that what might be called 'the minimalist conception' of facts endorsed by Strawson and mentioned above according to which a fact is a true proposition, is a viable conception of facts. Thus, if it is true that Madrid is closer to Paris than Moscow, then it is a fact that Madrid is closer to Paris than Moscow. And if it is true that it is wicked to cause unnecessary pain, then it is a fact that it is wicked to cause unnecessary pain, etc.

If so, and on this minimalist conception of facts, then those things mentioned above can be regarded as facts, and hence there seems to be no objection to the view that reasons are facts.

I say that there seems to be no objection to the view that reasons are facts. Nonetheless, some have denied that they are, or at least denied that all reasons are facts. This is denied by some who believe that there are different kinds of reason and hold that reasons of different kinds belong to different ontological categories, and in particular that our reasons for acting are mental states.

2.2.1. *Reasons and mental states*

One important motivation for the thought that different reasons belong to different ontological categories is connected to the popular view that some reasons are mental states of agents. Many philosophers argue that the reasons for which we act, and indeed the reasons that explain our actions—what I have called 'motivating' and 'explanatory reasons' respectively—are desires and beliefs, which they in turn conceive of as mental states. So they think that different reasons are ontologically different. They argue that, while all justifying reasons are, or may be, facts (if only in the minimal sense outlined in the previous section), motivating or explanatory reasons are not: they are mental states. Again, I shall have more to say about this claim in the coming chapters: here I shall only briefly outline some of the grounds for questioning it.

First, not all reasons that explain why someone ϕ-ed, even when ϕ-ing is an action, make reference to the agent's believing or wanting something (or to his hoping, suspecting, etc.). There are many different possible explanations of why someone ϕ-ed (such as that his mother asked him to do it, that he forgot, that he is in the habit of doing so, etc.) that do not make reference to the agent's wanting or believing anything.

Second, the claim that the reasons that motivate or explain some-one's ϕ-ing are his beliefs and desires is ambiguous. There is an act/object ambiguity in the term 'belief', for this term can be used to refer to my believing something, or to what I believe (what is often called 'the content' of a belief).[12] If 'a belief' is given the second use (i.e. to refer to what is believed), then to say that reasons are beliefs is not to say that they are mental states, because, even if believing that p is a mental state, what is believed (that p) is not itself a mental state. (And the same is true of the term 'desire', which may refer to what I desire: money, to save the world, an ice cream; or to my desiring it. I'll have much more to say about this issue in following chapters.) So reasons might be beliefs and desires and yet not be 'believings' and 'desirings' and therefore not mental states.

Thus, though popular, the doctrine that some reasons are mental states is not obviously true and it is therefore not clear that it gives us grounds for accepting the view that different reasons belong to different ontological categories.

In fact, I think we have reason to reject that conclusion. For, as we saw above, one and the same reason can play different roles. And this makes the suggestion that different reasons belong to different ontological categories implausible. In other words, it is implausible

---

[12] Perhaps it is not quite right to say that this is an act/object ambiguity, since believing something is not an act or occurrence—though coming to believe is. Nonetheless, the contrast intended, between believing and what is believed, is clear enough and so, for the sake of simplicity, I shall continue to refer to it as an 'act/object' ambiguity.

to suggest that if the fact that there has been a drop in temperature can be a reason to believe that my tulips will die (justifying), can be Mrs B's reason for bringing in her tulips (a motivating reason), and also the reason why my tulips died and why Mrs B brought her tulips in (explanatory), the ontological character of that reason changes depending on which of these roles we focus on.

This response may not satisfy those who are committed to the view that at least motivating and explanatory reasons must be mental states and hence ontologically different from justifying reasons (which they may be prepared to regard as facts). And they may say that, if the argument in the previous paragraphs appears to succeed, this is because I have misidentified the relevant motivating and explanatory reasons in my examples. For, they may say, the reason that motivated Mrs B to bring in her tulips cannot be just that there was a drop in temperature but rather it must be *her believing* that there had been, and that is also what explains her action of bringing in her tulips. And her believing that *is* a mental state. And this, the objection concludes, shows that motivating and explanatory reasons are mental states. But this argument fails.

First, the view that motivating reasons are mental states depends on the view that what motivates agents to act is their believing and wanting certain things. But this view has been disputed, and in the following chapters I shall argue that it is mistaken.

Moreover, the fact that there was a drop in temperature is a reason that explains why my tulips died—and that is surely an explanatory reason that is not a mental state, which implies that not all explanatory reasons are mental states. And it won't do here to say, as one might be tempted to, that since the death of my tulips is not an action, the fact that there has been a drop in temperature is not a reason but a *cause*. As I explained in Chapter 1, this would be to conflate two levels of relationship: that of causation and that of explanation. So, suppose that the drop in temperature caused the death of my tulips, then, *the fact* that there was a drop in temperature (causally) explains the fact that my tulips died, and therefore the fact that there was a drop in temperature is an explanatory reason.

It may be objected that that is true of the explanation of 'mere' events but that actions can only be explained by reasons such as that A believes that p, and these are not facts but are rather mental states.

As I shall argue in Chapter 6, I do not think that it is true that actions can only be explained by reasons of that kind, for it is possible to explain actions by citing the reason that motivated an agent, which might be simply that the temperature has dropped, or that her sister is ill. Nevertheless, it is true that sometimes we explain actions by saying things of the kind 'A ϕ-ed because A believed that p', or 'A ϕ-ed because A wanted to ψ'. And this means that 'A believed that p' or 'A wanted to ψ' are explanatory reasons. However, that A believed that p, or that A wanted to ψ are facts, we might say 'psychological' facts, and not mental states.

But my opponents will say that I am mischaracterizing what they claim is an explanatory reason here, which is not (the fact) that I believe that p, but rather *my believing* that p. And, they will add, my believing that p *is* a mental state, so some reasons are mental states.

But, in fact, the claim that my believing that p is a mental state needs careful scrutiny. The expression 'my believing that p' is a nominalization of the sentence 'I believe that p'. Some people think that the nominalized form can be used to refer to an entity (perhaps a 'trope'), which is a mental state of mine.[13] But even if there are such mental entities and even if these nominalizations *can* be used to refer to them, these nominalizations have other uses. For instance, they can also be used to refer to facts, as in 'The fact of his leaving so early was rather disconcerting'.[14] Thus, the expression 'my believing that she is ill' can be used to refer to the fact that I believe that she is ill. Consider what Strawson says about the expressions we use to refer to events and facts respectively:

We use nominal constructions of the same general kinds—nouns derived from other parts of speech, noun clauses, gerundial constructions—to refer both to terms of the natural and to terms of the non-natural relation [i.e. to events as the terms of the natural relation (causation), and facts as the terms of the non-natural relation (explanation) respectively].   (1987: 110)

And he goes on to say that in the sentence 'His death's coming when it did was responsible for the breakdown of the negotiations', the

---

[13] For a discussion of these issues see Lowe (2000: esp. chs. 10–11). For arguments that we ought to be cautious about the claim that 'my believing that p' denotes a (mental) state, see Steward (1997).

[14] I use 'refer to' here as used in 'I am referring to the fact that she left you', without commitment to the view that there is some *thing* that these expressions refer to.

expression 'his death's coming when it did' does not refer to an event in nature, i.e. to his death. Rather, it refers to *the fact* that his death came when it did. For, as Strawson says, his death's coming when it did, unlike his death, 'did not come at any time. It is not an event in nature. It is *the fact* that a certain event occurred in nature at a certain time' (ibid).

So, even if a particular nominal expression can be used to refer to an event (or, according to the objector, to a mental state) it can also be used to refer to a fact. And, in 'Her believing that p explains her ϕ-ing', the nominalization 'her believing that p' refers, not to a mental state, but to the fact that she believes that p. And, more generally, when we say that the reason that motivated an agent and that explains her action is her believing that p, this gerundial construction is a nominalization that must be construed as referring to *the fact* that she believes that p.

To see why, consider the following example. Suppose that I believe (falsely, and as a result of my suffering from paranoid delusions) that I am being followed by MI5. My believing that I am being followed by MI5 may explain why I go about incognito, so we can think of it as an explanatory reason.[15] And so, according to my opponents, my believing that is a mental state.

However, since I am not being followed, my believing that I am being followed is actually also a reason for me to visit a psychiatrist. And this is a justifying reason: it is a reason *for* me to visit the psychiatrist, i.e. a reason invoked for its normative force about what I ought to do. But if it is a justifying reason, then it must be a fact, and not a mental state, because it is wholly implausible to say that mental states have normative force—i.e. that they make it the case that anyone ought to ϕ, or make ϕ-ing right or appropriate: my being in a mental state, for instance, my believing that I am being followed by MI5, may have normative force, but the mental state I am supposed to be in itself cannot. So the justifying reason is, then, the fact that I believe that I am being followed by MI5.

However, as we just saw, my believing that I am being followed is also a reason that explains why I go about incognito. And it is also

---

[15] See Raz (1999a), Dancy (2000: 125) and esp. Hyman (1999: 444), from whom I have borrowed and adapted the example. I discuss this kind of case further in Chapters 5 and 6.

implausible to say that a reason changes ontology depending on the role it plays. Thus, if my believing that I am being followed is a fact when it plays a justifying role, it must also be a fact when it plays the role of explaining why I go about incognito.[16] And if that is right, then the explanatory and the justifying reasons here belong to the same ontological category, namely that of facts—and the expression 'My believing that p' in an explanation 'My believing that p explains why I ϕ' refers to a reason: to the fact that I believe that p.

So it is true that sometimes we explain actions by citing psychological facts about an agent: that they believe that p, that they are shy, etc. But what this suggests is that, in so far as it makes sense to say that a reason is a mental state, what this means is not that this reason belongs in a particular ontological category (for example, that of 'psychological entities', whether events or states), but rather that this is a reason that concerns a mental state of the agent: a fact about how things are, psychologically speaking, with him. And we can call these 'mental' or 'psychological' reasons. But then, all sorts of facts can be reasons, that is, facts about all sorts of things can be reasons. Some reasons concern the fact that the person believed and wanted certain things while others concern the fact that they are blonde, rich, or diabetic. We can call these psychological, physical, financial, and medical or physiological reasons respectively, but in doing so, we are not allocating each of those reasons to different ontological categories.

The idea that reasons are mental states seems, then, encouraged by a confusion concerning the use of imperfect nominal expressions such as 'his believing that p'. This is how the confusion arises. Explanations of an agent's ϕ-ing often cite the fact that the agent believed that p: 'He abandoned the game because he believed that she had cheated'; or 'The fact that he believed that she had cheated explains why he abandoned the game'. Such explanations can be given in a variant form involving the corresponding gerundial nominal: 'His believing that she had cheated explains why he left the game'. Here, this gerundial nominal clearly refers to the corresponding fact that he believed that

---

[16] This is not to say that the reason that motivates me to go about incognito is also that I believe that I am being followed. If asked what my reason was, I'd say that it was that I was being followed by MI5. See Chapter 5 for further discussion of this point.

she had cheated. However since, according to some, this nominal can also be used to refer to an entity (a mental state), it is easy to reach the conclusion that these explanatory reasons are mental states. But, to repeat, the grounds for saying that 'his believing that p' is an explanatory reason are also grounds for saying that this expression here refers to a fact and not to a mental state.

As I say, the idea that reasons are mental states is encouraged by this confusion. But it is motivated by something different, namely, a commitment to the doctrine, made popular by Davidson among others, that the reasons for which we act are the causes or, at any rate, the causal conditions of our actions. For, on the most prevalent views of causation, if reasons are to be causes or, causal conditions, of actions, they must be mental events or states and not facts or true propositions. This doctrine is widely, though not universally, accepted in contemporary philosophy.[17] But, in the absence of commitment to the doctrine, and given what we have seen about the different roles that the same reason can play, there seem to be no grounds for accepting the view that some reasons are mental states.[18]

2.2.2. *Motivation in error cases*

I now turn to the second route that might lead one to the conclusion that reasons belong to different ontological categories, a route that is related to the first type of error case discussed in the introduction to this chapter.

The thought is the following. Sometimes an agent can be motivated to act by something that is not the case (which would be captured in a false proposition).[19] But, the thought goes, what motivates someone

---

[17] Apart from the Wittgenstein-inspired anti-causalists that Davidson took himself to be arguing against (Anscombe, Kenny, Taylor, etc.) there are some contemporary non-causalists, see e.g. Bittner (2001); Ginet (1993); Haldane (1994); Hutto (1999); Rundle (1997); Schueler (2003); Sehon (1994, 1997, and 2000); Stoutland (1998); Tanney (1995); Wilson (1989). See also Alvarez (2007).

[18] It should be noted that the commitment to a causal picture is compatible with the acceptance of the view that reasons are not mental states. Stout, for example, holds that reasons, which he takes to be facts, are causes (see Stout 1996). Others have argued that reasons may cause actions, not directly, but in some indirect way. For instance, Crane and Mellor (1990) talk about mental entities that may be 'causal surrogates' for our reasons.

[19] And this in turn might lead one to think that the statement 'His reason for ϕ-ing was that p' is 'non-factive', i.e. that the statement may be true while p is false (Dancy, for

to act is a motivating reason. Therefore some motivating reasons are something that is not the case and are, therefore, not facts. Thus, the conclusion would go, although all justifying reasons are facts, some motivating reasons are not, and therefore not all reasons belong to the same ontological category.

Now, it is true that what motivates someone to ϕ, whether ϕ-ing is acting, believing, deciding, wanting, etc., may be something that is not the case—something that is in fact false, for example, that it is raining when it isn't. But this does not license the conclusion that some motivating reasons are not facts. As I said above (and will explain in more detail in Chapter 5), a motivating reason can be characterized as something in the light of which one acts. But it does not follow that *anything* in the light of which one acts is a motivating *reason*. Sometimes people are motivated to act by something that is only an apparent fact, and hence only an apparent reason. Therefore, the fact that people act motivated by apparent reasons, or endorse beliefs on the basis of grounds that turn out to be false, does not show that some reasons are not facts, because these motivating considerations are not reasons. And hence it does not support the view that there is ontological variety among different kinds of reason.

So we have seen that neither of the routes examined leads to the conclusion that reasons belong to different ontological categories. Rather, it seems that all reasons are facts, in the minimal sense outlined above.

Conclusion

In this chapter, I have argued that classification of reasons into kinds is role-dependent, and have distinguished three main roles that reasons can play: a justifying, a motivational, and an explanatory role. I have claimed that reasons can consequently be classified as justifying, motivating, and explanatory, depending on what role they play in a particular context.

example, says some things about reason explanations that appear to commit him to this view, see 2000: 131–7 and 146–7, and my Section 6.2.3 for a discussion of Dancy's view).

I have also argued that, since this classification is role-dependent, and since one and the same reason can play all of these roles in relation to a particular action, the classification of reasons into those three kinds does not correspond to any ontological difference between them. Finally, I have examined and rejected two routes that seem to lead to the conclusion that different reasons belong to different ontological categories. In the next chapter I begin to explore the role of reasons in motivating action.

3

Motivation and Desires

Introduction

The aim of this and the following two chapters is to offer an account of the concept of motivation in action, and of the relation between motivation, motivating reasons, and desires. In this chapter, I start with a brief exploration of these concepts and then move on to a detailed examination of desires.

My discussion of desires in this chapter focuses on two important distinctions concerning desires, which I explore in Sections 3.3 and 3.4. The first is the distinction between rational and non-rational desires. The second concerns the act/object ambiguity of the term 'desire', mentioned in Section 2.2.1: viz., the fact that this term is sometimes used to refer to my desiring something and sometimes to what I desire. The discussion of these issues prepares the ground for the question at the heart of the following chapter, namely the relation between desires and motivating reasons.

3.1. The Concept of Motivation

In philosophical discussions of action, the concept of motivation is often associated with that of a motivating reason. However, although both the terms 'motivation' and 'motivating reason' are widely used in those discussions, neither their meanings, nor the relation between them tends to be made explicit.[1] On the one hand, the meaning of the term 'motivation', as used in philosophical discussion, is fairly

---

[1] A recent attempt to clarify the notion of motivation can be found in Mele (2003). For an older attempt see Peters (1958).

closely connected to its meaning outside of philosophy, although there are differences I shall come to shortly. On the other hand, the term 'motivating reason' does not have much currency outside of philosophy and can rightly be regarded as a term of art.

The philosophical notion of motivation shares with the ordinary notion the connection with the idea of being moved or led to act, but the philosophical notion is more capacious. The etymology of 'motive', and of the related 'motivation', originates in the Latin verb *movere*, meaning 'to move', and its related particles, for instance *motivus* (and, post-classical Latin, *motivum*). In ordinary speech, the idea of 'being motivated' tends to be associated either with the concept of a motive—so people are said to be motivated by greed or jealousy, which are motives; or with a particular kind of attitude of enthusiasm or drive in situations that require effort or sustained determination. In this sense, people are said to be very motivated in their jobs, or motivated to win an Olympic medal. In philosophy, by contrast, the notions of motivation and of being motivated are applied more widely to include any context where someone is inclined to act, or where they do act, intentionally or voluntarily, regardless of whether the relevant action involves effort and determination or not. In this sense, one can be motivated to walk to the kitchen, to go to a party, to wave at someone, etc. And, in this sense, one might be motivated to act and yet not act.

Although the concept of 'being motivated to' is applied more widely in philosophy than in ordinary use, even in philosophy its application tends to be restricted to human agency: as we saw in Chapter 1, philosophers talk about 'motivating reasons' to refer to a person's reason for acting but not (or not typically) to refer to a person's reason for believing and wanting things. Whether this restriction in philosophical usage is rooted in any significant difference between believing and wanting, on the one hand, and acting, on the other, is not clear. The restriction may be no more than a terminological quirk for, after all, talking about being motivated to believe or want things is perhaps no more of a philosophical turn of phrase than talking about being motivated to act—at any rate when the latter is as widely used as it is in the current philosophical literature. Besides, a person's reason for wanting something, for instance for wanting to do some thing, may very well be also his reason for doing that thing. For instance, Brian's reason for wanting to watch TV—say, that he finds it relaxing—may also be his reason for actually watching TV. And the same is true of reasons for believing. For instance, Amy's reason for believing that her boss is angry, say that he has shut his door, may be the reason that leads Amy to do something, say, to open the window; and this is a reason which philosophers tend to refer to as Amy's 'motivating reason' for opening the window.

Be that as it may, since my focus in this book is the relation between reasons and action, I shall confine my investigation here to the concept of motivation as it applies in contexts of action.

In this philosophical sense, someone who is motivated to perform an action is *inclined* to perform it, though not necessarily *habitually* inclined: motivation is often episodic.

Although being motivated and hence inclined to do something often involves wanting to do it, this need not be so. For someone may be inclined to perform an action without wanting to perform that action, not even in the sense of 'wanting' which might be called a 'thin' sense and which includes anything that is willed, and not just what one feels like doing, or has a liking or preference for. This thin sense of 'want' is the sense in which most of us might sometimes be said to 'want' to go to the dentist, or to have an injection, etc., even when what is so wanted is not remotely appealing and may even be repugnant. There is another common sense of 'wanting', associated with preference and likes, and contrasted with, for example, duty or requirement.[2] In that sense, we do not always want to do the things we do, but we do those things because we (think we) must, or because (we think) they are a necessary means of achieving some other end that we want in the fuller sense.

And, to return to the connection between being inclined and wanting, it is possible to be inclined to act without wanting to act, even in the thin sense. For instance, someone who has a habit or tendency he is not aware of, or has an urge to do something which he repudiates, might be inclined to do those things but have no corresponding want. But more often, the things we are motivated to do are things that we want to do, at least in the thin sense outlined above; and in my discussion here I shall focus on the more common

---

[2] Schueler (2003: ch. 2) calls desires of this second kind 'proper desires'.

case where having an inclination to act implies some degree or sense of wanting.

Some things one is motivated and wants to do, one wants to do because of a reason one takes oneself to have to so act.[3] When this is so, the motivation to act arises from some perceived good or value in the prospective action. Being motivated to do something for a reason is being inclined to do that thing for a reason one (believes one) has; a reason that makes the relevant action worth doing in one's eyes. Another way of putting this point is to say that being motivated to do something for a reason is wanting (at least in the thin sense) to do that thing for a reason; that is, being inclined to do that thing on account of a reason one takes oneself to have for doing it.

So there seems to be a close connection between taking oneself to have a reason to ϕ and being motivated and wanting to ϕ. But how close is this connection? Is it so close that, if one takes oneself to have a reason to ϕ, then one is, thereby, motivated to ϕ? At first blush, the answer seems to be 'No', since it seems surely possible to take oneself to have a reason for doing something and yet not be motivated to do it, that is, have no inclination to do it. For example, I may take myself to have a reason to exercise or to get on with some chore but have no motivation to do so. Indeed, this is precisely what *akrasia* typically seems to involve.

Whether this is right would require a proper analysis of the nature of *akrasia* and related phenomena (for instance listlessness) and such an analysis is beyond the confines of the issues at hand. However, I should say something about this.

First, a terminological clarification. One can take oneself to have *a* reason to ϕ but not be motivated to ϕ *all things considered* because one takes oneself to have a better reason not to ϕ. But when I say that there is a close link between taking oneself to have a reason to ϕ and being motivated to ϕ I mean that if one takes oneself to have a

---

[3] Note that my discussion here is concerned with the relation between being motivated and *taking* oneself to have a reason to do something. I said in Chapter 1 that I take the expressions 'X has reason to ϕ' and 'There is a reason for X to ϕ' to be equivalent. But I don't take the former to be equivalent to, or to be implied by, the expression 'X takes herself to have a reason to ϕ'. While, in my view, a person has no special authority on whether she has a reason to ϕ, what she says does have special (though still corrigible) status concerning whether she *takes* herself to have a reason to ϕ, and on *what* reason she takes herself to have.

reason to ϕ, then one is, at least, pro tanto, motivated to ϕ, though one may take the reason to be defeated by reasons against ϕ-ing. For the sake of simplicity, my discussion in the next few paragraphs will concern someone who takes himself to have an 'all things considered' reason to ϕ. With this clarification, let me return to the question whether there is the kind of close link I have suggested between the two concepts we are examining: taking oneself to have a reason to ϕ and being motivated to ϕ.

Consider someone who takes herself to have reason to ϕ but who nonetheless does not ϕ, even though she is not prevented from ϕ-ing by any external force. Does it follow that the agent is not motivated, does not want to, or has no inclination to ϕ?

Different kinds of cases are possible here. On the one hand, there is the kind of case where the agent thinks that she has reason to ϕ and does decide to ϕ, or forms the intention to do so—and yet, when it comes to it, she does not ϕ. On the other hand, there is the kind of case where, though the agent takes herself to have reason to ϕ, the agent does not decide to ϕ nor has any intention of ϕ-ing. Some cases of inveterate smokers are surely such: the smoker sees that health, financial, and social considerations, etc., speak in favour of her giving up but she does not form the intention to give up. And though sometimes such a smoker may think that she has better reason to smoke than to give up (for instance, think that the pleasure of it outweighs all other considerations), there are cases where a smoker thinks that, overall, her reasons favour giving up—and yet she does not even form the intention to try to give up. It is tempting here to think that such an agent *must* take herself to have better reason not to ϕ; in our example, not to give up, for instance, that she takes the pleasure of smoking to outweigh the benefits of health. But while some smokers may indeed reason thus, this need not be so. For it is possible that an agent should not take herself to have any *reason* for smoking and take herself to have every reason to give up and yet have no desire or intention to do so. Of course, such an agent is likely to find some pleasure in smoking (though even this might be outweighed by the unpleasantness of the side effects and consequences). But she may not even regard that pleasure as a reason *for* smoking (though no doubt the pleasure will contribute to explain why she smokes).

So we seem to have at least two kinds of case where an agent takes herself to have reason to do something, or to stop doing something, but where she is not motivated to do it. And this seems to show that the link between taking oneself to have reason to ϕ and being motivated to ϕ is much looser than I suggested above. But is that right?

First, the fact that an agent who takes herself to have reason to ϕ does not ϕ does not imply that the agent has *no* motivation to ϕ. In the kinds of case discussed, it needn't be true that the agent doesn't *want*—at least in the sense outlined above—to ϕ; what is true is that she does not *feel* like ϕ-ing: but feeling like doing something is not necessary for being motivated to do it. And what is often true is that the agent *is* motivated—only she's not sufficiently motivated. Indeed this seems to capture what is so striking about weakness of will: the motivation that the agent has, such as it is, is not translated into action, sometimes not even into decisions or intentions, even though reason and the will still point in that direction, and there is no external coercion.

Moreover, it is worth remembering that, as the gap between what an agent claims to take herself to have a reason to do, and what she's motivated (however minimally) to do widens, then, at least in many cases, the agent's claim that she *takes* herself to have a reason to ϕ will come under threat—sometimes to the point of being wholly undermined, precisely because of the connection between taking oneself to have a reason to ϕ and being motivated to do it. The more appropriate description of that situation may be that the agent is aware that *others* take her to have a reason to ϕ, and that she can see why they do; but this may fall short of *her taking herself* to have such a reason.

But though many cases may fall within the descriptions given in the above paragraphs, and hence preserve the link between reason and motivation, it would be absurd to deny that there are hard cases, where an agent's reason points in one direction but where the will does not follow, that is, where motivation and desire, in any form, fail to materialize. And these cases seem to undermine the view that there is a close connection between taking oneself to have a reason to ϕ and being motivated to ϕ. In my opinion, however, these hard cases do not undermine the view that there is a very close connection—first, because what these cases show is that the connection, though very close, is not a 'logical' connection, and that it must be acknowledged to be loose enough to allow for these hard cases; and second, precisely because these are 'hard cases', often cases in the borderline between normality and pathology.

It seems, then, that the notion of having a reason to act—or more precisely, of taking oneself, rightly or wrongly, to have a reason to act—*is* closely connected to the notion of being motivated to act: someone who takes herself to have a reason to do something is, therefore, typically motivated to do it. (I may, of course, regard myself as having more than one reason to do something and be therefore motivated by more than one reason; but that need not detain us here.) And the question arises: 'What, then, are these reasons that motivate us to act'? Before attempting to answer this question, though, I need to say something about what I take it to mean.

So far, and indeed in the discussion that follows, the question has been: 'What motivates us to act?', asked with a view to finding an answer to the related question: 'What kind of thing are our reasons for acting?' But, as I said above, in ordinary usage the concept of motivation is associated with that of a motive, and so the intuitive response to the question 'What motivates us to act?', would seem to be, precisely, 'Our motives!': we are motivated to act by prudence, greed, self-interest, pity, and other motives. This is clearly right but it is not, however, inconsistent with the idea that we are also motivated by reasons.

A motive, I shall argue, is different from a reason, even though the two are conceptually connected, and even though motives are sometimes called 'reasons'—for instance, we often say that A's reason for killing B was revenge or compassion, which are motives, and conversely we sometimes refer to reasons as 'motives'. This usage, however, does not show that there is no conceptual difference between reasons and motives; rather, I think what this usage shows is that these concepts are closely related to each other, a relation that I shall seek to elucidate below. So, although motives are not strictly speaking reasons, the concept of acting out of a motive is closely connected to that of acting for a reason. And, because of this close connection, both motives and reasons can be said to motivate.

However, motives and reasons motivate in different ways. I shall say something about motives here, before returning to the question of motivating reasons. However, it is only when we have answered the question about what motivating reasons are, which will have been done by the end of Chapter 5, that we shall be in a position to understand fully how motives and reasons motivate and, hence, explain actions.

3.1.1. *Motives and motivation*

The concept of motive is, I think, complex and I do not propose to provide a detailed account of it here but only to say as much as necessary to proceed with our question about motivating reasons.[4]

In *The Concept of Mind*, Ryle famously characterizes motives as dispositions whose logic, he says, is captured by law-like generalisations: so if we say that a man boasted from vanity, Ryle suggests this should construed as:

He boasted . . . and his doing so satisfies the law-like proposition that whenever he finds a chance of securing the admiration and envy of others, he does whatever he thinks will produce the admiration and envy of others. (1949: 89)

Anscombe (1957: 21) argues that Ryle's account cannot be right because, she says, it implies that it is not possible to act out of a motive only once, which is clearly false. A person can act out of vanity once without being a vain person, that is, a person disposed to act out of vanity. And one can be motivated by greed now and then without being a greedy person, that is, a person disposed to be motivated by greed.

But perhaps there is another way of interpreting Ryle's remark so that his claim is not that one cannot act out of vanity only once. Perhaps Ryle's point is that vanity is a character trait that involves a tendency to act in ways that fall under the kind of law-like proposition he states, even if it is not the case that one cannot act once out of such a motive (see Wilkins 1963).

---

[4] In *Intention* Anscombe says that 'motive-in-general is a difficult topic' (1957: 20) although her discussion of motives there (1957: 18–23) is very illuminating. See also Kenny (1989: ch. 4).

So, although Anscombe is right that a motive for someone's action need not be a disposition of the agent's, there are nonetheless close conceptual links between motives and dispositions. First, many of the terms we have for motives—for instance, 'jealousy', 'ambition', 'humility', 'greed', 'compassion'—have cognates used to designate character traits that describe people precisely in terms of their behavioural dispositions; so people can be said to be jealous, ambitious, humble, greedy, compassionate, etc. And, as Ryle points out, to say 'that a certain motive is a trait in someone's character is to say that he is inclined to do certain sorts of things, make certain sorts of plans, indulge in certain sorts of daydreams' (1949: 90). So motives are not dispositions but we might say that many character traits, which are dispositions, can provide the motive for an action, for instance, a compassionate man is someone who tends to be motivated by compassion.

Not all motives have cognates that designate character traits: hatred, anger, admiration, pity, etc. can be motives but there are no corresponding terms for character traits: being hateful is not having the disposition to act out of hatred, and being angry is not having the disposition to act out of anger, nor is being full of admiration being disposed to act out of admiration. Being angry, or full of hatred, or of admiration seem to be states rather than character traits. However, a person who is often motivated by anger is likely to be an irascible person, that is, a person who is *disposed* to be angry. Likewise, a person may be filled with hatred once in his life (I don't mean just an instant); however a person who is often filled with hatred is a person who is likely to be malicious, that is, disposed to being motivated by malice. And so on.

Although many motives—for example, joy, avarice, generosity, humility, love, contempt—are feelings or emotions, not all motives are. For example, punctuality, fastidiousness, tidiness, dutifulness, can be motives but they are neither feelings nor emotions.

What all motives have in common is captured by Alan White, who says that 'to give the motive for a deed is to indicate a desire for the satisfaction of which the deed was done' (1968: 14). And this seems right. To say that the motive for an action was, for example, avarice, is to indicate a desire of the agent's, viz. to amass money, which he pursued in acting. If the motive was pity, the desire is to help; if vanity, to shine or to gain admiration; if revenge or hatred, the desire is to harm the other person. And so on. So the motive for an action indicates a desire (something wanted) for the sake of which the agent acted.

So motives are closely connected to desires in two ways. First, some motives (for example, revenge) are the *desire* itself for the satisfaction of which the agent acts. For instance, A may kill B in order to satisfy his desire for revenge, which is also his motive. Second, some motives indicate a desire. For instance, if one's motive in voting a certain way is ambition then the desire for the satisfaction of which one votes that way is, for example, to further one's career, or to increase one's power. Unlike revenge, ambition is not something the agent desires, but it gives an indication of what he desires.

Motives are also related to motivating reasons. First, since having a motive is having some desire one wants to satisfy, then, given that desire, certain facts (or apparent facts) will seem to the agent to be reasons for him to act. For example, to be motivated by avarice is to take certain facts (or apparent facts) as a reason for acting; and one takes those facts as a reason because what one desires is to amass money. These facts make the relevant action appear as a means, or as somehow contributing, to the satisfaction of a desire one has—in our example, the desire to amass money.[5] Moreover, given an agent's desire, taking certain considerations to be reasons, perhaps conclusive reasons, for doing something is constitutive of acting out of a particular motive: a desire to harm might constitute a motive of revenge against the background of a (perceived) past wrong. But that same desire might result in an action performed out of malice, if the agent regards the act of inflicting harm as worth doing for its own sake; or out of sadism, if the agent regards inflicting harm as worth doing for the sake of the pleasure it gives him. This explains why motives are sometimes called 'reasons' (and vice versa), for there is an internal connection between having a motive, having a desire, and taking certain considerations as reasons to perform an action.

As mentioned earlier, it is true that we often call reasons 'motives'. For instance, the police or crime detectives will say that a suspect had

---

[5] Whether one acts out of avarice or not depends at least partly on the extent to which the consideration that a particular action will be financially profitable is a *conclusive* reason for one to do it—whether, for example, it trumps other considerations that one takes to be reasons not to do that thing, for instance, that it is risky, that it will harm others, etc.

a *motive* to kill the victim, namely, that the victim had murdered the suspect's father. But it is worth noting that, while the mere fact that the victim had murdered the suspect's father implies that the suspect had *a reason* for killing the victim, that fact alone is not enough to make it true that the suspect had *a motive*. For, unless the fact that the victim had murdered his father made the suspect feel hatred, or a desire for revenge, or something like that, it is not true that the victim's actions gave the suspect a *motive* for killing the victim. And that seems to suggest that when we say that a reason someone had (that the suspect's father had been murdered by the victim) was his motive, what is meant is that the reason engendered a motive, for instance, a desire for revenge.

So, motives do indeed motivate our actions, and in Chapter 6 I shall explore how they can also explain them. But this fact about motives leaves open the possibility that something else also motivates, namely, *reasons*. And so I shall now turn to the question what these motivating reasons are.

3.2. Are Desires Motivating Reasons?

I said above that the term 'motivating reason' is a term of art that has gained currency in philosophical discussions in recent years. However, although the term is widely used, there is a deep disagreement about what a motivating reason is. Or rather, while all parties agree that motivating reasons are 'the reasons for which we act' or, as I shall also call them, 'our reasons for acting',[6] they disagree about what kind of thing these reasons are.

Many philosophers hold the view that our reasons for acting are mental states, in particular, states of believing and desiring.[7] This

---

[6] But, by 'our reasons for acting', I do not mean the reasons there are for us to act, but rather the reasons (or apparent reasons) for which we actually act.

[7] This view is held by many philosophers and it is often thought to be enshrined in this well-known passage of Davidson's: 'Giving the reason why an agent did something is often a matter of naming the pro attitude (*a*) or the related belief (*b*) or both; let me call this pair the *primary reason* why the agent performed the action. (. . .) *R* is a primary reason why an agent performed the action *A* under description *d* only if *R* consists of a pro attitude of the agent towards actions with a certain property, and a belief of the agent that *A*, under the

view is central to what has become known as the Humean view
of motivation—one of whose basic tenets is that all motivation is
dependent on desires.[8]

In recent discussions of this topic, a minority of philosophers have
presented a number of arguments against this Humean picture of
motivation.[9] On the one hand, some have questioned the prominence
that this picture gives to desires over beliefs in motivation—for one
thing, they argue, there seems to be no reason to claim, as Humeans
often do, that beliefs cannot motivate. Moreover, if it is admitted
that both beliefs and desires motivate, it is questionable that desires
are the fundamental motivators. In addition, many have challenged
the idea that our reasons for acting are mental states (whether beliefs
or desires) since, they point out, our reasons for acting are, at least
sometimes, things such as that I am late for a meeting, that there is
famine in Africa, or that my sister is moving house. And these, they
argue, whatever they are, are clearly not mental states.

My own views are decidedly on the side of this minority. The view
that desires are our reasons for acting seems to me mistaken. I shall spell
out my arguments in relation to this claim in the following chapter,
and my discussion will engage fairly directly with the debate about
motivating reasons as found in the contemporary literature. However,
I am unhappy with the way some of these issues are set out in the
literature because the terms in which the debates are framed seem to
me often unsatisfactory. In particular, the question whether desires are
motivating reasons is ambiguous and hence hopelessly unclear.[10]

On the one hand, there are different kinds of desire. For instance,
there are desires that we share with other animals, such as hunger

description d, has that property' (1980: 4-5). It is worth noting, however, that Davidson is
here talking about the reasons that explain an action and perhaps not about the reasons that
motivated it. See Section 4.2, note 9.

[8] Audi calls it 'the conative groundedness view' (2001: 66). See also Mele (2003: ch. 1).
[9] Bittner (2001); Dancy (2000); Hyman (1999); McDowell (1978); Nagel (1970); Schueler
(2003); Stout (1996); Stoutland (1998).
[10] In the contemporary literature on normativity there has been much discussion whether
desires are *normative* reasons (see Raz 1999a; Korsgaard 1996, 1997; Quinn 1993; Scanlon
1998; Schroeder 2007, etc.). The arguments rehearsed in that debate are relevant to our
question, which is whether desires are *motivating* reasons. Our question, however, needs to
be addressed in its own right because it seems possible, at least prima facie, that a desire
should not be a reason there is for someone to act and yet be the reason for which someone
acts: the reasons for which we act are not always reasons for which we should act.

and thirst; and there are desires that only creatures capable of abstract reasoning can have, such as the desire to become more generous or to buy a PlayStation. And again, there are things that one wants for their own sake—health is normally so wanted—and things that are wanted for the sake of something else—wanting a new tooth-filling is, for most people, such a desire.

Given this variety of kinds of desire, it should not be assumed that, if desires of one kind are not motivating reasons, desires of other kinds are not either. Therefore, the question whether desires are reasons must be explored in relation to desires of each kind.

Moreover, the question whether desires are motivating reasons is further complicated by the act/object ambiguity in the term 'desire' already mentioned.[11] The ambiguity is created by the dual use that the term is put to: to refer to someone's desiring something, on the one hand, and to what is desired, on the other. For example, 'my desire to go on holiday' is sometimes used to refer to *my desiring* to go on holiday, and sometimes to *what* I desire, namely to go on holiday. These are quite different: my desiring to go on holiday, but not what I desire, may be predictable, intense, uncharacteristic, etc. What I desire, but not my desiring it, may be unattainable, expensive, worthless, etc. So, in addressing the question whether desires are motivating reasons we also need to bear this ambiguity in mind.

I shall, therefore, devote the remainder of this chapter to exploring the concept of desire, the different kinds of desire and, briefly, the ambiguity inherent in the term. This will enable me to address the question whether desires are motivating reasons properly in the following chapter.

3.3. What Is a Desire?

In much contemporary philosophy, the concept of desire is introduced alongside the concept of belief, as two fundamental kinds of mental

---

[11] As I said earlier, there is a corresponding ambiguity concerning the term 'belief', which I'll explore in detail in Chapter 5.

state that are distinguished from each other in terms of the notion of 'direction of fit'. The idea is that, while to believe something is to be in a state with a 'mind-to-world' direction of fit, to desire something is to be in a state with a 'world-to-mind' direction of fit. While I don't have any substantial objections to this metaphor in itself, I doubt it is in fact very illuminating, not least because, as I shall argue, it encourages the idea that beliefs and desires are more alike than they really are, and it fails to emphasize a crucial aspect of desires, namely their connection to behaviour.[12]

Attempts to unpack the metaphor of 'direction of fit' often involve the idea of a 'defect', or of the 'onus of match' that each state has. So, a belief is said to be a state with a propositional content, such that if is there is a mismatch between the content of the state and the way things are in the world, then the defect rests with the belief (as it is often put, 'the onus of match is with the belief'); and contrariwise for desires: desires are said to be states with propositional content so that, when there is a mismatch here, the defect, and hence the onus of match, lies with the world. But, on examination, this way of unpacking the metaphor in terms of 'defect' and 'onus of match' does not seem to work for desires as it might work for beliefs, for two reasons. One is that the content of desires is different *in kind* from the content of beliefs. The other is that there is an important disanalogy between desires and beliefs.

According to the view under examination, both the contents of beliefs and those of desires can be thought of as propositions—hence both beliefs and desires are often called 'propositional attitudes'. The idea here is that to believe something is to have an attitude to a proposition, perhaps the attitude of taking it to be true; while to desire something is to have a different attitude to a proposition, for instance, perhaps a 'pro attitude' to it. So, on this view, to believe that my husband is at home is to take the proposition 'My husband is at home' to be true; and to want my husband to be at home is to want that proposition to be true.

However, although the idea that it is possible to express what it is to believe something in terms of having an attitude to a proposition may

---

[12]   See e. g. Platts (1979) and Smith (1987 and 1994). For some trenchant criticisms of this conception of desires see Zangwill (1998) and Schueler (1991).

be fine, the same is not true of desires. First, this way of characterizing desires does not cover the desires of non-human animals because, since it is implausible that these animals can entertain propositions, it is not possible that, for them, to desire something is for them to have a certain attitude to a proposition. One could reply that the 'propositional attitude' characterization was always meant to apply to human desires only, so that the fact that it does not apply to the desires of non-human animals is not a defect of the view. The problem with this response is that some of our desires, such as hunger, thirst, etc., are desires that we share with some other animals. But if these desires consist in having attitudes to propositions in our case, while they consist in something quite different in the case of other animals, then it is not clear what grounds we have for saying that these are desires that we *share* with other animals. I return to desires of this kind below.

But the problems for the propositional attitude view of desires do not end here. For even if we consider desires that only humans have because they require the capacity to manipulate abstract concepts, such as the desire to become prime minister, the claim that to have such a desire is to have an attitude towards a proposition is not free from difficulties. When one tries to express what is desired by means of a proposition the results are often forced and clumsy: 'I want that she goes to the cinema tomorrow', 'I want that my husband is at home', etc., sound odd and are barely grammatical, if at all.[13] It seems that, in order to express the content of a desire by means of a grammatical 'that'-clause, the latter needs to be in the subjunctive mood: 'I want that she go to the cinema tomorrow', '. . . that he be kinder', '. . . that my horse win the Grand National'; '. . . that the pound rise', etc. But it is not clear that such 'that'-clauses express genuine propositions—among other things, they do not seem to be capable of being true or false. Moreover, it is much more natural to express what is wanted by means of an infinitival phrase: 'I want her to go to the cinema', 'I want my horse to win', etc.[14]

---

[13] For similar criticisms see Ben-Yami (1997).

[14] Although desires can be expressed by using the optative mood, e.g. 'Would that I became a good tennis player', 'May you enjoy good health', *what* is desired is typically stated by means of an infinitival clause, e.g. 'to become a good tennis player', 'for you to enjoy

Consider what Michael Smith, a champion of the 'direction of fit' characterization of beliefs and desires, says about them:

The difference between beliefs and desires in terms of direction of fit comes down to a difference between the counterfactual dependence of a belief and a desire that *p*, on a perception that not *p*: roughly, a belief that *p* is a state that tends to go [out?] of existence in the presence of the perception that *not p*, whereas a desire that *p* is a state that tends to endure, disposing the subject to bring it about that *p*.   (1987: 54)

But does this way of characterizing desires work for all desires? There seems to be a problem in specifying what I want as *p*—a problem that, I think, tends to be obscured by the fact that the English language does not have a specific form for the subjunctive mood.[15] Let me explain.

Suppose that it is now October and I decide that I want my son to buy a house this coming December. On the 'state with direction of fit' view, I am in a state that is a desire that my son *buy* a house this December—what I desire is expressed with a clause in the subjunctive mood. But it is not clear that I could have the perception that it is not the case 'that my son buy a house this December' (even understanding 'perception' in its widest possible sense). One perception I could have that is relevant to whether my desire is satisfied or not is that December comes and goes and my son has not bought the house. Faced with *that* perception, I cannot, on pain of irrationality, retain the desire for him to buy a house this December—as that is, now, impossible. But, on Smith's criterion, since this would be 'a state that tends to go [out?] of existence in the presence of the perception that

good health'. The latter can also be stated by means of nominal expressions: 'proficiency at tennis', 'good health', 'having more money', etc., but it is not clear that it can be also expressed in propositional form.

[15] Even native speakers of English seem unsure about how and when the subjunctive ought to be used, and tend to avoid constructions that call for it. This may have contributed to the fact that many philosophers seem happy to use the indicative form where grammar requires a subjunctive in their characterization of desires. For example, Smith writes: 'Ascriptions of desires, unlike ascriptions of sensations, may be given in the form "A desires that p", where "p" is a sentence. Thus, whereas A's desire to ϕ may be ascribed to A in the form *A desires that he ϕ-s*, A's pain cannot be ascribed to A in the form *A pains that p*'. (1987: 47). But contrary to what Smith says, A's desire to become a pianist is ascribed to A as 'A desires that he *become* a pianist', that is, using the subjunctive and not the indicative form of the verb, as he suggests; and 'he become a pianist' is *not* a complete sentence, and it cannot be used alone to express a proposition.

not p' this would make my desire into a belief, which seems absurd. Moreover, the belief I would now have, that my son did not buy a house in December, does not have the same content as the desire I had that my son buy a house this December.

But suppose that we put this difficulty aside and agree, for the sake of argument, to express the content of desires by means of such 'that'-clauses. There is still a disanalogy between beliefs and desires that is masked by the characterization of both in terms of states with 'direction of fit'. It is a defect of a belief that its content does not match the way things are, for it makes the content of the belief false. But it is not a defect of desires that what is desired should be something that is not the case; on the contrary, far from being a defect, it is characteristic of a formally non-defective desire: we don't normally want what we know to be already the case (although we may want something that is the case to continue being the case, for example, I may want him to continue being happy). If a mismatch between mind and world were a defect of desires, the only non-defective desires we could have would be desires for things we falsely believe not to be the case, such as someone's desiring to see Mount Teide, while looking at it but not being aware that what he is seeing is Mount Teide.

It might be thought that this point is not very important because the idea behind the 'direction of fit' metaphor is clear: if there is a mismatch between what is believed and the way the world is, then the belief ought to change; whereas if there is a mismatch between what is wanted and the way the world is, then it is the world that ought to change in order to fit with what one wants—as Smith puts it, having a desire is 'being in a state the world must fit' (1994: 92 and 116). But in fact there is something very odd in this thought—for whether the world 'must fit' one's desire surely depends on what one desires. Some desires are foolish or evil and it is wholly implausible to say that having such a desire is being in a state that the world 'must' fit.

Moreover, Smith's characterization of the desire that p as a state that tends to endure 'in the presence of the perception that *not p*' is itself problematic. For suppose that I want to be now driving towards Seville and believe that I am. But suppose that I see a sign that shows that I am actually driving away from Seville and towards Granada. As Schueler points out (2003: 34), there is no reason to assume that, faced with this fact (this 'perception'), I shall not abandon my desire to drive to Seville and adopt instead one to drive towards Granada and hence bring it about that not *p*. Whether the desire to drive to Seville tends to endure when faced with the fact that I'm not driving to Seville will depend on a number of issues, not least of which are my beliefs about the relative merits, in the circumstances, of going to Seville vs. going to Granada—circumstances that include the discovery that as it happens I'm now on my way to Granada.

In fact, what is distinctive about desires is not so much that the world must fit with the content of the desire but rather that if one has a desire one has an inclination to *act* in the way that one believes will satisfy the desire (something Smith also mentions). In other words, what is distinctive about the concept of desire is its conceptual relation to *agency*, for an important criterion for the attribution of a desire to a person is whether that person is inclined to act so as to satisfy the relevant desire. And the characterization of desires as states with a mind-to-world 'direction of fit' takes the focus away from the all-important conceptual connection between desiring something and agency.

As far as I am aware, the metaphor of direction of fit originates in section 32 of Anscombe's *Intention* (although she doesn't use that expression), where she distinguishes between a shopping list that a man uses as an aid while doing his shopping—which can be seen as an expression of his intention to buy the things on the list—and a list of things bought by the man compiled by a detective who has been following him—which can be seen as a record and hence more akin to belief. However, when discussing the possibility of mistakes vis-à-vis the first list, that is, the possibility of a mismatch between the shopping list—considered as an expression of intention—and what the man actually buys—seen as the execution of the intention—Anscombe says that, if there is a mismatch, 'the mistake is not in the list but in the man's *performance*' (1957: 56, my italics). She refers to this as 'Theophrastus' principle', and she points out that if, on seeing a mismatch between the list and the shopping, the man thought that the way to resolve 'the mistake' would be to cross something off the list, this would suggest that the man does not understand the role of a shopping list (that is, the concept of intention). If he understood it properly, he'd realize that the mistake consisted *in his not having bought* that item, which resulted in the mismatch. And the significance of this point is that the concept of intention is tightly bound up with the concept of *acting*—as is the concept of desire. And this is something that the characterization of desires as 'states with direction of fit' does little to bring out. Or to put the point differently, if there is a mismatch between a desire and the way the world is, any onus of match that there might be is *with the agent*.

Thus, the metaphor of 'direction of fit', even if not misleading, is certainly not illuminating and it is not an improvement on Anscombe's other idea that 'the primitive sign of wanting is *trying to get*' (1957: 68); which means that, typically, someone who wants something is inclined or disposed *to act* in order to satisfy that desire (according to their beliefs about how to do that, of course). To be sure, desires come in different kinds and in different degrees of intensity, and the inclination to act to satisfy them varies accordingly. Moreover, the inclination to act may be outweighed by an inclination to do something else, or by a reason not to do it. But this does nothing to undermine the point that there is a fundamental conceptual link between desiring and acting.

It may be objected that this is too narrow a conception of desire. Many desires are desires we never act upon. Moreover, we may want things that nothing we could do would count as our trying to get because they are things that we know to be beyond our control, such as wanting that the weather should be sunny tomorrow. But, first, such wants are more akin to hopes and wishes. And second, for a want whose satisfaction one knows to be beyond one's control to be rightly attributed to someone it must be true that, had the agent believed that something he could do could contribute to bring about what he wants (for instance, pray, or do a little dance), then he would be inclined to do that thing. The inclination would, of course, be proportional to how much or how seriously one wanted that thing and how firmly one held the relevant beliefs about how to achieve it, and it might be outweighed by the cost of trying to get that thing, by conflict between it and other things wanted, etc. But nonetheless, the point remains that wherever there is desire, there is the inclination to act in order to get or bring about what is desired. As Aristotle says, what is desired is 'the realisable good'; and he adds that in order 'to produce movement the object [of appetite] must be [. . .] good that can be brought into being by action' (*De Anima*, Book I, 10; 433a, 28-30).

Because of this, and because I do not think much is gained by conceiving of desiring as involving a propositional attitude, or as being in a state with a 'world-to-mind direction of fit', I shall not characterize desires in this way.

As well as this way of characterizing desires in general, it is also common to find in the literature several kinds of distinction concerning desires. For instance, a distinction is often made between an 'intrinsic' desire (something wanted for its own sake) and an extrinsic or 'instrumental' desire (something wanted for the sake of something else to which this is a means). Another distinction often invoked is that between 'occurrent' and 'standing' desires.[16] These distinctions are more or less important and useful for different purposes. For my purposes, however, I should like to focus on another distinction, namely that between what I shall call 'rational' and 'non-rational' desires.

The distinction I wish to focus on is related to Nagel's distinction between motivated and unmotivated desires (1970: 29 ff.), although it does not altogether coincide with it.[17] Nagel characterizes the former as 'desires *arrived at* by decision and after deliberation' which, he says, is true of many beliefs also. These are contrasted with unmotivated desires: desires that 'simply assail us', 'like the appetites and in certain cases the emotions' (1970: 29).

Motivated desires, Nagel says, unlike unmotivated ones, can be given rational explanations. Indeed, they can be given the same explanations that would explain the relevant desire-satisfying action. So if I go to the shop in order to buy groceries because I am hungry, this implies that I have a motivated desire, namely to buy groceries, and an unmotivated desire, namely hunger. My desire to buy groceries is motivated by hunger but my hunger is not motivated by anything. And, Nagel says, both the motivated *desire* to buy groceries, and the *action* of going to the shop to buy groceries can be explained rationally, by reference to the fact that I am hungry.

While I think Nagel is right that the appetites and in certain cases the emotions simply assail us (though I don't think that emotions are desires, even if some may be accompanied by them, and necessarily

---

[16] See Mele (2003: ch. 1) for an account of some of these distinctions.

[17] Another closely related distinction is Scanlon's between 'judgment-sensitive' desires and those that are not (1998: ch. 1).

so), I think Nagel is wrong in saying that some desires, or beliefs, for that matter, are arrived at by decision. Decisions concern possible courses of action, and neither desiring nor believing are courses of action. One cannot simply decide to want something, though one can decide to try to obtain it.[18] But, although we cannot decide whether to desire something, Nagel is right that many desires (and beliefs) are arrived at after implicit or explicit deliberation—though not all desires that can be given rational explanations are arrived at by deliberation. For my desire to play the piano can be given a rational explanation, namely that I enjoy playing the piano, but my desire need not be arrived at by deliberation, whether explicit or not, even if it is an 'occurrent' desire.

I think that a more illuminating way of putting the kind of distinction that Nagel has in mind is in terms of rational and non-rational desires (which are not to be equated with irrational desires. The latter are against reason, while non-rational desires are neither irrational nor rational, just as there are actions that are neither voluntary nor involuntary—if the latter is taken to mean against one's will—but are simply non-voluntary).[19] The crucial distinction between rational and non-rational desires is that only the first are had for reasons.

Rational desires are desires we have for reasons and therefore only a creature with the capacity to reason can have such desires. Examples of rational desires are the desire to write a novel, to go on holiday, or to paint a window. Non-rational desires are not had for reasons, and at least some of them we share with other animals. Particularly important among non-rational desires are the appetites, such as hunger, thirst, etc.—which I shall refer to as 'bodily appetites', since the term 'appetite' alone tends to be used in either a wider sense (for any desire) or a narrower sense (for hunger alone) than I intend here.[20] These

---

[18] Likewise, it is not at all clear that it is possible to decide to believe something. But, as Raz (1997) points out, this does not mean that we are passive when it comes to beliefs, among other things because which beliefs we end up with depends partly on how we deliberate; and whether we deliberate and how carefully can be up to us.

[19] An alternative term might be 'arational' which, for instance, Hursthouse (1991) uses to refer to some actions, as she says, on the model of 'amoral' and in contrast to both moral and immoral.

[20] See Kenny (1989: 35 ff.), to which my discussion is indebted. Kenny uses the term 'desires' where I use 'non-rational desires'—and in particular 'bodily appetite'—and 'volition' where I use 'rational desire'; and he points out that 'some languages have a special

desires are typically felt, in the sense that, normally, having them involves experiencing certain characteristic bodily sensations.

There are other non-rational desires that we share with animals but which do not have characteristic sensations associated with them. For instance, the desire to play, to do things that feel good, to avoid what is painful, or to take action to diminish pain or to remove the cause of pain, etc., can be had by creatures that are not capable of abstract reasoning. These desires are connected to pleasure and the avoidance or assuaging of pain but they do not have characteristic sensations.

These non-rational and all rational desires *may* be accompanied by sensations, but those sensations need not be characteristic of the desire. So, while hunger is characterized by certain sensations, there is no bodily sensation that is characteristic of the desire to eat chalk or to go on holiday, and the having of such a desire need not be accompanied by any bodily sensation.[21]

Let me note briefly a point which I shall explain in detail below: what makes a desire non-rational is not its content, that is, not what it is a desire for but, rather, the fact that it is a desire not had for reasons and that it is felt. Hence, although thirst is a felt desire to drink, it is also possible to desire to drink because drinking is healthy and not to feel any desire. *That* desire to drink is, therefore, a rational desire. So animals can feel thirst but they cannot want to drink because drinking is healthy.

Although the distinction between non-rational desires, and in particular bodily appetites, and rational desires was given prominence by Aristotle and his medieval followers, it is a distinction that tends to be neglected nowadays. This neglect has been, I think, deleterious for discussions of the connection between desires and reasons, because such discussions tend to overlook the fact that desires of each kind seem to stand in a quite different relation to reasons. And this means

---

word for the kind of desire which is common to humans and animals: in classical Greek philosophers called it *"epithumia"* and in medieval Latin the scholastics called it *"concupiscentia"* ' (1989: 36).

[21] My distinction is not the same as Schueler's distinction between 'desires proper' and 'pro-attitudes', because for him a 'desire proper' is 'one where it makes sense to say that someone acted even though she had no desire *at all*, in *this* sense, to do so, as I might attend what I know will be a really boring meeting even though I had no real (that is, 'proper') desire to go' (2003: 24). All bodily appetites are 'proper' desires, in Schueler's sense, but so are some rational desires. For instance, my desire to go on holiday can be a proper desire.

that sometimes generic conclusions are drawn about the connection between desires and reasons which are, in fact, true only of desires of one of those two kinds.

Both kinds of desires share many features. But there are also important differences between them. Here, I shall start by examining non-rational desires, focusing on the bodily appetites, which include the desire for food, drink, sleep, and sex. I shall focus on them because, while much of what I say about their relation to reasons is also true of other non-rational desires, the bodily appetites are both very important and familiar among our desires. (And, as I have done up to now, I shall follow the common practice of using the terms 'desire' and 'want' roughly as synonyms, and will not use them to mark the distinction between bodily and rational desires.)

3.3.1. *Non-rational desires: bodily appetites*

The importance of the bodily appetites is nicely summarized by Thomas Reid in the following passage:

Though man knew that his life must be supported by eating, reason could not direct him when to eat, or what; how much, or how often. In all these things appetite is a much better guide than our reason. Were reason alone to direct us in this matter, its calm voice would often be drowned in the hurry of business, or the charms of amusement. But the voice of appetite rises gradually, and, at last, becomes loud enough to call off our attention from any other employment.

Every man must be convinced that, without our appetites, even supposing mankind inspired with all the knowledge requisite for answering their ends, the race of men must have perished long ago; but by their means, the race is continued from one generation to another, whether men be savage or civilised, knowing or ignorant, virtuous or vicious.   (1969: 120)

In this section I shall explore the nature of bodily appetites by focusing on two distinctive features they have: one is that desires of this kind are closely associated with particular bodily sensations which have a certain duration; the other is that, unlike rational desires, these are desires we do not have for reasons and indeed having them does not require the capacity to reason.

Before elaborating on these distinctive features of bodily appetites, it is important to note that, as I mentioned a few paragraphs earlier, for adult human beings, the desires for food, drink, sleep, etc., can actually take two distinct forms. They may take the form of a bodily appetite, such as hunger, thirst, sleepiness, etc., or they may take the form of what I called rational desires. Thus, thirst is a bodily appetite, but the desire to drink water need not be: it could be a desire that is not felt but arises from some consideration about the importance or goodness of drinking water, in which case it is a rational desire. As Reid says:

A man may eat from appetite only. So the brutes commonly do. He may eat to please his taste when he has no call of appetite. I believe a brute may do this also. He may eat for the sake of health, when neither appetite nor taste invites. This, as far as I am able to judge, brutes never do.   (1969: 122)

It might be tempting to think that a desire for food or drink that is not felt should also be regarded as a bodily appetite since it is a desire whose satisfaction necessarily involves changes in one's body, unlike, say, the desire for world peace. But what makes a desire bodily is not the nature of what is desired (for instance, some bodily activity or the enjoyment of some sensation) but rather whether having that desire typically involves experiencing certain characteristic bodily sensations and whether it is had for reasons. The bodily appetites are the kinds of felt desire that we have and that are also had by creatures that cannot reason.

So one distinctive feature of bodily appetites is that they are felt, that is, that there are certain bodily sensations that are characteristic of the appetite. For example, when the desire for food is a bodily appetite, it is characterized by the feeling of certain more or less unpleasant sensations located roughly around the stomach, oesophagus, etc.; the felt desire for drink is characterized by a sensation of dryness in the mouth and throat, and so on. A desire for food characterized by these sensations is what we call hunger, and a desire for drink characterized by those sensations is thirst. I may, to be sure, feel hungry and yet not want to eat—because, for instance, I know the food to be poisoned. Nonetheless, feeling hungry is still feeling a desire to eat, even if, in spite of my feeling this desire, I do not, all things considered, want to eat.

Because of the sensations that typically accompany them, feeling these desires involves more or less intense experiences of bodily discomfort and even pain, and they have what, following Wittgenstein, can be called 'genuine duration': their duration can be measured by the clock more or less precisely. Moreover, these sensations are fairly well localized in the body.

It is said that bodily appetites are characterized by their requiring 'prompt satisfaction' (see Kenny 1989: 36) and this feature of bodily appetites is precisely connected to the sensations that they are characterized by, because part of what is involved in satisfying the desire is assuaging the accompanying sensations.[22] And it is also this feature that makes it difficult for the person who experiences the desire to attend to anything else when the desire is sufficiently acute. Indeed, the intensity of a desire is partly measured precisely by whether the person *can* attend to anything else if he or she tries; to quote Reid again, 'the voice of appetite rises gradually, and, at last, becomes loud enough to call off our attention from any other employment' (1969: 120).

Some of the desires under discussion, such as the desire for food, water, and sleep—but not sex—have the character of a need, not merely in the sense that they are desires that require immediate satisfaction (which is true of all of them when sufficiently intense, and this includes sex), but also in the sense that some of them are desires for things that are needs for the human organism, things the absence of which will harm the organism.

The connection between these sensations and the desire they characterize is not that of symptom and condition; that is, those sensations do not constitute for their owner *evidence* that he has the relevant desire; rather, to experience those sensations *is* to feel the desire, and indeed the behaviour that the desire naturally leads to, that is, the behaviour that is characteristic of that desire (for instance, seeking to drink water, moistening one's lips), is behaviour that tends to assuage the relevant, more or less uncomfortable, sensations. (But note that feeling the relevant sensations is not all that there is to having the desire, because having the desire involves also an inclination to act in certain ways; rather, experiencing the sensations is all that there is to *feeling* the desire.)

---

[22] Thus these desires are presumably always what are called 'occurrent desires', if the latter means desires present to consciousness, given that bodily desires are present to consciousness for as long as they are felt.

Desires of this kind can be brought about by, or intensified or weakened through, stimulation of the senses, including the so-called internal senses: memory and imagination. But these desires can also be the upshot of physiological changes and states in us whose occurrence or obtaining has little or nothing to do with the senses. To the extent that the stimulation of the senses is under the agent's control, the bringing about or modification of those desires also is, and this is something that an agent might do more or less deliberately, and perhaps for a reason. But even then, as we shall see, it does not follow that these desires are had for a reason.

This brings us to the other distinctive feature of bodily appetites I want to highlight, namely that, unlike rational desires, bodily appetites are not desires we have for reasons, though there are reasons why we have them. Thus, the question: 'why do you feel a desire to ϕ (that is, why do you feel a desire to drink, to eat, etc.)?' makes sense only if it means something like: 'What is the reason that explains why you feel this desire?' and it does not make sense if it means: 'What is *your* reason for feeling this desire?' And when it means the first, the answer won't be your reason for feeling the desire; rather it will be some fact about the physiological, chemical, etc., state of your organism, or about your history and constitution, that explains why you feel this desire. Depending on the domain of interest, the having of these desires can be explained by reasons related to biological needs; to chemical states and changes in us; to genetic factors, to evolution, etc. But these are all *reasons why* we have those desires and not our *reasons for* having them; in other words, these are reasons that explain why we have these desires but they are not the reasons that motivate us to have the desires.

Someone's having a bodily appetite may be, for example, pre-dictable, or incomprehensible, given his or her circumstances. For instance, it is unsurprising that someone who hasn't eaten for two days should feel very hungry but odd that someone should still be hungry only two hours after a heavy meal, or thirsty having just drunk a litre of water. But the predictability or oddness of the desires, or the difficulty in understanding why these desires are present, has nothing to do with understanding the cogency or soundness of the agent's reasons for having the desires—it is, rather, related to understanding the reasons *why* he has them (to reasons that explain his having them), and these might be things such as that he had a salty dinner; that he has a metabolic dysfunction, etc. Such reasons are clearly not *the agent's* reasons for having those desires.

However, although bodily desires are not had for reasons, they are not altogether outside of the domain of reason, that is, not outside of the domain of the normativity of reasons; and this is so whether there is an obvious reason (explanation) why one has them or not. So, there is some connection between desires of this kind and reasons for ϕ-ing, which is that we generally have the capacity to reason about desires of this kind in at least two ways. First, we may reason about the appropriateness or otherwise of satisfying a bodily desire, and might decide to refrain from seeking to satisfy it—though the latter might sometimes require a huge effort and might, in some cases, have deleterious consequences for our health, particularly when the desires are linked to physiological needs. And second, we can reason, in a means-ends manner, about how to satisfy these desires.

In order to reason about whether to satisfy a bodily desire, it is necessary to be able to have the thought that one has such a desire. It may be that, given our natures as rational creatures, the experience of a bodily appetite is often accompanied by such thoughts, regardless of whether we are reasoning about whether or how to satisfy it.[23] Thus, I may feel thirsty and this feeling may be accompanied by the thought that I am. However, that does not mean that the appetite ceases to be a bodily appetite and becomes a rational desire. This is so because what makes a desire bodily is that it is felt and that it is not had for reasons, and the mere fact that the thought 'I am very thirsty' accompanies my feeling thirsty does not imply that I now have the desire for a reason.

We saw above that the things we desire in this bodily way, namely, to drink, to eat, to have sex, to sleep, etc., are things we can also desire rationally. And we saw that whether a desire for any of these things is bodily or rational depends on whether it is felt and whether it is had for reasons. Of course it is possible for us to have both a bodily appetite and a rational desire to drink at the same time: thus we may feel thirsty and also have a rational desire to drink—for example,

---

[23] Perhaps it is rare for us to feel a bodily desire without its being accompanied by such thoughts—the exceptions may be those instances when a bodily desire is extremely intense.

we may feel thirsty and at the same time want to drink water on the grounds that it is good for one's liver. In such a case, we have both a bodily appetite and a rational desire to do the same thing, viz. to drink.

When one reasons about whether to satisfy a bodily appetite, one may reach the conclusion that one has reason not to satisfy such a desire, for instance, because one is on hunger strike, about to have an operation, or married to someone else. Reasoning about the appropriateness of seeking to satisfy these desires can easily lead to self-deception and *akratic* action. Among other things, because these desires are intimately linked to our most fundamental physiological (and psychological) needs; because they can be very intense and powerful and demand immediate satisfaction; and because there are often strict conventions, moral injunctions, social imperatives, and taboos attached to them (especially, but not exclusively, in relation to sex). These are, however, very complex issues that I cannot and need not go into here.

As well as reasoning about *whether*, we can reason about *how*, to satisfy these desires. The satisfaction of a bodily appetite might be a straightforward matter, because what will satisfy my desire is obvious and easily available (say drinking water from a fountain), and the behaviour in which a creature engages to satisfy these desires may be instinctive or learnt or a combination of both. But satisfying the desire might involve more or less complicated ways of doing so, which may in turn require careful means–end reasoning.[24] I shall discuss the relation between reasoning about whether and how to satisfy a bodily appetite and motivating reasons in the following chapter. I now turn to rational desires.

3.3.2. *Rational desires*

As I said above, rational desires are desires had for reasons and hence having rational desires requires the exercise of the capacity to use abstract concepts. Rational desires are desires for things we want either in themselves, or instrumentally; while non-rational desires are

---

[24] Non-human animals also do things in order to satisfy their bodily desires, and they use tools in these activities. But it is, at best, controversial whether their doing this involves any reasoning.

always desires for things wanted in themselves.[25] I want to become famous because fame will bring me wealth, which I want because it will allow me to pursue my passion, which is to collect Indian sculpture. My desires to become famous and wealthy are instrumental; my desire to collect Indian sculpture is not. As has often been pointed out, every instrumental desire must be eventually grounded on a desire that is not itself instrumental, on pain of vicious regress: if nothing were wanted for its own sake and everything were wanted only in so far as it is a means to something else, then we would not want anything.[26]

A rational desire may be accompanied by more or less intense sensations and feelings. However, those sensations are not defining of the desire: there is no sensation or feeling that characterizes the desire to redecorate one's bathroom, or the desire to park a little closer to the shops. Moreover, although the intensity of such feelings and emotions may be indicative of the strength of a rational desire, they are not the criterion for the desire's strength; rather, the latter is determined by the lengths to which one is prepared to go in order to try to satisfy the desire. Thus, one's desire to beat a rival at tennis may be accompanied by an intense feeling of excitement, but the criterion for the strength of that desire is not the intensity of that feeling (though the latter may be a good indication) but rather what one is prepared to do in order to satisfy it: train intensely, take extra lessons, sabotage one's rival's racquet, or whatever.

This relation between rational desires and sensations and feelings explains also why rational desires, unlike bodily appetites, do not have what Wittgenstein called 'genuine duration'. I may want to go on a journey and feel very excited by the thought. But the excitement may pass and the want remain, and the want may remain even though I do not think about it at all or am in no way aware of it, indeed even while I am asleep—the same is not true of bodily appetites.

Like bodily appetites, rational desires can be brought about or intensified by stimulation of the senses: by sight, memory, imagination, etc. Desires of both kinds can be spontaneous, that is arise either 'just like that', or at the sight, memory, image, or thought of an object

---

[25] Some, e.g. Mele (2003), call this distinction 'intrinsic' vs. 'extrinsic' desires.
[26] See, e.g. Aristotle, *Nicomachean Ethics*, Book I.

or activity (cf. Anscombe 1957: 67). And both bodily and rational desires can be the subject of reasoning about whether and how to satisfy them. But only rational desires can be brought about through reason. This is because rational desires have a connection to reasons that bodily appetites do not have, namely that they are had for reasons: if one has a rational desire then one has some conception of what one desires that presents it as, in some respect, good. And the fact that the thing wanted is good (in that respect) is one's reason for having that desire.

The idea that some desires are had for reasons can be found in Aristotle and Aquinas, in the thought that what is wanted is always wanted *sub ratione boni* ('under the aspect of the good', Aquinas's *Summa Theologiae* 1a2ae, 8, 1. See also Aristotle's *Physics* II, 3, 195a26; and *Nicomachean Ethics* I, 1, 1094a3). This thought has been emphasized in different ways by recent philosophers.[27] For instance, in *Intention*, Anscombe talks about the 'desirability characterisation' of what is wanted: some aspect of what is wanted that captures what the good of it is in the agent's eyes. As Anscombe puts it, 'good is the object of wanting' as 'truth is the object of judgment'; and she adds: 'it does not follow from this that everything judged must be true, or that everything wanted must be good [. . .] the notion of "good" that has to be introduced in an account of wanting is not that of what is really good but of what the agent conceives to be good' (1957: 76). And Aristotle says that the object of desire 'may be either the real or the apparent good' (*De Anima* III, 433a28). This, Anscombe says, means that the desirability characterization picks out a feature that makes it intelligible to others that the person should desire it: 'the good (perhaps falsely) conceived by the agent to characterise the thing must *really* be one of the many forms of good' (1957: 76-7); the latter being things such as health, virtue, friendship, pleasure,[28] etc. (or that the thing wanted is a means to such goods).

---

[27] For contemporary discussions, see Anscombe (1957); Quinn (1993); Raz (1999a); Scanlon (1998).

[28] The relation between pleasure and reasons is somewhat problematic. Someone's claim that his reason for doing something is that it is pleasurable is generally intelligible, at least to the extent that it is intelligible that he should find it pleasurable. However, if we are concerned with normativity, things are more complicated. For while the fact that something is, say, an act of friendship is obviously always a reason in its favour, even if it is defeated by another reason against it, the same does not seem to be true in relation to pleasure. For

Thus *rational* desires are grounded in, that is, motivated by, the fact that we find some aspect of the thing or the activity wanted valuable because it seems good to us in some respect. The way in which it seems good is, precisely, our reason for having that desire, that is, our reason for wanting what we want.[29] To be sure, what one desires through bodily appetites is also appealing to one, but the difference is that in order to feel a bodily appetite it is not necessary to have the capacity to *conceive* of what one wants at all and, a fortiori, not necessary to conceive of it as good or worthwhile, and to be able to want it for that reason; whereas a rational desire requires the exercise of that capacity.

It has been objected that this claim, viz. that there is a connection between having (rational) desires and conceiving the wanted thing as good, is, at best, exaggerated.[30] After all, it is argued, we want to do things that we do not believe to be good, or even things that we believe, or know to be bad, even when we know or believe the bad in them to outweigh the good (see Heuer 2004). The response is that this is true, but nonetheless we always want to do them 'under the aspect of the good', that is, because of some good we see in them—for instance, we want to smoke, if we do want to in spite of knowing that it is extremely harmful, because we find it pleasant or relaxing. *What* we want, we might say, is the pleasure of smoking, not the harmful effects of it (or if someone wants the harmful effects, it will be for some 'good' to be derived from them).[31] But surely, it will be objected, we can want what is bad *because* it is bad. But

---

it is not obviously true that the fact that something is found to be pleasurable by someone is a reason for that person to do it (albeit a defeasible one), regardless of what it is that is pleasurable. For it seems arguable that there are things one ought not to take pleasure in, and that therefore the fact that one takes pleasure in them would not be a reason *at all* for doing them. Because of this, it is not clear to me whether the fact that something is pleasurable is a reason so long as the pleasure is not 'corrupt' (in which case it would be a reason for *not* doing it); or whether the truth is rather that the fact that something is pleasurable is always a reason but is often (and perhaps easily) defeated by other reasons.

[29] Dancy says: 'To desire is to be motivated by some conception of how things are' (2000: 91). If one restricts this to rational desires, this seems a close enough characterization of them.

[30] See Stocker (1979 and 2004); Raz (1999b); and Velleman (1992).

[31] The philosopher Francis Bacon says that 'There is no man doth a wrong for the wrong's sake, but thereby to purchase himself profit, or pleasure, or honours, or the like' (1909–14: bk IV).

again, if we want something because it is bad, this is because of some characterization that 'its being bad' has that makes it seem good. For example, we want to do what is morally bad for the thrill of it, or as a way of defying authority, and thus showing that we are free, or powerful, etc. As Anscombe puts it, the exhortation 'Evil be thou my good' is open, in order for it to be intelligible, to the question: what is the good of evil's being your good? (And she suggests that a plausible answer might be 'the condemnation of good as impotent, slavish and inglorious' (1957: 75).)[32]

But, one might insist, surely this is just a stipulation, for we might want to do something without being capable of saying what the good of doing that thing is; indeed perhaps we see no good in it at all. So, although, in general, the things we want we want because of some good we see in them, it is surely possible to want to do things for no reason—one may just have the sudden desire to do certain things such as pull a face at an important interview, or do a cartwheel down a corridor. Well, first, if something is wanted in that way, that is not a rational want and hence, although there may be no connection between what is wanted and a conception of the good, this is no objection to my claim that, in all that is rationally wanted, there is such a connection. Besides, very often we might find it difficult to say why we want to do something, that is, what the good of it might be. And this could be a matter of a failure of self-knowledge, honesty, or courage (the kind of thing for which we need siblings, friends, or, failing that, psychoanalysts). But that does not mean that the wanted thing is not regarded as somehow linked to the good, and it is perhaps arguable that many of those apparently pointless things one wants to do are things that we have some reason for wanting to do (for instance, to relieve boredom, to show to ourselves that we are still free spirits, and so on).[33] Finally, to the extent that one is wholly unable to specify what the good of what one wants to do

---

[32] Velleman makes an objection to this claim of Anscombe's that seems to me to depend on implicitly thinking that the good must be some kind of 'ethical good', for he says: 'Anscombe's Satan can desire evil only by judging it to *be* good, and so remains at heart, a lover of the good and the desirable—a rather sappy Satan' (1992: 119). But this objection only has bite, as far as I can see, if a lover of the good must be a lover of what is *morally* or *ethically* good, which Anscombe is not committed to: her Satan loves power.

[33] For a plausible argument to this effect see e.g. Quinn (1993: 246–52).

is, it becomes questionable that one does *want* to do that thing, as opposed to having an urge to do that thing, *having* to do that thing, feeling an impulse to do it, etc.: for, to the extent that something is not wanted for a reason, that desire has more the character of an urge, an impulse, a yen, etc. Thus, the compulsive hand-washer may see that there is no good whatsoever to be derived from his excessively frequent hand-washing and may be incapable of saying anything in its favour.[34] However, first, there is some good that he sees in washing his hands, for example, that it helps prevent infections, is a symbol of moral purification, or whatever—what he may not see *any* good in is the inordinate repetition of this act. But does the compulsive hand-washer actually *want* to wash his hands so frequently, as opposed to, say, feeling a compulsion to do it?

So just as there seemed to be a connection between taking oneself to have a reason to do something and being motivated to do it, there seems to be a connection between taking oneself to have a reason for wanting something, and wanting that thing (as opposed to *feeling* a desire to do it), and the reason is something that, in the agent's eyes, picks out some feature of what is wanted as good.

As I mentioned above, a rational desire may be instrumental or it may be a desire for something wanted for its own sake. It is important to note, though, that a rational desire for something wanted for its own sake is still a desire I have for a reason. Something I want for its own sake is something that I regard as good in itself, where its goodness may be in respect to a variety of criteria: moral, prudential, aesthetic, hedonic, legal, etc. And this good that I see in what I desire (that it is pleasant, my duty, elegant, an act of friendship, etc.) is my reason for wanting it: it provides the desirability characterization of the thing wanted, and, because it is wanted for its own sake, it is something I see as, somehow, an instance of some form of the good. Because of this, when one gives a non-instrumental reason for wanting something, as

---

[34] Such urges or impulses (for instance a pregnant woman's craving to eat chalk) share with bodily appetites that they are not had for reasons and that both require prompt satisfaction. But these urges and cravings differ from bodily appetites in that they do not have characteristic sensations associated with them. It is possible to characterize a sensation as the sensation felt in one's stomach when one is hungry but not as the sensation one feels when, to use Davidson's example, one feels a yen to drink a can of paint, or to eat chalk. See Hursthouse (1991) for an interesting discussion of a variety of actions, which she calls 'arational', some of which are respones to such impulses.

Anscombe says, 'Here we have arrived at a desirability characterisation which makes an end of the questions "What for?" '(1957: 72).

When reasoning about whether and how to satisfy a rational desire, several kinds of consideration come into play. First, if a thing is wanted for its own sake, a central consideration is whether it is something that is really worth wanting. On reflection one might realize that, say, celebrity is worthless, while domestic happiness is worth pursuing. Another kind of consideration is whether the satisfaction of one desire is compatible with the satisfaction of another desire that, in the circumstances, may take precedence for the agent. Yet another kind of consideration concerns the means that are available to achieve what one wants. One might reason that one's desire is almost impossible to achieve, or conclude that achieving it is feasible but the means required to bring it about are not acceptable (morally, legally, etc.), or one may conclude that, to paraphrase Dr Johnson, a thing is worth having but not worth trying to get. And so on. In all these ways one may come to think that there is no good reason, all things considered, to (try to) satisfy a desire, or perhaps that there is good reason not to (try to) satisfy it.

This susceptibility of desires to reasons does not mean we can choose what to desire; it does, however, mean that we have some control over our rational desires: we can reflect on the reasons why we have the desires we have, and decide that the reasons (and hence perhaps the desires) are inappropriate or bad, or conclude that there is better reason to have other desires one doesn't have. Such reasoning might result in our losing some desires and acquiring others, or, if we cannot rid ourselves of a desire, we might try to ignore it, or try not to let it affect our behaviour, etc.[35]

Having explored the notion of a desire and the distinction between bodily and rational desires, my next task is that of examining the relation between desires and motivating reasons, and in particular

---

[35] Harry Frankfurt (1988) has characterized the distinction between desires that are genuinely one's own and those one repudiates in terms of first- and second-order desires, where to have a desire that is genuinely one's own is to have a second-order desire to have the first-order desire. There is a huge literature on this topic and I cannot go into it in any detail here but, like many, I am not convinced that the idea of a second-order desire is the most illuminating way of characterizing this phenomenon. (For persuasive criticism of Frankfurt's position, see Watson 1975).

whether desires, be they bodily or rational, are motivating reasons. However, before undertaking that task, I need to return to an issue that I have mentioned several times but which, for the sake of simplicity of exposition, I have had to suppress so far in my discussion of desires, namely the ambiguity of the term 'desire'.

3.4. The Ambiguity of 'Desire'

As already noted, many discussions about desires and reasons have been dogged and obscured by an ambiguity that arises because the term 'my desire' (or 'my want') has two possible uses: one to mean my desiring something (or my wanting something), and the other to mean what I desire (or what I want).

The difference between my desiring something and what I desire is captured by the act/object distinction, and it can be brought out by considering, first, that there are things which are true of the one that need not be true of the other. As I said above, what I desire may be unusual, very expensive, and even very desirable, while my desiring it need not be any of those things. So, a teenage boy may desire to own a limited edition Ferrari: what he desires is rare, but his desiring it may not be, at least not among his peers. This difference is sometimes reflected grammatically, in that, when qualifying a desire, we may use an adverb if we are qualifying the act (that is, the desiring), but must use an adjective when qualifying what is desired. For instance, if I have an intense desire to see the sea, it is my desiring, not what I desire, that is intense. And this is expressed by means of an adverb that qualifies the act: 'my *intensely* desiring to see the sea' (and not my desiring to intensely see the sea). However, if I have an unattainable desire, for example, to win an Olympic medal, then it is what I desire, not my desiring it, that is unattainable, and this is expressed by means of an adjective that qualifies the 'object': 'I desire something unattainable, namely to win an Olympic medal'. This could not be expressed by saying that I unattainably desire to win an Olympic medal.

This dual use of the word 'desire' is also relevant when considering the differences between the kinds of desire mentioned above, such as that between intrinsic and extrinsic desires, that between occurrent and standing desires, or the distinction I drew between bodily and rational desires. These distinctions apply to one's *desiring*—they are distinctions about the manner in which something is desired. For instance, the distinction between bodily and rational desires is a distinction concerning *desiring*, for they refer to the manner of desiring: as we saw, what is desired, for example, to drink, could be the same whether the *desiring* is bodily or rational.

In drawing attention to the act/object ambiguity, I don't pretend that it has gone altogether unnoticed in discussions of reasons. In fact, the distinction between my wanting something and what I want is often mentioned under the headings 'a desire' (a state of desire) and 'its content'—though it must be noted that if 'a desire' refers to what is desired, then these are the same: the content of my desire to meet the Dalai Lama is, precisely to meet the Dalai Lama, which is what I desire or 'my desire'.[36] Although the distinction is acknowledged, it is, however, seldom given much importance when articulating arguments, and both defenders and attackers of the view that desires are motivating reasons tend to use the term 'desire' to mean now one thing, now the other. So, the ambiguity resulting from the failure to specify whether one is focusing on a desiring, or on a thing desired, when arguing for or against the view that desires are motivating reasons, can have the effect of hopelessly compromising the conclusions of those arguments. In general, then, we must be clear whether claims and arguments about desires refer to what is desired, or to our desiring it.

Given these complexities concerning the concept of desire, it seems that the question whether desires are motivating reasons must first be disambiguated, so that the resulting questions can be addressed separately. This is what I propose to do in the following chapter.

Conclusion

The focus of this chapter has been the concept of motivation in action and the relation between motivation and desires.

---

[36] And that content is my desire rather than, say, my fear, simply because I desire rather than fear to meet the Dalai Lama.

I acknowledge the common-sense view that among the things that motivate us to act are, precisely, our motives. Having briefly explored the notion of a motive and its connection to desires, I noted that, although we are moved to act by our motives, that does not mean that we are not also moved to act by reasons.

I have argued that there is a close connection between being motivated to ϕ, taking oneself to have a reason to ϕ, and wanting to ϕ. Being motivated to ϕ involves having an inclination to ϕ. If one has such an inclination typically, though not always, one wants to ϕ, either because one *feels* an inclination to ϕ, or because one takes oneself to have a reason to ϕ. This led to the question whether desires are among the reasons that motivate us to act.

I argued that, given the complexity of the concept of desire, that question about motivating reasons requires a better understanding of what desires are, of the different kinds of desire, and of the significance of the fact that the term 'desire' is ambiguous.

After exploring the connection between desires and agency, I focused on the distinction between bodily appetites and rational desires which lies partly in their relation to bodily sensations, and partly in their relation to reasons: bodily appetites, unlike rational desires, are felt and are not had for reasons. I examined some of the distinctive features of desires of each kind, and argued that they stand in importantly different relations to reasons.

I then emphasized the act/object ambiguity inherent in the term 'desire', which serves to refer either to what is desired, or to one's desiring it (whether one desires it bodily or rationally).

With these distinctions in place, we can now turn to the question concerning the relation between motivating desires and reasons. And it becomes clear that the question: 'Are my desires motivating reasons?' can be construed in two ways. One construal yields the question: (1) 'Is what I desire a motivating reason?' On the other construal, the question is: (2) 'Is my desiring something, whether I desire it bodily or rationally, a motivating reason?' And these are quite different questions, each of which I shall examine in the following chapter.

4

Desires and Motivating Reasons

Introduction

Much recent literature about reasons and action has focused on the relation between desires and reasons. One question that has been widely debated recently is whether desires constitute or provide reasons for acting, that is, whether desires are normative reasons.[1] I shall have little to say about that, since my focus in this chapter is whether desires are *motivating* reasons.

As I said at the end of the previous chapter, given the dual use of the term 'desire', this question can have two construals: one is whether *what* is desired is a motivating reason; and the other is whether desiring something is a motivating reason. I shall examine them in that order. And, for the second question, it will be necessary to determine the answer depending on whether we are dealing with a rational or with a non-rational desire respectively.

My answer to those questions will be negative. So, one of the central claims of this chapter, which I shall outline in Section 4.1, is that what I desire, whether we're dealing with a rational or a non-rational desire, is not a motivating reason. However, as I shall show, that does not mean that what is desired plays no role in *motivation*. It does. But the role that it plays is not that of *a reason*. Thus, part of the task of Section 4.1 will be to explain the sense in which what is desired can be said to motivate without being a motivating reason.

---

[1] For a summary of some of the main positions in this debate, as well as references to some of the most influential contributions, see Chang (2004).

Another main claim that I shall be defending in this chapter is that my desiring something is not a motivating reason either, and that this is true whether we are dealing with rational or non-rational desires. In Section 4.2, I argue that having a rational desire is not a motivating reason. And in Section 4.3, I argue that the same is true if we are dealing with non-rational desires. In the final section, 4.4, I explore the relationship between desires (in both uses of the word) and motivation.

4.1. What Is Desired and Motivating Reasons

When I introduced the distinction between bodily and rational desires, I pointed out that what we desire in a bodily way, say to drink or to have sex, can also be desired rationally; and I argued that something is a rational desire when it is desired for a reason. The desire to have sex, for instance, may not be a bodily desire, since it is possible to desire to have sex for a reason, for instance, because having sex is a means of conceiving a child. This, I also argued, shows that the distinction between rational and non-rational desires applies not to what is desired but to the desiring. Because of this, in investigating whether *what* is desired is a motivating reason, we can disregard whether this is a rational or non-rational desire. In other words, for the purposes of this question, it is safe to ignore that distinction.

In order to decide whether what is desired is a motivating reason, we need a clearer idea of what kinds of thing are the things we desire.

We saw in earlier chapters that the kinds of thing that we desire can seem to be very varied. We desire objects (money, a nicer garden); to do something (to sing, to learn to rollerblade); something or someone else to do something (the weather to change, the postman to arrive soon); oneself or others to be a certain way (to be more agile, my neighbour to be more considerate); or just things to be a certain way (tomorrow to be less humid than today; life to be simpler); and so on.

On closer examination, however, there is more uniformity in the nature of what is desired than it first appears. For the variety of things we desire can be expressed by means of an infinitival clause whose subject is either oneself, or something or someone else. So what is desired can be expressed as 'I want to ϕ', or as 'I want x to ϕ', where the value of 'x' need not be an agent, and that of 'ϕ' need not be an action verb.[2] Thus I can want to be more patient; to own a horse; to run a mile in four minutes; my daughter to come home; cold-callers to stop calling; people to be more polite; poverty to become history, etc.

The exception to this might seem to be that we can desire things: inanimate objects, animate things, and people. But in fact, to desire an object is to desire to own, or consume, or somehow to use or interact with that object. And, *mutatis mutandis*, the same is true of our desiring people and other living things. So to desire something is, necessarily, to desire to ϕ that thing (where ϕ stands for a verb signifying anything one can do with a thing, including merely owning or contemplating it; see Kenny 1963: 112 ff).

It seems, then, that there is no obstacle to the claim that what we desire is always either for ourselves, or for something or someone else to ϕ, namely, to (not) do something or to (not) be a certain way.

The issue, then, is whether the things we desire are reasons that motivate us to act, whether these things desired are mundane, such as to drink some water, James to come to the cinema with me, etc.; or more of an aspiration, such as to become an opera singer, the UN to be more effective, or to do my bit for the environment.

Now, when I act for a reason, the reason for which I act is what I have called a 'motivating reason', which, we saw, is something that in my eyes makes it right for me to act in that way, and in the light of which I act. A reason that motivates is a reason that *leads* the agent to act, in the sense that it presents a course of action to the agent as something right or good so that the agent acts in the light of that reason. Given this, it seems implausible that what is desired could be a motivating *reason* because what is desired is neither something that makes acting right, nor something in the light of which one acts.

For suppose that I want to have a pint of bitter and go to the pub in order to do so. It is not what I desire, namely, to have a pint of bitter,

---

[2] Not everything that I desire involves agency on my part although, as I said above, my taking action to bring about the desired outcome if the opportunity arises (or seems to me to) is one of the criteria for the attribution of that desire to me and for the intensity of my desire.

that I take to be the good of my going to the pub. Rather, for me, the good of going to the pub is the fact that they serve bitter there. And that fact is not what I desire.

Again, if what I want is to see my supervisor and I know she's in the library, then, what speaks to me in favour of going to the library is that my supervisor is there. It is true that this speaks in favour of my going to the library *because* I want to see my supervisor; but this does not mean that what speaks in favour of my going to the library is what I want—that is, to see my supervisor—rather it means that the fact that my supervisor is there speaks to me in favour of going to the library because I want to see her.[3] Thus, it is not what I desire that speaks in favour of acting but the fact that acting in that way is a means of getting what I desire.

Thus, if I go to the library in order to satisfy my desire to see my supervisor, then I go to the library in the light of the fact that my supervisor is there. And *what* I desire, viz. to see her, is not something in the light of which I go to the library; rather it is something *for the sake* of which I go: I go to the library *in order to* see my supervisor (or for the sake of seeing her), and in light of the fact that she is there now.

So what is desired is not a reason that motivates us to act. However, this does not mean that what is desired plays no role in motivation. Indeed, what is desired plays an all-important role in motivation.

What is desired plays the role of a *purpose or goal* for the sake of which we act. An agent's purpose or goal is that for the sake of which the agent acts and towards which his action is directed. And this is the sense in which what is wanted motivates: as a goal.

4.1.1. *Desires, goals, and intentions*

A goal or purpose is an end for the sake of which an action is performed. Goals are ends not only in the sense that, when all goes well, one's goal is what is achieved in or through one's action but

---

[3] One might argue that my reason, that is, what speaks to me in favour of going to the library, is *that I want to* see my supervisor. But that is a different claim from the one under examination, which is that my reason is what I want, namely, to see my supervisor. The other claim I examine in the following section.

also in the sense that a goal is that towards which action and activity are directed. As Aristotle emphasized, plants and animals, both human and non-human, can direct their actions or activity towards specific ends (such an end he called a *telos*). But there are important differences between the sense in which plants, non-human animals, and humans respectively, can be said to direct their actions or activity to ends (see Aristotle, *Physics* 198a,18 ff).

First, most if not all animals, but no plants, have some awareness of the world around them.[4] Plants do not have senses and hence do not have the capacity to be aware of their surroundings, while animals do: a cat is aware of the mouse it is about to catch; a gazelle is aware of a lion; and a dog can smell a bone. So a dog can dig in order to find a bone, of which it has some awareness, through the sense of smell or through memory. And when an animal does something in order to do something else, the end towards which it directs its actions is what the animal's purpose or goal in acting is: in our example, the dog's purpose or goal in digging is to find the bone.

What is distinctive about human agency is that, in addition to having awareness of the world around them, humans have the capacity to conceptualize their goals, and they also have the capacity to conceive of them as *goals*, that is, as that for the sake of which they act and towards which they direct their actions.[5] Thus for humans a goal or purpose can be an end the agent is aware of as an end, and something towards which he can direct his actions. Moreover, human agents can think of their goals as good: they can think of a goal as something that is appealing or somehow valuable and therefore wanted. So for us a goal is typically something wanted as good or valuable (in some respect), and conceived of as an end towards which we direct our actions.

The human capacity to conceive of goals as ends for the sake of which we can act and towards which we direct our actions is central to the notion of acting for a reason. A human agent who pursues a goal can direct his action guided by reasons: that is, can pursue his

---

[4] If there are creatures which fall on the borderline of this division, then they may also fall on the borderline between having and lacking these capacities.

[5] See Aquinas's discussion of this in the *Summa Theologiae* 1a, 2ae: q.1, a.2; q.6, a.2; q.13, a.2, *et passim*.

goal in the light of reasons. When he does so, he acts for a reason. Thus, acting for a reason is a special and rather sophisticated way of acting for a purpose: what makes it so is that an agent who acts for a reason takes into account reasons about whether and how to achieve his or her goal, and also reasons about the latter, which may include calculations about the intrinsic or relative value of the goal he or she is pursuing.[6] Thus, while many animals act for purposes, that is, in order to bring about a certain end, only creatures capable of reasoning are capable of acting both for a purpose and for a reason.

Our goals are things wanted and for the sake of which we act. Since things may be wanted either in themselves or instrumentally, something wanted may be a goal in itself, or only instrumentally, for the sake of some other goal. For instance, for someone who wants to play tennis for its own sake, because he enjoys it, playing tennis is a goal in itself. And it will be the final goal of a number of other things he does, for example, travel to the tennis club, or change into his tennis clothes, since he does those things in order to play tennis. Those other things he does may also be goals relative to yet other things, such as calling a taxi, or getting his tennis clothes out of the bag, which he does in order to achieve those intermediate goals. But all these are goals he adopts for the sake of that further goal: to play tennis. So they are not things wanted in themselves but only for the sake of something else. By contrast, the action of playing tennis is something he does for its own sake, and so not something done for a further goal: here the goal and the action are one and the same, namely to play tennis.

The goals we adopt which are things wanted in themselves (intrinsically) are wanted in the fuller sense of 'want' described in Chapter 3; while the goals we adopt which are things wanted only instrumentally are wanted at least in the 'thin' sense of that word described there, the sense in which wanting something is compatible with finding it tiresome, unpleasant, and even repugnant. For instance, in the example above the person wants to play tennis in the fuller sense of 'want' but he may only want to do those other things required for playing tennis (take a taxi, change into this tennis clothes, etc.) in the thin sense.

[6] See Anscombe (1957: 65), where she explains that practical reasoning requires calculation about how to achieve an end.

So what is wanted motivates by being a goal in action. When what is wanted is to do something, then one's goal is, precisely, doing that thing. But we saw that one can also want for someone or something else to do something, or for things to be a certain way. In that case, one's goal can be thought of as achieving something and acting will be directed at bringing about the thing wanted. For example, if I want my neighbours to turn down their music, then my goal in acting will be to make them do so, and I shall act so as to bring it about that they do, for example by asking them to do so or by knocking on the wall.

In humans, not everything that one wants to do or achieve is made into a goal of action. I may have a bodily desire to eat but reason that I ought not to, because I need to fast for an operation. In that case, so long as I keep to my decision, eating will not be a goal for me, even though I feel the desire to eat. Or I may have a desire to visit Rome in August but reason that it will be too hot and decide against visiting it then. Here again, something wanted, to visit Rome in August, is not adopted as a goal (at least pro tem).

However, when something one wants to do or achieve is adopted as a goal, then it can be the beginning of practical reasoning about how to achieve that goal. As Anscombe, paraphrasing Aristotle, puts it: 'the $\alpha\rho\chi\eta$ (starting point) [of practical reasoning] is τo $o\rho\epsilon\kappa\tau o\nu$' (the things wanted) (1957: 63).[7] And Aristotle says the following about the source of (local) movement for animals:

Both of these then are capable of originating local movement, thought and appetite; thought, that is, which calculates means to an end, that is, practical thought (it differs from speculative thought in the character of its end); while appetite is in every form of it relative to an end; for *that which is the object of*

---

[7] Anscombe says that what makes practical reasoning distinctive is not merely that its subject matter is practical: 'I have always objected to accounts of practical reasoning which reduce it to theoretical reasoning, i.e. to the argument from the truth of the premises to the truth of a conclusion implied by them [. . .] My own view is that the conclusion of a practical syllogism is an action or decision—that a man draws this conclusion shows that he wants to have or avoid something mentioned in the premises, and that the premises show what the point of the decision or action was' (1974: 19). I agree with Anscombe that practical reasoning presupposes a goal (or goals) in the person who engages in the reasoning; and the goal gives the *point* of the reasoning. However, as she also says, the goal itself is not a premise, although the goal is often actually mentioned in, or indicated by, the premises.

appetite is the stimulant of practical thought.   (*De Anima*, Book III, section 10;
433a 13–18, my italics)

Here Aristotle is drawing a distinction between two things that can be
regarded as 'sources of movement'. On the one hand, there are goals,
which are the objects of appetite. On the other hand there is practical
thought, which involves means-ends reasoning about how to achieve
those goals, including reasoning about how the satisfaction of a given
goal may affect other goals one also has.

The reasons that guide purposive actions can be reasons the agent
rehearses in practical reasoning, which is reasoning about one's goals
and about how to achieve them. In these actions, what is wanted
is the beginning of practical reasoning and it is also the end of
action (see also Aquinas, *Summa Theologiae* 1a2ae, q.1). Thus, what
is wanted is clearly crucial in motivation but its role is, as Aristotle
suggests, that of a starting point of practical reasoning, and the
goal towards which our actions are directed. And this also helps
to link the concept of goal with that of intention, since our goals
in acting are precisely what our actions *tend* towards—that is, our
intentions in acting: goals are intended ends for the sake of which
action is undertaken. In other words, our goals are our intentions in
acting.

Just as with things one wants to do or achieve, goals and intentions
are typically captured by infinitival clauses: 'to ϕ'; for example: 'to
grow stronger', 'to catch a train', 'to kill a mouse', 'to get John to
help me'. And, like wants, goals and intentions may also be expressed
with nominals: 'a quiet evening', 'world peace', 'friendship', etc. But
just as to desire a thing is to desire to get, have, enjoy, etc., that
thing, to have something that is expressed by a nominal as a goal or
as an intention is also to have the goal or intention of getting, having,
enjoying, etc., that thing.

A statement like 'It would be good to catch the train' or 'I ought to
kill that mouse' can express one's goals. However, one may entertain
such thoughts without being motivated to act, and without engaging
in practical reasoning about how to pursue those goals. But someone
who *is* motivated by those things, so that those statements would be
expressions of his adopted goals and intentions, will typically engage
in action to achieve those goals.

Thus, a goal is not a reason because, as we saw above, a goal is not what, to the agent, speaks in favour of ϕ-ing, what seems to her to make her ϕ-ing right. What seems to me to make it right to give my daughter antibiotics is not my goal, namely, to combat her pneumonia, but rather some facts: that she has pneumonia, that antibiotics are efficient at combating pneumonia, etc. And these are my reasons for giving her antibiotics. It may be true that these facts are *reasons* for me only because I have the goal of curing my daughter's pneumonia; but given that I do have that goal, my reasons are those facts.

It is true that goals, as well as intentions, etc. are sometimes called reasons. This is partly because a question 'Why are you ϕ-ing?' can be answered by citing one's goal: 'in order to ψ'; it is also partly because, although my goal is not itself what speaks to me in favour of ϕ-ing, it often gives a pretty good indication of what that might be; and so, if something is done for a reason and in pursuit of a goal, knowing the goal enables one to infer at least one desirability characterization of the action, that is, one motivating reason. Thus, in the example above, if one knows that my goal in giving my daughter antibiotics is to combat her pneumonia, then one can infer my reason for giving her antibiotics: namely, that antibiotics are efficient at combating pneumonia. Moreover, if goals were reasons, it would follow that any animal that acts in pursuit of a goal would also act for a reason. But whereas it is fairly uncontroversial that a dog who digs in order to find a bone acts in pursuit of a goal, it is much more controversial to say that the dog acts for a reason: that what motivates the dog to dig is a reason, namely that digging is a means to find the bone, and that the dog acts guided by that reason. So calling goals reasons is not helpful, as it suggests that wherever there is purposive action there is rational action, that is, acting for reasons, and even action involving practical reasoning, both of which seem doubtful.

I conclude, then, that what we desire is not a motivating reason; rather what we desire may be adopted as a goal and thus be one's intention in action. In that way, what is desired plays a very important role in motivating action: it is a *sine qua non* for intentional action and it is the beginning of practical reasoning. Thus, what we desire moves us to act but not as a reason, rather as a goal or purpose, and when we act with a purpose, our purpose is also our intention in acting.

So we have established that a desire, in the sense of what is desired, may be a goal and an intention in acting—but it is not a motivating reason. I now turn to the question whether *my having* a desire is a motivating reason for action.

We saw, when exploring whether what is desired is a motivating reason, that there was no need to distinguish between rational and non-rational desires. However, as I pointed out in the preceding chapter, rational and non-rational desires stand in quite different relations to reasons. Because of this, it is necessary to examine the question whether having a desire is a motivating reason for desires of each kind separately. I shall start with rational desires, as they are more closely connected with reasons.

Before doing that, though, I need to make a point of clarification. In Chapter 2, I noted that, according to some, the gerundial expression 'my believing that p' can be used to refer to a mental state of mine. But I added that, whether that is true or not, such expressions can also be used to refer to facts: to the fact that I believe something. Clearly, this applies also to the expression 'my wanting x': if it can be used to refer to a mental state, as it is claimed, it certainly can also be used to refer to the fact that I want something.

Since our question is whether having a desire (bodily or rational) is a reason, and since, as we saw in Chapter 1, reasons are facts, if desires are to have any chance of being motivating reasons, the expression 'having a desire' in this context must be construed as referring to a fact. So in the coming sections, I shall take the expressions 'my desiring something' and 'the fact that I desire something' to be equivalent, and shall use either, depending on the grammar of the context, to refer to the fact that I desire something. That is, I shall take 'His wanting to improve his game' and 'the fact that he wanted to improve his game' to be merely stylistic variants, each of which I shall use according to the grammatical or idiomatic requirements of the relevant context.[8]

---

[8] This is an issue I shall discuss again and in more detail when I talk about beliefs as reasons.

4.2. Having Rational Desires and Motivating Reasons

It has seemed to many philosophers that, typically, our reasons for acting are, at least partly, our wanting to do something (the other part of the reason being some belief about how to satisfy that want).[9]

According to this, if I revise hard in order to pass my exam, my reason for revising hard is my wanting to pass my exam and my believing that my action under the description 'revising' is a means of ensuring that I pass my exam. And this view, or versions of it, is the orthodoxy in contemporary theory of action.

But the popularity of the view notwithstanding, I think it is mistaken: my wanting something is not my reason for acting. To see why not, we need to consider the connection, examined in the previous chapter, between having a rational desire, reasons, and the good.

As we saw there, rational desires are desires we have for reasons. When I have a rational desire, that desire is grounded on a reason, which is also the 'desirability characterization' of what I desire: the good, in my eyes, of what I desire (a good that may be intrinsic or instrumental). In other words, I want what I want for a reason, and that reason is the good that I see in the thing I want. But the good I see in what I want is not the fact that I want it, for that does not give a desirability characterization of what I want. Such a characterization must pick out some feature or aspect of what I want that makes it desirable to me, and the mere fact that I want something simply does not do that: things do not seem desirable to me because I desire them; rather I desire them because they seem desirable to me—even when

---

[9] As was mentioned earlier, Davidson argued that 'R is a primary reason why an agent performed the action A under description d only if R consists of a pro attitude of the agent towards actions with a certain property, and a belief of the agent that A, under the description d, has that property' (1980: 4 ff.). Davidson did not, in that paper, specify whether he took the 'reason that explains why an agent performed' an action to be also the agent's reason for acting. If one takes the latter to be the reasons that figure as premises in practical reasoning, given Davidson's account of practical reasoning, the answer may be 'no'. Nonetheless, many who have endorsed Davidson's conception of a primary reason do take that reason to be the agent's reason for acting—what I am calling the 'motivating reason'.

it might be quite difficult to articulate precisely what makes them seem desirable.

Thus, suppose I want to invest in an ISA. Then it follows that there is something good I see in investing in an ISA—for instance, that ISAs are safe and tax-free investments. This is the desirability characterization that investing in an ISA has for me, and this is therefore my reason for wanting to invest in one.

Now, suppose that, in those circumstances, I invest in an ISA. Then, my reason for doing so will be my reason for wanting to invest, say, that ISAs are safe and tax-free. For the good I see in investing in an ISA is what motivates me to invest, which is also what motivates me *to want* to invest. And the good I see in investing cannot merely be that I want to invest. To borrow an example from Anscombe, what makes my acquiring a pin desirable to me cannot simply be that I desire to acquire one: there must be something about acquiring a pin that makes it seem good because fun, reassuring, etc.—which is my reason for wanting it. (And although I may say that the reason why I acquired a pin was that I wanted to, this is a way of saying that I acquired it for no reason, or it is a way of implying that there is a reason that I am not willing to disclose or something similar. I develop this point in the next section.)

Just as the mere fact that I want something does not capture a desirability characterization that I take as a reason for wanting it, the mere fact that I want *to do something* does not capture a desirability characterization that I take as a reason for *doing it* either. The mere fact that I want to invest in an ISA says nothing about what, in my eyes, the good of investing in an ISA might be, for the good I see in investing in an ISA is not that I want to invest; rather the reverse is the case: I want to invest because I see some good in investing. Therefore, my reason for acting is not my wanting to act so but rather whatever reason I have for wanting to act so.

What is true, however, is that if A has a rational want to ϕ, then A takes ϕ-ing to be, in some respect, good. Thus, the claim that A has a rational want to ϕ implies that, in A's eyes, there is something good about ϕ-ing. But, to repeat, this is not because her wanting it is the reason she takes herself to have but rather because *if* she has such a rational want to do something, then she must at least believe that there is something about doing that thing, some feature or aspect of it, that makes it good in her eyes and hence desirable.

I have argued that wanting something is not normally a motivating reason. However, we sometimes say things such as 'I acted because I wanted to', and this appears to suggest that wanting to do something *can* be a motivating reason. In the next section I provide an account of how to understand such claims and show that the appearance is deceptive.

4.2.1. *Doing things 'because I want to'*

Suppose that someone says that they returned some stolen property 'because they wanted to'. One thing he might mean by this statement is that nobody is forcing him to do it. To say this is not to give his reason for returning the money, it is rather to exclude a range of reasons or explanations of why he acted that are connected to external coercion, or commands, etc.: it tells us that the agent did not act because he had been commanded to do so, or threatened, or in some other way externally compelled to act. Thus, if there was a reason that motivated him to do it that reason was not something such as that he'd been told to do it, or that he would be punished if he didn't.

Another thing one might mean, which is compatible with the above, is that one is not doing it for some ulterior motive, for example to avoid jail or to appear to be good, but rather one is doing it 'for its own sake'—one sees a point in returning the stolen stuff which is not instrumental to some other end, for instance, that it was wrong to steal it in the first place. (More on this shortly.)

Finally, in saying that he returned some stolen property because he wanted to, someone might mean that he is returning the money simply because he feels like it, that is, because he feels an impulse to do so. In saying this, he would be explaining *why* he is returning the money and also probably implying that he did not do it for any reason at all. If you do something simply because you feel like doing it, then it follows that you did not do it for a reason: your feeling like doing it is not your reason for doing it although it is the reason why you did it.[10]

---

[10] As Anscombe points out, the question 'Why?' is not refused application (that is, one is not rejecting the implication that this was a voluntary action) 'because the answer to it says

It may appear that this is just a stipulation and that, in fact, wanting to do something, or feeling like doing something, can be reasons for doing that thing.[11] Thus, suppose that Ann feels a desire to sing, and consequently breaks into song. She doesn't sing in order to show that she is happy, nor to exercise her voice, etc. She simply sings because she has a desire to sing. Surely, my opponent will argue, in such a case her wanting to sing is her reason for singing. A. Mele (from whom I've taken the example) gives the following argument to support this claim:

singings motivated by such desires are intentional actions; it is standardly held that intentional actions are done for reasons; this wholly intrinsic desire is the best available candidate for a relevant reason; the desire plays a central role in explaining the action; and the role is very similar to that played by typical Davidsonian reasons.   (2003: 82)

Even if we accept the first of Mele's claims (that such a singing is an intentional action), there is still the question whether to accept that every intentional action is done for a reason. For it seems plausible to argue that some actions are intentional but not done for a reason, for example actions that are under one's control and done knowingly but for no purpose, such as whistling, or skipping along the road; or actions that are pure manifestations of emotions.[12]

However, if we accept that all intentional actions are done for reasons, then someone who thinks this singing was not done for a reason will conclude that it was not intentional. This is not as problematic as it might seem, because to say that the singing was not intentional does not imply that it was *un*intentional, or accidental, or coerced. We might say that it was not intentional but voluntary,

that there is *no* reason, any more than the question how much money I have in my pocket is refused application by the answer "None" ' (1957: 27).

[11] Chang (2004) argues that it is, for instance, in a Buridan's ass type of case: where one is faced with a choice between two identical options. But her argument only shows that whatever one chooses can be explained by saying that one felt like choosing that option, and not that wanting it was one's reason for choosing that option. In fact, it is not clear that in such cases one can choose one option rather than another *for a reason*.

[12] See Hursthouse (1991) and Alvarez (2009). There are also actions that are under the agent's control but are not fully intentional. See e.g. Aquinas, *Summa Theologiae* Ia, 2ae, q.1, a.1, ad 3, where he says that these actions do not belong 'properly to man' qua rational being; and also O'Shaughnessy (1980: vol. 2, ch.10).

in the way in which many animal actions are surely voluntary (they do what they do because they want to) but not intentional if that means 'done for a reason', since (at least) many animals do not act for reasons.

So the question here is whether the singing Mele describes is done for a reason. I don't think it is, nor do I think that his argument shows that it is. First, it is not clear that the role that Ann's desiring to sing plays in *explaining* her singing fits the Davidsonian model. And second, and more importantly, the fact that a reason explains an action does not imply that that was the reason for which the agent acted.

The reason why this example does not seem to fit the Davidsonian model is this. Strictly speaking, the Davidsonian explanation should be something like: 'Ann had a desire towards actions with a certain property (namely, being a singing), and she also had a belief that A, her action, under description d (namely 'singing'), had that property.' (See Davidson 1980: 4 ff.) But this barely makes sense, and the only reason to claim that Ann had such a belief is that then the example will fit the Davidsonian model.[13]

Second, even if the case could be said to fit that model of explanation, that would not show that wanting to sing was the reason that motivated the agent to sing. It would seem that behind the view that Ann's reason for singing was that she wanted to sing might be the thought that, since Ann's singing can be explained by her wanting to sing, then it follows that her wanting to sing was her reason for singing.[14] But it doesn't. What follows is that her wanting to sing was *the reason why* she sang. As we saw in Chapter 1, a reason can explain an action without being the agent's reason for acting: some fact can be a reason why Ann ϕ-ed without being her reason for ϕ-ing.

I must emphasize that I am not claiming that people never do things just because they want to, or because they feel like doing them. My claim is that, when they do, and there is no more to say about their

---

[13] And one could not substitute 'her action of moving her lips as she did, etc.' for 'her action of singing' because that would explain why Ann moved her lips as she did but not why she sang. For, in my view similarly unsuccessful, attempts to argue that Davidson's model can fit all cases of voluntary action, see Smith (2004), and Harcourt's reply (2004).

[14] Some arguments to the effect that our wanting something, or our feeling like doing something, can be reasons seem to depend on this thought: since our wanting something makes it intelligible that we should do that thing, then our wanting it must have been our reason for doing it. But that conflates explanatory and motivating reasons.

reasons for wanting to do the relevant thing, their action will be an action not done for a reason, even though it was voluntary and even though there was a reason why they did it—namely that they wanted to do it.[15]

It should be noted that doing something because you want to, or feel like doing it, is different from doing something because you *like* doing that thing. If you give as your reason for doing something that you *like* doing that thing, then your reason for doing that thing is that you like doing it, that you will enjoy it, which is perfectly intelligible as your reason for acting—though, as Anscombe says (1957: §39), there are limits here. The limits are not those of morality or propriety but of intelligibility, for sometimes it is difficult to see what the pleasure of doing a particular thing might be—for instance, the pleasure of sitting through an eight-hour speech by Fidel Castro. (Of course, it is true that if one *feels* like doing something this may well be because one imagines that doing that thing will be in some way pleasant or agreeable. If so, then perhaps the reason for doing it is that it will be pleasant and not that you feel like doing it. But that would be different from the case where one simply does it because one wants to, or feels like it, while not having anything to say about what the good of doing that thing might be.)

Let me mention a kind of example that I think is the closest to a case where wanting to do something is your reason for doing it. Suppose that you have a persistent want to do something—to straighten a picture, or to remove a thread from the jacket of the person sitting in front of you at a lecture. Now, you may or may not be able to give a desirability characterization for it (it could be an aesthetic desirability characterization, or the thought that the world will be a tidier place if you remove the thread). But what matters is that, although initially you decide against doing it (perhaps you don't know the person at all), the desire to do it is so persistent and is so distracting that eventually

---

[15] Perhaps many or all things that we do ostensibly for no reason, or claim to do just because we feel like it, are in fact always done for some reason—only these are reasons that the agent is *unable* (psychologically, not epistemically, speaking) or unwilling to identify; reasons that may require a great deal of soul-searching or professional help to unearth (a project which in most cases is unlikely to be necessary or profitable). If this is right, then there may be reasons for which we do those things but, if so, our reasons for doing those things are not that we want to do them but rather those other facts that psychoanalysis will help bring to light.

you conclude that unless you do it you won't be able to concentrate on the lecture, and you end up removing the irritating thread. Here it seems plausible to say that your only reason for removing the thread was that you wanted to, and indeed that you wanted to do it very much. But in fact that is not quite right. Your reason for removing the thread, if we agree that you did it for a reason, is that the desire to do it is so distracting that, unless you do it, you will not be able to focus on the lecture. That is the desirability characterization that you could give of doing that thing (given that we agree that you did it for a reason), and not the mere fact that you wanted to do it; for your wanting to do it, no matter how intensely you want to do it, does not give the desirability characterization that doing that thing had for you. A desirability characterization that an action has for you is precisely what makes doing that thing desirable for you; but the fact that you very much want to do something does not make doing that thing desirable, it makes it *desired*—which is a different thing.

To sum up, on none of the interpretations of doing something 'because one wants to' that we have examined have we found that one's reason for acting was wanting to do that thing: things done genuinely and merely 'because one wants to' are either things not done for a reason—and hence the fact that one wanted to do it was not one's reason for doing it; or they are things done for some reason that has not been stated, and is perhaps obscure and subconscious—and hence, a fortiori, not for the reason that one wanted to do them.

There is another source for the view that the fact that one wants to do something is one's reason for doing it, which depends on a misunderstanding of the concept of doing something for its own sake—a misunderstanding that in fact consists partly in assimilating the concept of doing something for its own sake to that of doing something because one wants to. I now turn to exploring actions done for their own sake.

4.2.2. *Doing something for its own sake*

There are things we do for the sake of other things we want, and there are things we do for their own sake. It seems clear that something done for the sake of something else is done for a reason: if you ϕ in order to bring it about that p, then your reason for ϕ-ing is the fact ϕ-ing will bring it about that p. For example, if I exercise for the sake of health, my reason for exercising is that it is a way of keeping healthy. And if I study law in order to become a barrister, then my reason for studying law is that it is the way to become a barrister. And so on. But what about things done for their own sake—are they also done for a reason? And if so, what is that reason?

Things done for their own sake are things done because one wants to do them on account of some good one takes the action to have, which is one's reason for wanting to do it. Hence, it seems that something done for its own sake is something done for a reason. And now it is tempting to think that the reason must be precisely that one wants to do those things—wants to do them for their own sake. But this is wrong and it is evidence of a misunderstanding of what doing something for its own sake is.

Doing something for its own sake is doing it for the reason that there is—in the agent's eyes—something good about the action that makes it worthwhile as an end in itself and not merely instrumentally as a means to some other end. For instance, if I go skiing for its own sake (and not in order to network with potential clients) then my reason is that in my eyes there is something intrinsically good about skiing, let's say, that it is enjoyable for me, that is, that I enjoy it.

Now, to say that my reason for going skiing is that I enjoy it is to give my reason for going skiing, namely, that I enjoy it—although it is not to give a further aim for the sake of which I go skiing. That is, I don't go skiing in order to enjoy myself, even though my reason for going skiing is that I enjoy it; indeed to say that I enjoy doing it is to explain why, or the sense in which, skiing is something I might do for its own sake.

But surely, someone might object, if you go skiing because you enjoy it then your reason for going skiing must be that you want to do something enjoyable (together with your belief that skiing is an enjoyable thing to do). This view, though popular, is I think mistaken: if I go skiing because I enjoy it, it does not follow that I go skiing because I want to do something enjoyable. I *can* go skiing because I want to do something enjoyable; for instance, if I reasoned as follows: 'I have been advised by my therapist to do more things I find enjoyable. Skiing is something I find enjoyable. So I'll go skiing.' In such a case it would be true that I go skiing for the sake of doing something enjoyable (that is, because I want to do something enjoyable). But note that, since my reason for wanting to do something pleasant would be that my therapist has advised me to do so, even in this case, my reason for going skiing would not be just that I wanted to do something pleasant but also that my therapist had advised me to do something pleasant, and that skiing is such a thing, etc. Moreover, in such a case I would not go skiing for its own sake but rather for the sake of doing something enjoyable, which I'd do for the sake of my mental health. So let us return to the example where I go skiing for its own sake, to see whether my reason there is that I want to go skiing.

It would be perverse, because it would get things the wrong way round, to say that if I go skiing because it is enjoyable, then my reason for going is that I want to go skiing. Rather, my reason for going skiing is that it is enjoyable, and that is also my reason for *wanting* to go skiing. The things one finds enjoyable are things that prima facie, and because one finds them enjoyable, one wants to do (though one may come to see that one has reason not to do them and hence, perhaps, to see that one has reason not to want to do them—for instance if they are harmful to others or to oneself).[16] But none of this shows that my reason for doing something I find enjoyable is that I want to do it. The fact that I enjoy it is my reason for wanting to ski, but that does not turn my wanting to ski into my reason for skiing.

The point here is not simply that it is *possible* to state my reason for acting without mentioning the fact that I want certain things. That may be true but it is trivial. The point is that, when I act in order to satisfy a want, the reason for which I act (if any) is the reason for which I want what I want (if any). And in things we want to do for their own sake, our reason for acting is not that we want to do them but the reason that we take ourselves to have for wanting to do them,

---

[16] A number of complex issues—some concerned with the normativity of reasons, some concerned with weakness of the will—are raised by this point but I cannot go into them here.

namely the good, the desirability characteristic, that we take doing that thing to have: that it is fun, an act of friendship, aesthetically pleasing, healthy, etc.

4.2.3. *Wanting to φ as an instrumental reason*

I have argued, then, that my wanting to ϕ is not my reason for ϕ-ing. I can ϕ simply because I want to—but then it is possible that I do not ϕ for a reason. And I can ϕ for its own sake where I ϕ for the reason that there is, in my eyes, something good about ϕ-ing. So, if ϕ-ing is something I do for its own sake, my reason for ϕ-ing is not that I want to ϕ. For example, my reason for spending time with a friend is not that I want to spend time with them; it is rather that that person is a friend—which is also the reason why I want to spend time with them. And if someone asked: 'But why do you want to spend time with your friends?' they would show that they do not understand what friendship is.

However, all the above may be right but it does not rule out the possibility that wanting to ϕ should be, not my reason for ϕ-ing, but my reason for doing something *else* (ψ-ing, say) which is a means of ϕ-ing. In other words, it does not rule out the most common interpretation of the orthodoxy I mentioned above: the view that, if the explanation of why I ψ is that I want to ϕ, then my reason for ψ-ing is that I want to ϕ, and believe that ψ-ing is a means of ϕ-ing. According to this suggestion, and to return to the ISA example above, my reason for investing in the ISA is not that I want to invest in an ISA but rather, say, that I want to improve my financial situation, and believe that investing in ISAs is a way of doing so. And, likewise, if I visit China to learn Chinese, my reason for visiting China is that I want to learn Chinese, and believe that . . . And so on. If this is right, then at least for things done for the sake of something else, wanting something is a motivating reason.

This suggestion seems plausible but, on examination, it is unconvincing. Remember that my reason for acting is the desirability characterization that an action has for me. But, if I want to ϕ and believe that ψ-ing is a means of ϕ-ing, what makes ψ-ing desirable to me is precisely *that*: namely, that my ψ-ing is a means of ϕ-ing (which is something I want). The desirability characterization that my ψ-ing has is that it is a means of ϕ-ing. Thus, in the example above, the desirability characterization that investing in an ISA has for me is not that I want to improve my financial situation but that investing in an ISA *will improve my financial situation*[17]—and improving my financial situation is something I want, a goal of mine.

It is true that the fact that ψ-ing is a means of ϕ-ing will only be a motivating reason for me to ψ if ϕ-ing is one of my goals. And as we saw in the previous section, for it to be my goal there must be something I see in ϕ-ing that makes it seem good or something that I see as somehow attractive. Hence, the fact that an ISA will improve my financial situation will only motivate me if I want to improve my financial situation; and for me to want that, there must be something good I see in it; for instance, that financial security contributes to a good life. Still, the reason that motivates me to invest is not that I want to improve my financial situation but that so investing will satisfy that want.

This may not seem right because we often say 'my reason for ψ-ing was that I wanted to ϕ'. For instance, my reason for running was that I wanted to catch the train; my reason for studying is that I want to become a barrister. And so on. And this suggests that my wanting those things are the reasons that motivate me to act.

However, this thought results from a failure to see that those expressions provide the agent's *goal*: for instance, to catch the train, to run a marathon, etc. These apparent expressions of reasons are distinctive: in general, the expression 'A ψ-ed because *she wanted to ϕ*' provides A's *goal or purpose* in ψ-ing, namely to ϕ. This is clear because 'A ψ-ed because she wanted to ϕ' implies 'A ψ-ed *in order to ϕ*'. For instance, if I lend you my car because I want to please you, then it follows that I lend you my car in order to please you (pleasing you is my goal or purpose); if I ran because I wanted to catch the train, then I ran in order to catch the train; and if I study because I want to become a barrister, then I study in order to become a barrister, etc. And so these expressions give one's goals, viz. to catch the train, etc. In short, my wanting something is not the reason that motivates me,

---

[17] In Chapters 5 and 6, I shall discuss the connection between beliefs and reasons, and explain what my reason is when things are not as I believed they were, for instance when, contrary to what I thought, investing in an ISA won't improve my financial situation.

and the fact that we use the expressions just examined does not show that it is.

To sum up the argument so far. The fact that rational wants are grounded on reasons means that when I act in order to satisfy a rational want, the reason that motivates me to act is whatever reason I have for having that want, whether my reason is instrumental (satisfying this want is a way of satisfying some other want) or intrinsic (some good that I perceive in what I want). My reason is not, in either case, what Humeans claim, namely my wanting something. I now turn to non-rational desires and in particular to bodily desires.

4.3. Having Bodily Desires and Motivating Reasons

In this section I shall examine the same question about wanting but concerning bodily desires; that is, whether if, for instance, I drink because I am thirsty then my *feeling* thirsty is my reason for drinking; and more generally, whether my feeling a desire to ϕ is my reason for ϕ-ing when I ϕ because I feel the desire.

Because of the fact that bodily appetites are not desires we have for reasons, we cannot say, as we did with rational wants, that we perform the desire-satisfying actions (that is, to eat, drink, etc.) for the reason that we have to have those desires: for there is no such reason. So it seems that perhaps our reasons for performing those actions is that we feel the relevant desires. But is this right?

It seems plausible at least prima facie that these desire-satisfying actions are in fact not done for a reason. So one way of deciding the question about whether having a bodily appetite is one's reason for acting to satisfy it, is to ask whether this is so, that is, whether when I drink because I feel thirsty, I drink for a reason. If I do, the next question is whether my reason is that I feel a desire to drink, or something else. I am inclined to think that, since bodily appetites are not had for reasons, when I drink because I feel thirsty I do not drink for a reason and, more generally, that when performing the desire-satisfying action, I do not typically act for a reason. If that is right, then it follows a fortiori that when acting to satisfy a bodily appetite my feeling the desire is not my reason for acting. But as we shall see, there are also arguments that suggest that when we act to satisfy a bodily appetite we do indeed act for a reason. I shall examine those arguments and show that, even if they are right, our reasons for acting in such cases are not that we feel the desire. Either way, the conclusion is that whenever I act to satisfy a bodily appetite, my feeling the desire itself is not my reason for acting.

Now, it seems clear that if I feel thirsty, I am inclined to drink, and if I do drink then, normally, I drink because of this desire I feel: I drink because I feel thirsty and in order to satisfy my thirst. But as we have seen, this does not make my feeling thirsty my reason. From the fact that I drink because I feel thirsty it is right to conclude that my feeling thirsty explains why I drink and, hence, that that is the reason *why* I drink. But from this, we cannot straightforwardly conclude that my desiring to drink is *my reason* for drinking because the reason why someone does something need not be his reason for doing it.

In order for my desiring to drink to be my reason for drinking it should be true that in such cases I drink for a reason—but it is not clear that I do.

It *is* clear that I *can* drink for a reason. For example, suppose that, while not feeling thirsty, I drink three glasses of water as part of what I regard as a healthy diet. If so, my reason for drinking is that drinking plenty of water is part of a healthy diet. In this kind of case, drinking is something I do for a reason—a health-related reason. So it is clear that I can drink without feeling a desire to drink, and do so for a reason. But the fact that sometimes I drink for a reason does not imply that whenever I drink, I drink for a reason; and, more importantly, it does not imply that when I drink because I feel thirsty, then my feeling thirsty is my reason for drinking.

Similarly, if I am thirsty but refrain from drinking, normally I refrain for a reason I have for not drinking, for instance, that I am fasting, or about to have an operation. But again, the fact that, if I am thirsty and refrain from drinking, I normally do so for a reason does not mean that when I drink because I am thirsty I also drink for a reason.

We saw in the previous chapter that bodily appetites are not had for reasons, even though there are reasons why we have bodily appetites (that is, our having those desires can be explained by those reasons). Since these desires are not had for reasons, it is at least plausible that the actions that are performed to satisfy them are not performed for reasons. To see the plausibility of this claim, consider the cases of some other animals.

4.3.1. *Bodily appetites in animals and humans*

Bodily appetites, like other non-rational desires, we share with many other animals. These animals eat and drink because they feel the relevant desires, and when they eat and drink they do so in order to satisfy their hunger and thirst. However, since (at least most of) these animals lack the capacity to reason and hence to act for reasons, they do not eat or drink for a reason. And in general, for them, the fact that they feel those desires, or their feeling those desires, is not *their* reason for doing what will satisfy them: eating, drinking, etc.

It is in the nature of bodily appetites, whether ours or those of other animals, that the actions for which they are desires are intrinsically attractive to the creature that has the desire—at the very least because they bring with them a degree of pleasure, if only that concomitant to the cessation or assuaging of unease, discomfort, or unpleasant sensations. Because of this, it is right to say that *the reason why* the creature performs the relevant actions is that it feels a desire to do it and that such actions are pleasant. And yet, that they are pleasant is not the creature's reason for doing them. For we have seen that this would require them to *conceive* of what they do to satisfy their desires as pleasant, or good in some other respect, but non-human animals do not have that capacity and hence do not act for the reason that it is good or pleasant. And the general point is that, in such cases, a creature (whether human or not) need not *think* of an action as good in any sense, not even as pleasant, in order to perform that action. I do not simply mean that they needn't consider that thought at the time of acting. I mean something more radical: namely, that it makes sense to attribute to them the capacity to experience the relevant pleasure, or to be attracted by the relevant good, without needing to attribute to them the capacity to *think* of the action as good. Thus, actions that are performed in order to satisfy a bodily appetite, whether in our case or in that of other animals, do not appear to be performed for a reason.

One might object that there is an important difference between animals on the one hand, and adult human beings, on the other, which is precisely that while creatures that cannot reason are aware of their desires, that is, they feel them, they are not aware of the fact *that* they feel such desires. A human adult, by contrast, not only feels the desire to drink but is also aware that he feels such a desire and can reflect on it. And it may seem to follow from this that, even if this is not so for animals and babies, when a human adult drinks because he feels thirsty, he drinks for a reason and that reason is precisely that he feels thirsty; in other words, his reason is his feeling the desire to drink, that is, the fact that he wants to drink.

It is true that human adults normally have the capacity to think about their desires, that is, to have awareness of them qua desires. But this fact alone does not show that the actions that satisfy a bodily appetite are performed for a reason, and even less that that reason is the fact that the person feels the relevant desire. This is so because, given what acting for a reason involves, in order for the desiring to be the agent's reason, two conditions would need to be met—but in fact neither is met.

One condition is that it should not be possible to explain the agent's behaviour without invoking his capacity to conceive of actions, of desires, of reasons, and of the relation between them. The other is that, in exercising that capacity, the agent must conceive of his feeling the desire as that which makes the relevant action good. And neither of those conditions is met when humans act in order to satisfy a bodily appetite.

In general, in order to understand the pattern of explanation exemplified by a felt desire and the corresponding action we do not need to invoke the agent's capacity to conceive any part of the process: feeling the desire, the action, etc. The point here is not that the agent may not actually or explicitly go through a process of reasoning (for example, 'I am thirsty, my being thirsty is a reason for me to drink, therefore . . . ') for he need not do that when he acts for a reason. The point is that an explanation of the behaviour that the satisfaction of such a desire involves does not require that the agent should *be able* to conceptualize the whole or even part of the process, and a fortiori it does not require the capacity to conceptualize it in terms of one's desiring being a reason.

It could be objected that, given our rational natures, it is actually impossible for us, except in very rare cases, not to conceptualize the process from felt desire to action. And if so, it seems that it is impossible for us not to act for a reason whenever we act in order to satisfy a desire. But the fact (if it is a fact) that whenever we act to satisfy a bodily appetite, we conceptualize the relation between desire and action does not mean that we thereby act for a reason.

When I drink because I am thirsty, this may be accompanied by a thought such as 'I'm very thirsty' or 'I really want some water'. Such thoughts can be present (it may even be rare for adult humans to feel the desire without the accompanying thought passing through their minds), but the presence of such thoughts is not required for desires of this kind to be felt and acted upon, nor for them to make the pattern of desire and action intelligible. Thoughts such as these ones, whether voiced or not, are a linguistic expression of the desire to drink. However, the mere fact that one can express the desire linguistically does not make the feeling of the desire into a reason, since the capacity for such linguistic expression is not necessary for experiencing such a desire, nor for engaging in the pattern of behaviour characteristic of such desires and their fulfilment. The linguistic articulation of the desire and of its connection to action is superfluous to the explanation of this kind of behaviour, as can be seen from the case of animals and human babies.

Generally, the connection between my feeling the desire and my performing the action that satisfies my bodily appetite is not mediated (implicitly or explicitly) by any thought to the effect that I have a reason to act, even less that my feeling that desire is a reason for me to act, for example that my feeling thirsty is a reason to drink.

When I drink because I am thirsty, I drink in order to satisfy my desire (to quench my thirst), but so do other animals and we saw that in doing this they do not, or need not, act for a reason. Acting for a reason is a (fairly sophisticated) way of acting for a goal. It is sophisticated in the sense that it requires awareness of one's goal as a goal, the capacity to evaluate one's goals, and the capacity for means-ends reasoning. But it is possible to act in pursuit of a goal without acting for a reason, as is the case of (most) other animals. And when our goal in acting is the satisfaction of a bodily appetite, it seems plausible to say that, in so acting, we need not be acting for a reason. If I feel the desire to drink, one might say, I do not need a reason for drinking, that is, I do not need any conception of what the good of drinking is to motivate me to drink.

So the fact that we can or even that we must think of these bodily appetites and perhaps even of the link between them and the actions that will satisfy them whenever we engage in the relevant behaviour does not mean that when we drink because we are thirsty we drink for a reason. To claim that we must do would seem an over-intellectualizing of the character of bodily appetites and of their relation to actions.

If this response is right, then when we drink because we feel thirsty we don't drink for a reason and, therefore, our feeling the desire to drink is not our reason for drinking. True, we drink *in order* to satisfy our desire, and that makes our action a purposive action that can be explained by reference to the goal or purpose for the sake of which we act. But this does not imply that we act for a reason.

4.3.2. *Bodily appetites and acting for a reason*

But perhaps the view I have been defending involves an exaggeration of the immediacy of the connection between the desire and the relevant action in humans—a kind of 'zoomorphizing' of our behaviour. Perhaps, one might argue, the truth is rather that actions such as drinking when thirsty, eating when hungry, etc., are so ordinary and ingrained, that we never rehearse our reasons for doing them. But we do still do them for a reason. Thus, sometimes I drink for an extrinsic reason, one unrelated to whether I feel thirsty, for instance that it will please my host, or that it will help swallow a pill. But in the normal cases my reason for drinking is intrinsic: it is simply the fact that I feel thirsty. And so on for other desires. In short, it might seem that the first response mistakes an implicit and default reason for no reason.

Suppose we accept that the actions that satisfy bodily appetites are performed for a reason. It is still implausible to say that in these cases, my reason for acting is *my feeling a desire* (or the fact that I feel a desire). For it is implausible that I think that the good of my drinking is that I feel thirsty; rather, if anything, what makes drinking good in my eyes is *that drinking will satisfy my thirst*. Admittedly, the fact that drinking will satisfy my desire will seem a reason for me to drink *only* because

I feel thirsty. But that does not mean that my reason for drinking is that I feel thirsty.[18]

So, even if we accepted that these actions are done for a reason, it does not seem that our reasons for doing them is that we feel those desires.

Towards the end of the section on rational desires we saw that some philosophers may argue that, although I am right in claiming that, in general, my wanting to ϕ is not my reason for ϕ-ing, nevertheless my wanting to ϕ is my reason for ψ-ing, if I regard ψ-ing as a means of ϕ-ing. In a parallel way, one may argue here that, although my feeling thirsty may not be my reason for drinking, it is nonetheless my reason for doing those things that are conducive to my drinking: for example, fetching a glass of water. The response to this is similar to that given to the corresponding point about rational desires. My reason for doing the things that are conducive to the action that will satisfy my bodily appetite (for instance, fetching a glass of water, preparing some food) is precisely that those things are, each in a different way, conducive to the action that will satisfy my bodily appetite (to drinking, eating, etc.). So I do those things for the reason that they are conducive to my performing the relevant action, and I do both (those preparatory actions and the desire-satisfying one) for the sake of satisfying my bodily appetites. Nonetheless, it remains the case that my reason for doing those things is not my feeling those desires.

So even if we accepted the view that when I act to satisfy a bodily appetite I act for a reason, it would not be true that my reason for performing the desire-satisfying action is that I feel the desire—the reason would seem to be, rather, that the action (for example drinking) will satisfy my desire, or that it (for instance fetching a glass of water) is conducive to my performing an action that will.

---

[18] It may be tempting here to add that the fact that drinking will satisfy your desire will be a reason for you to drink only if you have a desire to satisfy your thirst. This thought may be encouraged by the fact that sometimes we have a reason for not wanting to satisfy a bodily desire: that one is fasting or trying to lose weight may be someone's reason for not eating when hungry. And, one may argue, in such cases you have a reason and hence a want not to satisfy the bodily desire. That seems right. The temptation is to go on to think that, when we have a bodily desire and have no reason (and hence no desire) not to satisfy it, then we must have a desire to satisfy it. But the temptation should be resisted.

As in the case of rational desires, there is a kind of case where it might seem that the fact that one feels a bodily appetite could be one's reason for acting. I have in mind cases where the desire, say your hunger, is so intense that you cannot think of anything else. In such a case you may reason that you ought to eat because otherwise you cannot get on with your work. What is distinctive about this case is that you eat not for its own sake but for an ulterior motive: to enable you to get on with work. Thus, in this kind of example, as was the case in the example of removing the thread from someone's jacket, your reason for doing that is, not your feeling the desire, but some means–ends reasoning: your reason for eating is that it will enable you to concentrate on your work.

We have seen that neither what is desired, nor our desiring those things, whether felt or not, are motivating reasons. What is desired is a goal, and as such it motivates though not as a reason. My desiring something is not a motivating reason either. In cases of bodily appetites, we either do not act for a reason, or if we do, the reason is not our feeling the bodily appetite but that performing that action will satisfy the bodily appetite, or will be conducive to performing another action that will. In the case of rational desires, my reason for acting is either the good that I see in the action itself, or its good as a means to another action that is my end and that I regard as good in itself. Thus, normally, when I have a rational desire, I am motivated to act by whatever reason I have for having that desire; and this is not normally the mere fact that I have the desire.

I shall finish this chapter by saying something about the relation between desires and motivation.

4.4. Desiring and Motivation

I have argued that my desiring something is not a motivating reason, a reason for which I act. And yet, many philosophers think it is. In this last section, I shall suggest that the arguments given to defend this Humean view of motivation are confused or unpersuasive.

First, many Humean arguments are flawed because they conflate the idea that we are motivated by the things we desire with the idea that we are motivated by *states* of desiring. Second, and relatedly, Humean arguments about motivation, when they succeed, succeed typically in showing only that if one is motivated to act, then there must be something that one wants—at least in the thin sense of 'want' in which one can want to go to the dentist because it is the only means of getting rid of one's toothache, while not fancying at all the idea of going. And this is sometimes expressed, in the preferred Humean terminology, as the claim that the agent must be 'in a state of desiring'. But this is a far cry from showing what such arguments are intended to show, namely that states of desiring motivate actions.[19]

Some defenders of the view that wanting is a reason talk about wanting something as a 'motivational state'. For instance, Audi says that wanting is 'the most representative element [of motivation]' (Audi 2001: 66); and Mele says that having a desire or having intentions are states 'that encompass motivation' (Mele 2003: 16). Such claims, however, are somewhat ambiguous as they can be read as a claim that wanting something is a *motivating* state, or as a claim that wanting something is *being in a motivated state*. Consider an analogy. As Aristotle pointed out, the term 'healthy' can be applied to something on account of its *promoting* health, or of its *having* health. Thus exercise is said to be healthy in the first sense, while people are said to be healthy in the second.

For a state of desiring to be even a candidate to be a motivating reason, the state must be motivating in the first sense, that is, it must be a state that motivates (in the same sense as exercise is healthy). However, it seems that a state of desiring, whether bodily or rational, is motivational in the second sense: it is a state of being motivated, rather than a motivating state. The state of wanting something, whether in a bodily or rational way, is a state someone is in when he is motivated.

The state of motivation that we are said to be in when we desire something can be said to be a state of being inclined to act in order

---

[19] As I showed in Chapter 3, Humeans also sometimes conflate motivating and explanatory reasons, and motivating reasons and goals; that is, they assume that if an action is motivated by a desire and it can (or must) therefore be explained by citing the fact that someone *desired* something, then it follows that the fact that they desired that thing was (part of) their reason for acting. See e.g. Pettit and Smith (1990).

to obtain what we desire. In other words, if I desire to eat, or to become prime minister, then I am inclined to act so as to satisfy those desires. When we have a bodily appetite, say, to drink, the state of desire involves the felt inclination towards drinking. When the desire is a rational desire, say to become prime minister, the state of desire involves an inclination either to do what is desired, or to do something else which is (or that seems to be) a means to what is desired, namely to becoming prime minister. In either case, what is desired (to drink, to be prime minister) is motivating: it is the goal towards which our actions aim. But the state of desiring is not; though it is a state of being motivated.

So, if you have a desire, you are motivated to act but what motivates you to act is not your having the desire, but the desire you have, that is, what you desire. And, if the desire is grounded on a reason, then what motivates you to act is the reason that grounds your desire. Thus, a state of being motivated is not what motivates and a fortiori it is not a motivating reason.

Mele thinks, rightly in my view, that one can cite the fact that someone had a desire in order to explain why he did something. It is precisely because being in a state of desiring something is being in a state of being inclined to act that it is possible to explain why someone acted by citing the fact that he desired something, that is, that he was in that state of being motivated. But this does not make wanting something a motivating reason; rather it makes it only a reason that explains why he acted as he did.

In his defence of the Humean thesis about motivation, David Lewis, for example, says:

A Humean thesis about motivation says that we are moved entirely by desire: we are disposed to do what will serve our desires according to our beliefs. If there were no desires to serve, we would never be moved more to do one thing rather than another.   (1988: 323)

To prove his point, Lewis describes a case where you are faced with a choice between two candidates for an academic job, Meane and Neiss, and where you vote for the better philosopher (Meane) over the one with the more likeable personality (Neiss). He says that, in doing this, 'you were moved entirely by your desires', as opposed to your beliefs, and he argues that the non-Humean may be inclined to disagree because she is (perhaps implicitly) restricting the concept of desire to things we *feel like* (what he calls 'warm desires'), as opposed to things we desire despite our inclinations ('cold desires'). He adds:

We [Humeans] are within our rights to construe 'desire' inclusively, to cover the entire range of *states* that move us, including for instance the state that moved you to vote for Meane   (Lewis 1988: 323, my italics).

But clearly Lewis's argument about Meane and Neiss does not show that we are motivated by states of desiring—at most it shows that we are motivated to act by the things we desire, for example *to hire the best available candidate*—however 'coldly' we desire those things. And, as we have seen, to show that you are motivated by things you desire is not to show that you are motivated by states of desiring.[20]

Michael Smith articulates a pro-Humean argument about motivation making use of the idea, discussed in Chapter 3, that beliefs and desires are states with 'direction of fit', according to which beliefs have a mind-to-world direction of fit, while desires have a world-to-mind direction of fit.

Here is how Smith argues in favour of the view that we are motivated by our desires:

(1) Having a motivating reason *is*, *inter alia*, having a goal
(2) Having a goal *is* being in a state with which the world must fit and
(3) Being in a state with which the world must fit *is* desiring. (1987: 55)

I have argued that (1) is not, strictly speaking true, because although if someone has a motivating reason for action then they have a goal, having the one is not to be identified, not even *inter alia*, with having the other. In any case, all that Smith's reasoning shows is that someone who has a motivating reason is someone who desires something. It

---

[20] The remaining and rather technical part of Lewis's paper is devoted to a discussion of decision theory that is clearly concerned with states of believing and desiring, since it is concerned with functions that measure the degrees to which agents believe (or desire) what they do.

does not show that his desiring something is the relevant motivating reason.[21]

Smith argues that states of desiring are motivating states and that, since states of desiring are states with a world-to-mind direction of fit, then anything that motivates must, like a state of desiring, have a world-to-mind direction of fit. Since a belief, Smith claims, is a state with a mind-to-world direction of fit, a belief cannot motivate because it has the wrong direction of fit.[22]

Even if one puts aside any of the reservations about characterizing believing and desiring as states with direction of fit as discussed in Chapter 3, Smith's argument fails. First, Smith's claim that states of desiring are *motivating* states is mistaken because a state of desiring is a state of being motivated, not a motivating state.[23] Second, this, if true, does not show that only a state with a world-to-mind direction of fit can motivate. In fact, all that follows from what Smith says here is that (i) if one has a motivating reason, then one has a goal; and (ii) that if one has a goal, then one is in *a motivated state*, that is to say, in a state with a world-to-mind direction of fit. His argument does not show that what motivates one to act is a state of desiring.

To desire something may be, or involve, an inclination to act in order to obtain what is desired. That, however, does not imply, as we have seen, that a state of desire is what motivates us to act.

Conclusion

The upshot of this discussion is that neither what is wanted, nor wanting something is, strictly speaking, a motivating reason. The qualification 'strictly speaking' is important because, both inside and outside of philosophy, wanting something is often called 'a reason'.

---

[21] For further criticisms of Smith's argument, see Dancy (2000: 91).

[22] He considers the possibility that a state could have *both* directions of fit but concludes that, 'taken quite literally', the idea that 'there may be a state with both directions of fit is incoherent' (Smith 1987: 56). This conclusion depends on his characterization of beliefs and desires as states with different directions of fit; a characterization that, I argued in the previous chapter, is not free from difficulties.

[23] As I argued earlier, his claim that a state of desiring is a state that motivates is akin to claiming that a healthy state is a state that *gives* health, as opposed to a state of being healthy.

But we have seen that in both of these contexts wants are in fact called reasons on either of three related grounds, none of which supports the claim that they are motivating reasons.

One ground is that, when dealing with rational wants, what is wanted is wanted for a reason and thus, when someone says that she wants something, we can presume that there is a reason for which she wants it (which may be fairly obvious, whether the thing is wanted intrinsically or instrumentally), and that will be a reason that motivates her to act. The second is that what is wanted is sometimes called a reason although not in the sense of a reason in the light of which one acts but rather as a *goal* or a purpose for the sake of which someone acts, which can also be the intention in acting. Finally, the fact that one wants something can be a reason that *explains* why that person acted and, in that sense, wanting something can be a reason but, as we have seen, this would not be the reason for which one acts (a motivating reason); rather it would be the reason that explains one's action (an explanatory reason).

Thus, despite the fact that wants are sometimes called reasons, we can conclude that they are not motivating reasons. In the following chapter I examine the relation between beliefs and motivating reasons, and shall defend a perhaps somewhat peculiar construal of the claim that motivating reasons are beliefs.

5

Beliefs and Motivating Reasons

Introduction

In the preceding chapters I have argued that, while what we desire can motivate by being a goal in action, desires in general are not motivating reasons. So the question remains what motivating reasons are. It is the task of this chapter to answer that question.

I shall start by outlining two conceptions of motivating reasons found in the literature, which I shall term 'the psychological' and 'the non-psychological' conceptions. In Section 5.1, I explain the shape of the disagreement over which conception is correct. In Section 5.2, I argue in favour of the second, the non-psychological conception. In Section 5.3, I address what is regarded as the most serious difficulty for this conception, namely, how it can account for a certain kind of error case, that is, a case where the agent acts on the basis of a false belief. I show that, contrary to what is often thought, these error cases do not favour the psychological conception of motivating reasons. In Sections 5.4–5.6, I develop in detail my non-psychological account of motivating reasons.

5.1. Two Conceptions of Motivating Reasons

In Section 3.2, I mentioned a disagreement among philosophers concerning what motivating reasons, our reasons for acting, are. I noted there that, on the one hand, there is the dominant view, the Humean conception, which says that a person's reasons for acting are his believing and desiring certain things. On the other hand, there is a minority view that rejects the Humean conception. I said there that in this debate I side with the minority. In this chapter I shall defend my own version of this conception of motivating reasons. Before outlining and defending my own account, though, I need to make some preliminary points.

First, the Humean view says that motivating reasons are combinations of beliefs *and* desires—or, to be precise, if less idiomatic, of 'believings' and 'desirings'. I argued in Chapter 4 that desires, whether in the sense of what is desired or in the sense of one's desiring something, are not motivating reasons. The arguments in that chapter undermine the standard Humean view but they leave room for a modified version of that view, which says that an agent's reason for acting is his believing something. This version of the Humean view, which I shall refer to as the 'psychological conception' of our reasons for acting, will be at the centre of the arguments in this chapter.

Second, the psychological conception of motivating reasons is sometimes expressed with the slogan 'our reasons for acting are *beliefs*'. However, the act/object ambiguity discussed in connection with the term 'desire' affects also the term 'belief'. For the term 'belief' can be used to refer to one's believing something or to what one believes. So the slogan just mentioned is ambiguous between two construals: 'our reasons for acting are what we believe' and 'our reasons for acting are our believing those things'. Since the psychological conception says that motivating reasons are *believings*, the slogan captures that conception only if it is construed as saying that a motivating reason is an agent's believing something, as opposed to what he believes.

Third, the majority conception of motivating reasons, whether in the full Humean version or in the modified version I have called the 'psychological conception', is normally interpreted as implying that motivating reasons are *mental states* of agents. So, the psychological conception says that, for example, if I run because I am late, my reason for running is *my believing that I am late*. And this is normally interpreted to imply that my reason is a mental state, namely, my mental state of believing that I am late. So most philosophers think that to embrace the psychological conception is to embrace the view that reasons are mental states.[1]

However, in previous chapters I argued that expressions such as 'my desiring x' or 'my believing that p' can be used to refer to facts—to the fact that I desire x, and to the fact that I believe that p, respectively—even if it is true that they can also be used to refer to mental states.[2] Therefore it is possible to hold the view that motivating reasons are 'believings' without endorsing the claim that they are mental states. For one could maintain that my reason for acting is my believing that I have been betrayed, and take this to refer to the fact that I believe that I have been betrayed. In this chapter, when talking about the 'psychological conception' I shall mean simply the view that someone's reason for acting is *his believing* something, leaving aside for the most part whether someone's believing something should in this context be taken to be a mental state, or to be the fact that he believes something. And, as before, my use of the locutions 'that he believes something' or 'his believing something' in this chapter will be guided by what is grammatically required or what is more idiomatic in the relevant context.

Fourth, as I said in Chapter 1, throughout my discussion of motivating reasons, the term 'belief' is used as a generic term for a range of related epistemic concepts such as knowledge, suspicion, consideration, supposition, etc., as is common practice in the literature. It is clear, however, that when explaining why someone acted, it can matter whether the reason that explains her action is that she knew, or that she merely suspected, or believed, or doubted it, etc. I shall have something to say about that issue in Chapter 6. However, the issue can be put aside for the purposes of this chapter, since the matter that concerns us here is whether the reason for which I act is *what* I believe (suspect, know, etc.), or *my believing* (suspecting, knowing, etc.) it.

Fifth, we often talk about '*the* reason' why someone did something, or '*my* reason' for doing something. For instance, I may say that my

---

[1] And many think that these mental states are realized in, supervene on, or are perhaps identical with, physical states of the brain or, more generally, of the central nervous system.

[2] I say 'even if' because it has been argued quite persuasively that the idea that believing something is a mental state is problematic. See Collins (1987); Hacker (1990: 28 ff.); Steward (1997); and Williamson (2000), for discussions of this issue.

reason for going to the shop is that it sells milk. However, for any one action, one may cite more than one fact as *the* person's reason for acting. So in our example I could also say that my reason for going to the shop is that I have run out of milk. And so on. Does this mean, then, that I acted for several reasons? And if so, how are these reasons related?

In a sense, the reasons just mentioned are, all of them, my reasons for going to the shop. But it would be misleading to say that I acted for several reasons. It would be misleading because this would normally mean that I acted for several *independent* reasons. For example, my reasons for walking rather than driving to work could be that walking is healthier, more sociable, and also more relaxing than driving. Each of these counts as my reason for walking independently of the others. And this is true even if any one of them would not have been enough by itself to make me decide to walk instead of drive. If that were the case, none of these reasons, taken alone, would have been a conclusive reason for me to walk. But each of them would still have been independent of the others, because each one would count as a reason (conclusive or not) even if the others were not assumed.

The example of the milk is different. Here the three reasons I mentioned are not independent of each other. The fact that the shop sells milk is a reason for me to go there *only* because I have run out of milk and need some. If I had plenty of milk at home, or if I didn't need milk, I would not have taken the fact that the shop sells milk as a reason for me to go there. And, conversely, if they didn't sell milk in the shop, I could not have taken the fact that I need milk as a reason for me to go to the shop. The facts themselves—that I have run out of milk or that the shop sells milk—are independent of each other. But they are interconnected with each other as my reasons for going to the shop.

So, what determines whether my reasons for doing something are independent of each other or not? It is the relation between reasons for acting and the goodness or value of the action for which I take them to be reasons that explains why sometimes my reasons for doing something are independent of each other and why sometimes they are not. In the example of the milk, the reasons I mentioned are not independent of each other because *together* they make my going to the shop a good or valuable action for me: the facts that I need milk, that

I have run out of milk, *and* that the shop sells milk together make my going to the shop a good thing they do in my eyes. By contrast, in the walking example, the reasons I mention are independent of each other: each one of them makes my walking to work a good thing to do in my eyes.

This independence, or otherwise, of our reasons for acting is also reflected in the pragmatics of explanation. In normal circumstances, if I say to someone that my reason for going to the shop is that I've run out of milk, they'll assume that I need milk, that the shop sells milk, etc., and so in most cases there is no need to make explicit the concatenation of reasons that makes the action good in my eyes, in order for my interlocutor to know that these are also my reasons. By contrast, if my reasons for walking to work are that it is healthier, more relaxing, and more sociable than driving but I only mention one of them, say that it is healthier, there is no implication (strict or pragmatic) that I also walk for the other reasons, and my interlocutor will not be in a position to know that I do: each reason would need to be mentioned explicitly.

Finally, a terminological point. The non-psychological view of motivating reasons is sometimes called the 'externalist' view but I shall not use that label. For one thing, it might encourage confusion with the externalist view about normative reasons famously attacked by Bernard Williams[3]—the view that the reasons an agent has for acting are not dependent on his desires (or, as Williams puts it, on 'the agent's subjective motivational set' (1981: 102)). But the externalist view attacked by Williams and the position I am defending, though by no means incompatible with each other, concern different issues.

For another thing, to call the minority view of motivating reasons 'externalist' and its opponent 'internalist' might suggest that the disagreement between them concerns the question whether motivating

---

[3] The labels 'internalism' and 'externalism' are also used for two competing views in the philosophy of mind on the question whether, or to what extent, the content of someone's beliefs, hopes, fears, etc., is determined by an agent's environment. Again, this dispute should not be confused with the disagreement about motivating reasons under consideration, as the latter is a disagreement about whether reasons are believings or what is believed, without commitment to any particular view about how 'what is believed' by someone is determined.

reasons are 'outside' or 'inside' the agent. But although some philosophers talk as if this is indeed the issue (for instance, Stout 1996), I do not think it is, not least because it is not clear what is meant by 'outside' and 'inside' in this context. One way to understand what is meant would be to say that 'internalism' is the view that, for something to be someone's reason for acting, that person must know or believe that thing. If that was what is meant, then that would obviously not be the same as the disagreement I am interested in examining, for even those philosophers who defend the minority view will accept that motivating reasons are *in that sense* internal: nobody disputes the point that, in order for an agent to be motivated by a reason, the reason must be something the agent is at some level aware of.

Another way of understanding the claim about externalism might be to say that the externalist believes that reasons are 'out there in the world', while the internalist denies this and claims that reasons are 'psychological entities'. But at least some of those who hold the minority, non-psychological conception think, as I do, that reasons are facts, or 'what is the case', or 'what is believed', etc. And although these are not 'psychological entities', neither are they 'out there in the world', if what is meant by that is that they have spatial location (see Section 5.5 for more on this issue).[4] There may be other senses in which a reason can be said to be internal, e.g. that it is in the agent's mind in the sense of being currently entertained by the agent. But that need not detain us here. Thus, the label 'externalist' does not seem to me to help elucidate the minority conception of motivating reasons.

With these clarifications in place, the stage is set for the debate about motivating reasons. On the one hand, we have the psychological conception, which says that someone's reason for acting is her believing something. On the other hand, we have the non-psychological view, which holds that the reason is what the agent believes, not her believing it. For instance, if I buy a magazine because I believe it contains the TV listings for the week, according to the psychological conception my reason for buying the magazine is *that I believe* (or

---

[4] It is true that those who think that an agent's reason for acting is his believing something tend to think that someone's believing something is a mental state of the agent's and that a mental state is something 'internal'. But this suggests that these so-called mental states have, literally, spatial location, which also seems doubtful.

my believing) that it contains the TV listings; while according to the non-psychological conception it is *that it contains the TV listings.*

One might think that the distinction between the non-psychological and the psychological conception of motivating reasons should be characterized as that between *oratio recta* and *oratio obliqua* reports of an agent's reason for acting. This, however, does not seem right because both *oratio recta* and *oratio obliqua* statements of, for example, what someone believes can be true regardless of the truth of their subclauses. Thus, the statements 'He believed: "It is a beautiful day" ' (*oratio recta*); and 'He believed that it was a beautiful day' (*oratio obliqua*) can both be true regardless of whether it was a beautiful day. Nonetheless, 'His reason for buying the magazine is that he believed that it contains the TV listings' can be true regardless of the truth of the 'that'-clause; while the statement 'His reason for buying the magazine is that it contains the TV listings', which corresponds to the non-psychological conception, can be true only if the magazine contains the TV listings. So the disagreement cannot be captured in terms of the difference between *oratio recta* and *oratio obliqua*.[5]

It is sometimes thought that the disagreement is superficial, since the psychological conception says that reasons are beliefs *with* contents. For example, according to the psychological conception, my reason for acting is my *belief*, whose content is, as the non-psychological conception says, that the magazine contains the TV listings. So, the thought goes, the psychological conception can embrace the non-psychological conception. This suggestion, however, is confused and it underplays the important difference between the two conceptions by trading on the ambiguity in the term 'belief' mentioned above. For my believing something and what I believe are different things, as is evident from the fact that one of the putative reason statements could be true while the other is false: I could believe that the magazine contains the TV listings (psychological) even though it does not contain them (non-psychological). So my believing that p and the fact that p are not the same reason. And the question is: Which conception of motivating reasons is right?

---

[5] What is true is that we can use both *oratio recta* and *oratio obliqua* respectively to report the reason. So if someone's reason for taking his umbrella was 'It is raining', we can report that reason in *oratio obliqua* by saying that his reason was that it was raining.

5.2. A Non-Psychological Conception of Motivating Reasons

As we saw in previous chapters, the question: 'What was the agent's reason for ϕ-ing?' is a question about what made ϕ-ing seem right, or appropriate, or desirable to the agent—as McDowell puts it, what shows the action in 'a favourable light' (1982: 302). We have also seen that this question is closely connected to practical reasoning because answers to it are statements that could appear as premises in a reconstruction of the agent's (implicit or explicit) practical reasoning. And these very rarely take the psychological form: 'that I believe that p' or 'my believing that p';[6] rather, they normally take the non-psychological form, 'that p': 'that she has fallen ill', 'that the train was about to arrive', 'that the weather won't hold', 'that it's great fun', 'that it may be dangerous', etc.

In general, then, what seems to me to make my action right or appropriate is what I believe, not my believing it. Consider an example. Suppose that I give my cousin some money because I believe what he tells me, namely, that he needs it to pay his rent. It would seem that what motivates me to give him the money is that he needs it: it is *that* that seems to me to make the action of giving him money right or appropriate and not *my believing* that he needs it. For, if my reason had been *my believing* that he needs the money, then, when deciding whether to give him the money, my concern would be with how things are with *me*, in particular, with my own state of mind, rather than with how things are with *my cousin*, in particular, with his financial situation. But in fact, my concern when deciding what to do is with my cousin's financial situation: with whether he

---

[6] Although, as some authors have pointed out, they may, occasionally, take the psychological form: see Hyman (1999: 444), and Dancy (2000: 125). For instance, to adapt Hyman's example, my reason for visiting a psychiatrist might be that I believe that I'm being persecuted by the security services (while also realizing, at least on occasions, that there's something wrong in my believing that). But it is worth noting that even in these cases we could formulate this kind of reason in the non-psychological form, e.g. my reason is that I am paranoid. In her paper 'Von Wright on Practical Inference', Anscombe points out that in that sense 'I want to ϕ' can also be a motivating reason: e.g. the fact that I want to kill my parents may be the reason that motivates me to visit a psychiatrist (1989: 381; she credits the example to A. Müller).

needs the money.[7] So it is that which motivates me to give him the money.

To see that this is so, suppose that he had deceived me and he didn't really need the money. Discovering that he had deceived me would be discovering, among other things, that I had been motivated to give him the money by something that was not the case. But what I would discover not to have been the case would be that he needed the money and not that *I believed* he did—for that *was* the case: I did indeed believe he needed it. And this shows that what motivated me was that which seemed to me to be the case, and to make it appropriate to give him the money, namely that he needed it.[8]

So it seems that we can conclude that a motivating reason is, typically, what the agent believes and not his believing it.[9] And this is what the non-psychological conception says motivating reasons are.[10] There are, however, three considerations that might lead one to think that this cannot be right—that motivating reasons cannot be what is believed.

Let me deal briefly with the first one, a point that refers back to desires. One might think that what motivated me is some desire I had, for instance, the desire to help my cousin. After all, had I not had that desire, I would not have been motivated to give the money to him by what I believed, namely that he needed it. But this, if true, doesn't show that what is believed does not motivate.[11] As we

---

[7] Bittner, who defends a similar view, says that 'to be a reason for which the action is done is to be something to which the action is a response' (2001: 66). He characterizes reasons as events, states of things, or states of affairs, and resists the idea that, strictly speaking, reasons are facts (2001: 69). However, he also says that it 'does not do any harm' to say 'that the reason for which I stopped was the fact that the lights were red' (2001: 70).

[8] Stout (1996: ch. 2), makes a similar point.

[9] In his paper 'How Knowledge Works', Hyman (1999) argues that the fact that p can be one's reason for ϕ-ing only if one knows that p, and not if one merely believes or suspects that p. If that is right, the claim above (and throughout this book) can be adapted accordingly: motivating reasons are things known by the agent. Moreover, since many (though arguably not all) things one knows are also things one believes, for all cases where knowing that p implies believing that p, motivating reasons are also things believed.

[10] These things believed, or known, may be facts about oneself. That is, my reason for going to the doctor could be that I have lost too much weight; or that I need psychiatric help because I (sometimes?) believe that I am Joan of Arc; or, the example Anscombe attributes to Anselm Müller mentioned above about my wanting to kill my parents. These, if they are my reasons, are all facts about myself that I am aware of.

[11] Nagel (1970) suggests that, in any case, the ascription of some of these desires is a purely formal matter and shows nothing about whether motivation is always desire-dependent. See also McDowell (1978).

saw in the previous chapter, the fact that our desires (what we desire) motivate us does not mean that these desires are motivating *reasons*: they are the goals we pursue in acting. So, in our example, I was motivated by my desire to help my cousin. But my desire to help him is not a motivating *reason*. Moreover, if, as the objection says, what I believe motivates me *only* because of my desire to help him, this does not show that what I believe is not what motivates me to give him the money. On the contrary: if anything it shows that what I believe motivates me to give him the money, even if it motivates me only because my goal is to help him. My belief that he was in need, coupled with a different goal, say to cause him harm, might have motivated me to withhold my help; just as the goal of helping him, coupled with another belief, say that he needed exercise, might have motivated me to propose a game of tennis. So this point about desires does not suggest that what I believe is not what motivates me.

The second consideration that appears to undermine the view that what motivates is what is believed is a thought analogous to the one about desires but concerning my believing what I believe. It goes as follows. In order for the fact that p to motivate an agent, that agent must believe (or know, suspect, etc.) that p. And this suggests that the reason that motivates him is not that p, but *his believing* that p. But the objection fails, and in fact the very way it is articulated undermines its conclusion. For the objection says that for the fact that p to be a reason that motivates an agent, the agent must believe that p (or be somehow aware of that fact). But this suggests that, if the agent does believe that p, then what motivates him is the fact that p, *what* he believes—and not his believing it.[12] Consider an analogy. Unless I have money, I cannot pay for my lunch with it. But if I *have* money and pay for my lunch, I pay with the money I have, and not with 'my having the money'. Likewise, in order for p to motivate me to act, I must believe (or know, suspect, etc.) that p; but it is a mistake to infer from this that the reason that motivates me to act is my believing that p; rather the reason that motivates me is that p, which I believe.

The third objection is more complex and has been thought to be decisive in showing that the reasons that motivate us must be our believing something rather than what we believe. The objection

---

[12] For a detailed discussion of this point see Dancy (2000: 127–30).

centres on error cases where what the agent believes is false. In the example above, I initially said that the reason that motivated me was *the fact* that my cousin needed the money to pay his rent. But suppose that he lied about needing the money and he just wanted it to buy a plasma TV. In that case, my reason cannot be the fact that he needed the money, for there is no such fact. But if my reason was not the fact that he needed the money, what was it? The most plausible candidate seems to be a factor that remains constant, whether my cousin needed money or not, which is my believing that he did. So this appears to be my reason.

The problem that seems to lead to that conclusion becomes apparent if we consider that I cannot, without an air of paradox because of the implicit contradiction, say something like: 'My reason for giving him the money is that he needs it, although he doesn't'. Statements like this are reminiscent of Moore's paradoxes of belief, though they also differ from them in important respects. For instance, unlike Moore's paradoxes, such statements remain paradoxical when recast in the third-person: 'Her reason for giving him the money is that he needs it, although he doesn't'.[13] And again, unlike Moore's cases, these remain paradoxical when they are put in the past tense. Thus compare 'My reason for giving him the money was that he needed it, although he didn't need it' and 'I believed that he needed money, although he didn't': the first retains an air of paradox that the second does not have.

The problem with this way of expressing what motivated the agent is not that it is impossible to think of a context in which such statements may be used appropriately. The problem is that, given the contradiction implicit in them, their use would always involve a note of irony that subverts the claim about the alleged reason, in the way in which a statement such as 'He's so laid back that even his cereal packets are arranged alphabetically' is ironic and subverts the claim about his being laid back.

This, it is thought, presents an insuperable problem for the non-psychological conception of reasons because it seems that that

---

[13] Compare such statements with Moore's paradox: 'I believe that p, although not p' and 'She believes that p, although not p', where only the first-person statement is paradoxical. The reason why in our examples above both first- and third-person statements have the air of paradox is, I shall argue, that both 'My reason is that p' and 'Her reason is that p' are 'factive': their truth implies the truth of the proposition contained in the 'that'-clause.

conception cannot accommodate error cases. For many, this has been decisive in adopting the psychological conception. The following section is devoted to a critical examination of this problem.

5.3. Error Cases and Motivating Reasons

The challenge that error cases present to the defender of the non-psychological conception of motivating reasons can be outlined as follows. According to that conception the agent's reason for acting is what he believes. But when what the agent believes is false, the non-psychological conception faces a choice between what seem to be three unpalatable options. One option is to say that in error cases the agent's reason is still what he believed, even though what he believed is false. Another option is to say that in error cases there is nothing that is the agent's reason for acting: in these cases the agent does not act *for a reason*. The third option is to say that in error cases the reason for which the agent acts is *his believing* something; but, of course, to opt for that option would be to embrace the psychological conception—at least for error cases.

The first two options seem unacceptable for different reasons. On the one hand, as we shall see, there are good grounds for rejecting the idea that a false belief, something that is not the case, can be a reason. On the other, it seems wrong to say that when I act on the basis of a false belief, I do not act for a reason—after all, my action is not mechanical, irrational, or arbitrary; and it can be explained by a 'rationalization': an explanation that, to paraphrase Davidson, shows what I thought there was to be said for that action. So, since neither of those options seems acceptable, the conclusion appears to force itself on us that in error cases the psychological conception must be right: in those cases my reason is *my believing* something, for instance, my believing that my cousin needed the money. And then it is tempting to argue that if this is so in error cases, it must be so also in veridical cases. And this would take us to the conclusion that, after all, the psychological conception is right for all cases: the reason that motivates me to act is not what I believe but my believing it.

Against this last conclusion, it can be argued that reasoning from error cases to a general conclusion about what motivating reasons are is a form of the 'argument from error' and that argument is, at best, unreliable. For, as has been pointed out, if critical examination of cases of error or failure (concerning, for instance, perception, knowledge, etc.) leads to some conclusion regarding what to say about *those* cases, it does not follow that we must say the same about *veridical* or *success* cases. That is, there is no a priori reason to rule out the possibility that some concepts (perception, knowledge, etc.) call for disjunctive accounts. And this applies also to reasons: it is possible that there should be a disjunctive account of motivating reasons so that in veridical cases, that is, when the agent acts on a true belief, the motivating reason is what the agent believes; while in error cases the motivating reason is the agent's believing what he believes.[14] So, even if the psychological conception is right for error cases, it does not follow that it is right for veridical cases too.

However, I think that it is possible to show that the psychological conception is not right even for error cases and that, contrary to what the reasoning about the three options rehearsed just now might appear to suggest, there is a viable alternative about how to understand those cases. To see this, we need to return to the reasoning sketched above that seemed to lead to the conclusion that in error cases we must embrace the psychological conception. According to that reasoning, error cases appear to favour the psychological conception because the other two options seem unacceptable. In order to resist that conclusion, then, we need to show that at least one of those two options is acceptable after all. I shall begin with the first option, which says that in error cases the motivating reason is a false belief.

5.3.1. *False beliefs and reasons*

According to the response under examination, a motivating reason is always what the agent believes, whether that belief is true or false. The problem with this response is that the idea that a false belief can be a reason is problematic.

The expression 'N's reason is/was that' is an operator that, it seems, can only form true sentences when attached to a true sentence (or can form a sentence that expresses a true proposition only when attached

---

[14] For discussion of disjunctive accounts of reasons see Stoutland (1998 and 2001); Stout (1996); Dancy (2000).

to a sentence expressing a true proposition).[15] For, as we saw, there is an implicit contradiction in claims to the effect that someone's reason is (or was) that p but not p, that is, claims such as 'Alice's reason was that her husband was at home, although he wasn't at home', or 'James's reason is that his car has been stolen, although it hasn't been stolen'.

We may wonder why this should be so. After all, reasons could be analogous to beliefs. Beliefs are said to aim at truth but this does not exclude the possibility of there being false beliefs. And the operator 'N's belief is that' can form true sentences regardless of the truth of the sentences to which it is attached. So it may be true that Alex's belief is that whales are fish even though it is false that they are. Likewise, one might think, reasons aim at what is the case but this should not exclude the possibility of there being 'false reasons': such reasons are things that are '*as such* suited to be the case'[16] but that are not the case, for instance, 'Alice's reason for going to his house is that he is at home' (although he isn't), 'James's reason for calling the police is that his car has been stolen' (although it hasn't), or even impossibilities, such as 'My reason for complaining about getting the wrong change is that $500 - 442 = 68$' (which is false). And this might make it seem that the claim that a false belief cannot be a reason is just a stipulation.

After all, if an agent says that her false belief that p *was* her reason, it would seem that she has a kind of authority on the matter: once the possibility of dishonesty, self-deception, or confusion has been excluded, if she says that her reason was that p, it seems that what she says goes: her reason *was* that p.[17]

---

[15] I shall drop this qualification as the issue whether truth attaches to sentences or propositions is not relevant to the discussion.

[16] I borrow this phrase from Dancy (2000: 149). Some of the things that Dancy says in (2000: 131–7 and 146–7) might appear to commit him to this view. However, I do not think that this is his view because, although Dancy is not explicit about what he takes the reason (if any) to be in error cases, he seems to think that what is not the case *cannot* be a reason, which I agree with; for example, he says that the reasons that motivate us must be capable of being good reasons. But what is false is not capable of being a good reason. Where I think he is mistaken, however, is in his view that 'a thing believed that is not the case can still explain an action' (2000: 134). This is at best a misleading way of putting a true point about the explanation of action. I will discuss this view in more detail in Chapter 6.

[17] For an illuminating discussion of the sense in which we have authority over our reasons, motives, intentions, see Anscombe (1957: 41, esp. §24). One is not incorrigibly right about what one's reasons, intentions, etc., are. Nonetheless, as Anscombe says, 'there is a point at which only what the man himself says is a sign' (ibid.).

There are three points to make in response to these remarks. One is that even if the agent has some kind of authority over *what* motivated her, this does not imply that she has this kind of authority over whether what motivated her was a *reason*. If someone says that what motivated her was that her cousin needed the money, then, barring confusion or deception (including self-deception), that *is* what motivated her.[18] But her authority here does not extend to the truth of her beliefs, and hence to whether what motivated her was a fact and hence a genuine reason. So this point about first-person authority over what motivates one does not show that false beliefs can be *reasons*.

The second point to make here is that when an agent insists that a belief of hers that others claim to be false was, nonetheless, her reason for acting, she will typically say so because she does not accept that the belief is false, perhaps because she thinks the arguments given against it are specious, or that the matter has not been settled, e.g. the evidence is not decisive either way, or because . . .

Finally, if an agent still insists that what she accepts to be a false belief is her *reason* we'll have to wonder what she means by 'a reason'. For, if the truth or falsehood of what is presented as one's reason for acting (or for believing) did not affect its status as a reason, then there would be no need to retract one's claim that one's reason for ϕ-ing was that p on being confronted with the fact that not p. But as we saw above, there is an implicit contradiction in claims that one's reason was something one knows to be false and, because of this, on finding out that it is not the case that p, one has to retract the claim that one's reason was that p. And this suggests that the false belief that p might motivate one but it cannot be one's *reason*.

The idea that what is not the case could nonetheless be a motivating *reason* may seem plausible if one conflates cases where an agent acts motivated by something that is a reason, but is not a reason *for her to do what she did*, with cases where she acts motivated by something that is not a reason because it is a false belief and so cannot be a reason for her or anybody else to do anything.

---

[18] I say 'perhaps' in order to allow for the possibility of being motivated by beliefs that were not really accessible to the agent's consciousness and where, therefore, it is not clear the extent to which the term 'self-deception' is appropriate to cover the case.

As we saw in Chapter 2, a fact can be a reason for ϕ-ing but not a reason for ψ-ing. For example, that A stole some money may be a reason for imprisoning him, but not a reason for stoning him to death. And something can be a reason for A to ϕ but not a reason for B to ϕ. For instance, that the stuff in this bottle is whisky may be a reason for A to drink it but not a reason for B to do the same if, for example, B is a child. But a false belief cannot be a reason for anybody to do anything: it cannot speak in favour of any action for anybody, for it cannot make any action right, appropriate, etc. If, for instance, 'that he committed a murder' or 'that the stuff in this bottle is wine' are false, then they cannot be a reason for anybody to do anything. What is not a reason for doing one thing because it is not the case cannot be a reason for doing something else. That there is life on the Moon cannot be a reason for anybody to do anything, for there is no life on the Moon. This is so, even if someone insisted that *his reason* for travelling to the Moon is that there is life on it. This would not be a reason for this person to go to the Moon, nor is there any agent for which that there is life on the Moon could be a reason for doing anything.

One might object that, although what is believed but is not the case is not a reason, there is nonetheless a sense in which it *can* be because it is the sort of thing that can be true. But this is wrong—or at least wrong without qualification. It is true that what is believed, even if false, is in 'better metaphysical shape' (as Dancy puts it, 2000: 149) than, say, trees and numbers, to be a reason. But the belief that p *can* be a reason for A to ϕ only *if it is the case* that p. And this 'can' is what Austin called a 'constitutionally iffy "can" ', that is, the possibility involved is a conditional possibility; in this case, conditional on its being the case that p (compare with 'I paid you yesterday, if you remember' where the 'if'-clause is not a condition of my having paid you yesterday[19]). And this means that if p is not the case, then the belief that p cannot be a reason, good or bad—although it can be mistaken for one.

So a false belief is not a reason, even when the agent mistakes it for a reason, and even when it is a belief that motivates one to act.

---

[19] An example that Austin credits to Peter Geach; see Austin (1956: 213).

In Chapter 1, I mentioned the view that a person who has a false belief has no 'objective' reason but does have a 'subjective' reason to do what she does. If we adopted that view, we might say that in error cases the agent acted for no objective reason but acted for a subjective reason. However, I prefer to put the point in terms of 'real' and 'apparent' reasons because 'subjective reason' suggest that it *is* a reason but a reason only for this particular agent, or only from his point of view—which is false. The term 'apparent reason', on the other hand, suggests, as I think is right here, that something appeared to the agent to be a reason but it was not really one.[20] Thus suppose that a woman kills her husband motivated by the belief that she would receive the money on his life insurance. But suppose that, unknown to her, her husband had cancelled the policy. The belief that motivated her was that she would receive the insurance policy money. This seemed to her to be a reason to kill her husband but it wasn't: it was an apparent reason.

One might insist that false beliefs that motivate are still reasons—only they are *false* reasons. But this is analogous to saying that a Vermeer that has been shown to be a fake is still a Vermeer—only it is a *fake* Vermeer. And clearly this is just a way of saying that it was not really a Vermeer, just as saying that something is a false reason is just a way of saying that it is not really a reason. Of course, one might, if one wishes, *call* false beliefs that motivate 'false reasons' but I think that is misleading as it suggests that they *are* reasons, which they are not. Because of this, I prefer to use the labels 'motivating false *beliefs*' or '*apparent* reasons' to refer to false beliefs on the grounds of which someone acts, as these labels do not suggest that we are dealing with genuine reasons.

This, however, still leaves open the question of what the motivating *reason* is in error cases. And, unless we are prepared to embrace the psychological view, at least for error cases, we have only one option:

---

[20] As I also mentioned in Chapter 1, the preference for the idea that she had a subjective reason arises from the thought that acting against what one believes one has reason to do is a form of 'irrationality' but that, since the agent was mistaken, the irrationality is subjective. I am not persuaded that the best way of putting the point about irrationality is in terms of subjective rationality. Another way of putting it is in terms of a principle of practical rationality that says that it is irrational not to take what one regards as feasible means to one's ends.

that in error cases the agent did not act *for a reason*. I now turn to that suggestion.

5.3.2. *Error cases and 'acting for no reason'*

The suggestion that someone who acted motivated by a false belief does not act for a reason might seem prima facie wrong. But, as I shall show, although it might be misleading to say that someone who acts on a false belief acts for no reason, the claim is strictly true, for the false belief is not a motivating *reason* even though, as we shall see, it is a motivating consideration. Let me explain.

One may be inclined to reject the suggestion that an agent motivated by a false belief does not act for a reason on the grounds that to say that the agent did not act for a reason implies that there is no reason *why he acted*. And if there is no reason why someone acted, then it seems to follow that his action cannot be explained. But surely, the thought continues, the action of someone who acted on a false belief *can* be explained, so we should not say that a person in that kind of case acted for no reason.

But as I hope might be clear by now, this argument depends on conflating the agent's reason for acting and the reason that explains why the agent acted which, as we saw, may but need not be the same. If we do not conflate the two, we shall see that to say that the agent did not act for a reason is not to say that there is no reason why he acted. Indeed, in error cases, the reason *why* he acted, that is, the reason that explains his action, is precisely that he (falsely) believed that p. For instance, if someone went home motivated by the false belief that her husband was at home, we can explain her action by saying that she went home *because* she believed that her husband was there: her believing that he was there was the reason *why* she went home. So, since saying that someone did not act for a reason does not imply that there is no reason why she acted, the objection just examined does not rule out the 'no motivating reason' response to our trilemma.[21]

---

[21] Williams seems to be making the same point, though he puts it differently, in his discussion of someone who drinks petrol because he wants to drink gin and believes the stuff in a bottle is gin when in fact it is petrol. In such a case, he says, we 'have an explanation of his [drinking] (a reason why he did it)' (1981: 102) and he adds that this consideration

Another reason for resisting the suggestion that in error cases the agent did not act for a reason is that this seems to assimilate the case under discussion with quite different kinds of case.

First, the phrase 'done for no reason' is used to describe cases where an agent was not motivated by any belief at all: he just did what he did. For example, if Carol does a cartwheel in her office corridor simply because she feels like it, without thinking that there is anything to be said for her action, she may not have been motivated to do it by any belief, whether true or false: she simply felt like doing it and just did it. This is quite different from the kind of case under consideration. In the kind of spontaneous action just mentioned, no belief need have made the action right in the agent's eyes, and there is no means-end reasoning, implicit or explicit, about what to do: the agent acts on impulse, because she feels like it. In error cases, by contrast, some belief makes it seem to the agent that her action is the right thing to do, perhaps after implicit or explicit deliberation, and that belief motivates her to act.

One way of avoiding the conflation of these two kinds of case is to say, as we sometimes do, that an agent who acts on impulse acts for no reason, whereas an agent who acts on a false belief acts motivated by something that was a reason albeit not a *good* reason to do what he did. However, *that* expression is also used for a different kind of case (already mentioned above), namely, when an agent acts in the light of something that is a reason but not a good reason *for that agent to do that thing*. Thus, if Stefano shoots Carlo because Carlo has looked at Stefano disrespectfully, we may say that Stefano shot Carlo for no good reason, even if it is true that Carlo gave the disrespectful look; for the fact that someone looks at you disrespectfully is not a good reason to shoot him, though it may be a good reason to do something else, for example, to return the disrespectful look. But again, there is an important difference between a case where someone acts for a reason, even if that reason is not a good reason to do what he does,

might lead us to conclude that 'he has reason to drink this stuff which is petrol'. But he goes on as follows: 'I do not think however that we should say this. It looks in the wrong direction, by implying in effect that the internal reason conception is only concerned with explanation, and not at all with the agent's rationality, and this may help to motivate a search for other sorts of reasons which are concerned with his rationality. But the internal reasons conception is concerned with the agent's rationality' (1981: 2–3).

and the case where someone acts motivated by a false belief, since a false belief is not a reason: not a reason to do that or indeed anything else. So the description of an error case as a case where the agent acts 'for no good reason' may invite confusion with the kind of case just described.

Moreover, it is not always clear that the right way of characterizing the kind of case just described is in terms of 'no good reason', as opposed to merely 'no reason'. For suppose that my reason for stabbing someone is, say, that I dislike his shoes. It seems wrong to say that I had *a* reason for stabbing him, only not a good reason. One might think that in this case I have no reason at all. Some writers disagree. For example, in his discussion of this issue, Bittner says that 'a reason I act upon is always a reason I have' (2001: 122). And he adds that in the sort of example just given, it seems wrong to say that I had *a* reason as opposed to no reason only because we hear 'I have a reason to stab him' as 'I have a *good* reason to stab him'—which, he agrees, I do not have. However, he thinks I still have *a* reason to stab him, even if it is not a good one (ibid.). I find this response unpersuasive: sometimes a reason for which someone ϕ-s may be a more or less good reason for ϕ-ing but not at all a reason for ψ-ing. So, in the example above, Stefano had a more or less good reason for giving Carlo a disrespectful look but, arguably, he had no reason at all to shoot him. Consider an analogy. If my proposed solution to world poverty is to jump up and down, this does not seem merely a *bad* solution: rather it seems simply *no* solution to world poverty (though it may be a solution to poor circulation). The same seems true of reasons. In the example above, my reason for stabbing my victim, namely that I don't like his shoes, is not simply not a good reason to stab someone—it is rather *no* reason to do so. That I dislike someone's shoes *is* a reason; for instance, it is a reason for me not to buy the same shoes. But my dislike of the shoes is simply no reason for me to stab their wearer, even if in my aesthetic fanaticism I believe it is.

Be that as it may, this kind of case is different from the false belief case, even though both can be described as cases where the agent acted for no reason, or for no good reason. And so it seems that resistance to saying that in error cases the agent acts for no reason arises from the fact that this may cause confusion with the different kinds of case just discussed. However the potential for confusion does not imply that it is inaccurate or wrong to say that in error cases the agent acts for no reason, or does not act for a reason. For, just as one can say that an action was not voluntary either when it was *in*voluntary or when it was *non*-voluntary, so an agent can be said not to have acted for a reason, either when he was not motivated to act by any belief, or was motivated by a true belief that was no reason to do that thing, or, finally, as in our case, when he was motivated by a false belief, and hence by what is not a reason.

It seems, then, that we have three different kinds of case of which it might be true to say that the agent acted for no reason. One is when the agent just acts on impulse or because he feels like it. Another kind of case is when the agent acted on a true belief which does not justify his doing what he did: his belief is a reason, but not a good reason or simply not a reason at all for doing what he did. Finally, there is the kind of case we are concerned with, error cases, where the agent acted motivated by a false belief that is neither a reason for him to do what he did nor a reason for anything: it is simply not a reason. But, then, so long as we are clear about what kind of case error cases are, and we do not assimilate them to these other two, it is right to say that in error cases the agent does not act for a reason. Or, another way of putting the point, which I have already used, is to say that in error cases the agent acts for what is merely an *apparent* reason.

But the issue is slightly more complicated than this discussion suggests. For when someone acts motivated by some belief, very often this belief plays the role of a premise in a piece of explicit or implicit practical reasoning which underwrites the agent's action. So for example, I may reason that, since I need some milk to bake a cake and there is none at home, and since they sell milk at the newsagent, I'll go to the newsagent. But suppose that I am wrong and there *is* milk at home. In that case, my belief that there is no milk at home is false and hence not a reason. Nonetheless, since the fact that I need milk to bake a cake and that they sell milk at the newsagent also motivated me to go there, I can cite them as my reasons for going to the newsagent and, since those beliefs are true, they are reasons. However, my belief that there was no milk at home was false and, so, in the circumstances and all things considered, I had no reason to go to the newsagent and hence I went there for no reason—but only for an apparent reason.

It is possible to think that the claim that someone who acts motivated by a false belief does not act for a reason results from confusing normative and motivating reasons. For, one might think, in cases of false belief, the agent had no 'normative' reason but he *has* a 'motivating' reason—namely the false belief on which he acts. This suggestion is defended by Michael Smith. Thus, in his discussion of Williams's example about someone who believes that the stuff in a bottle is gin when in fact it is petrol, Smith says:

> Though prudence does not require my mixing the stuff before me [viz. petrol] with a tonic and drinking it, and hence there is a sense in which I do not have a reason to do so, yet it seems entirely correct to suppose that I now have a motivating reason to do just this.   (1987: 41)

But I think Smith is wrong and indeed I think *his* view stems from confusing motivating and *explanatory* reasons.

What seems entirely correct to say in the example is that (i) I have a *belief*, namely that the stuff is gin, that gives me a motivation to mix the stuff with tonic and drink it; and (ii) that if I mixed the stuff with tonic and drank the mixture, my doing so can be *explained* by reference to my wanting a gin and tonic and *my believing* that the stuff in the bottle is gin.

But the fact that my action can be explained by reference to my believing that the stuff in the bottle is gin only means that my believing that is an explanatory reason.[22] That fact has no tendency to show that my believing that the stuff is gin was a motivating reason, nor that what I falsely believed was a reason. What motivated me was my false belief, viz. that the stuff in the bottle was gin; and being false, although it was a motivating belief, it was not a motivating *reason*. So, contrary to what Smith suggests, it does not seem right to say that, in believing the stuff to be gin, I have a motivating reason to drink it.

There is a different kind of consideration that suggests that it is not right to say that someone who acts on a false belief does not act for a reason. For someone who acts on a false belief will typically also act *for a purpose*. Thus in the example of my cousin, we said that what motivated me to give him the money was my false belief that he needed it; but we also said that this implied that I must have wanted

---

[22] For Williams's own view of this example, see n. 21, above.

to help him: my goal or purpose in acting was to help him. And, since acting for a purpose is surely acting for a reason, and often this will involve practical reasoning, then someone who is motivated by a false belief still acts in pursuit of a purpose and, hence, he acts for a reason.

This reasoning needs to be unpicked. It is not true that anyone who acts for a purpose acts for a reason (as the case of most animals and some of our own actions show). What is true, however, is that someone who acts for a purpose often acts after (implicit or explicit) deliberation which may involve a combination of true and false premises. Thus, as we saw above, the true premises are indeed reasons. Nonetheless, someone who acts on a false premise does not, all things considered, have a reason to do what he did, though he thought he did. This is the case in the example of my cousin: my purpose was to help him. Among my motivating beliefs there were some true ones (say, that money could help someone in need), and at least one false one (that he needed money), which was only an apparent reason. So, although I acted for a purpose and thought I had a reason to give him money, in fact I didn't. And, in general, a person who acts motivated by a false belief acts for a purpose but had not, all things considered, reason to do what he did, and hence did not act for a reason.

Thus all these considerations that lead us to resist the idea that someone who acts on a false belief does not act for a reason fail. So long as we keep the necessary distinctions in mind, it is right to say that an agent who acts motivated by a false belief does not act for a reason; rather he acts for a purpose and is motivated by an *apparent* reason.

So the conclusion that, since the two other responses are not tenable, the only viable option in error cases is to embrace the psychological conception of reasons was too hasty. On examination, the second response turns out to be not only acceptable but in fact accurate. And the claim that motivating reasons are beliefs in the sense of 'what is believed' does not lead to any implausible conclusions in error cases because in such cases the agent acts only for an apparent reason—and the apparent reason he acts for is not that he believes that p, but rather what he believes, namely that p. And this means that error cases do not, after all, favour the psychological conception of motivating reasons.[23]

---

[23] For a similar view that an agent who acts on a false belief does not act for a reason, see Bittner (2001: 112–18), though I suspect that Bittner would probably object to my

I have argued in this section that we are motivated by what we believe, whether that is true or false, and that, given the dual use of the term 'belief', we can say that motivating reasons are true beliefs.[24] I have claimed also that this differs importantly from the dominant psychological conception of motivating reasons, as that conception is captured by the slogan that 'reasons are beliefs' only if 'beliefs' is construed as 'believings'; whereas my view is captured by the slogan only if 'beliefs' is construed as what is believed (or known, etc.). This point bears emphasizing. Dancy, for example, discusses a version of what he calls a 'psychologistic account of motivating reasons' according to which 'it is the psychological state plus content that together constitute the motivating reasons and the content alone that constitutes the normative reason, if there is one' (2000: 113). If believing something is rightly characterized as a state with content, then my view is that the motivating reason (and the normative reason, if there is one for that action) is the content alone. And the content alone—what is believed—is also called 'a belief'. And it is in that sense, and only in that sense, that motivating reasons can be said to be beliefs.[25]

However, it might be tempting to think that my view of motivating reasons is, if not the dominant psychological view, certainly a psychological conception of motivating reasons—for to say that reasons are beliefs, even if that means 'what is believed', is surely to allocate reasons to a psychological category. An exploration of the concept of 'belief' in the sense of what is believed will help to show why that supposition is wrong.

5.4. What Is Believed

The distinction between my believing something and what I believe is a familiar distinction—as we saw, it is an instance of the act/object

suggestion that reasons can be thought of as 'what is believed' since he thinks of reasons as things we encounter in the world, such as events and states of things, to which the action is a response. See Bittner (2001: ch. 4). On this issue, see below, Sections 5.4 and 5.5.

[24] Although, as I said in the introduction to this chapter, 'to believe' is here a generic term for a range of epistemic verbs. But see n. 9, above.

[25] For a number of reasons, however, I prefer not to use the characterization of believing in terms of state and content.

distinction found elsewhere, for instance, in the distinction between the act of stating something and what is stated when that act is performed.

But although discussions of the notion of belief often acknowledge the distinction, its significance goes easily out of focus. As a result, the term 'belief' is sometimes used to refer now to one, now to the other, indiscriminately, thus generating an entity called 'a belief' which is a kind of hybrid of the two, with the logical features of both, and which is therefore capable of playing very different roles.[26] This practice, however, often leads to confusion and poor arguments—as we shall see.

We saw earlier that what is believed can also be suspected, thought, stated, etc.; and, if what is believed is true, it can also be known. Let me, for the moment, call what is believed, suspected, etc., 'a proposition'—by which I mean simply something that can be thought, and can replace 'p' in 'John believes that p', 'Mary doubts that p', 'Fred stated that p', 'Angelina implied that p', ' the proposition that p is true', etc.

A proposition is called 'a belief', or 'a thought', or 'a suspicion' on account of its being something that can be believed, thought, or suspected respectively. I say that *can* be believed, rather than that *is* believed, because for the proposition that p to be called 'the belief that p', or 'the suspicion that p', it is not necessary that anyone actually believe or suspect, or have believed or suspected, that p. Even if nobody has ever believed that the Earth is made of cheese, we can talk about 'the belief that the Earth is made of cheese' and say, for instance, that it is a belief that nobody has ever held. All that is required for the proposition that p to be called 'the belief that p' is for the proposition to be considered as a possible object of belief: as a 'believable'. And so on regarding other epistemic terms.

Now, if John believes that p, the proposition that p can be referred to as 'John's belief that p'. If, instead, John suspects that p, then the proposition can be referred to as 'John's *suspicion* that p'. In either case it is the same proposition that is being talked about—what varies is John's epistemic state.

---

[26] See Price's 'Self-Verifying Beliefs' (1969) for an interesting discussion of how the failure to note the distinction can lead to apparent paradoxes.

What John believes, Mary can suspect, and Angelina can know. Suppose that John believes that Andrew has eloped, that Mary merely suspects it, and that Angelina, with whom Andrew has eloped, knows that he has. John's believing that Andrew has eloped is different from Mary's suspecting it; and Angelina's knowing it is different from both. However, what is believed, suspected, and known by each is the same, namely, that Andrew has eloped.

So one person can believe what another person knows. And, of course, two people can believe the same thing, that is, have the same belief. If I believe that the Earth is round and you also believe it, then we have the same belief, namely that the Earth is round.

Some may want to qualify this claim by saying that what we have cannot be 'numerically' the same belief; rather we must have two 'tokens' of the same belief 'type'. Accordingly, your belief that the Earth is round and mine would be two beliefs, not one, and they would differ in that mine is had by me, and yours is had by you. But this is surely wrong. For it seems that in the case of beliefs, unlike the case of, say, noses (putting aside conjoined twins), the fact that the same belief can be had by two people does not imply that we are dealing with two items, that is, two instances of the same kind (or tokens of a type). It is not clear that what is believed is the kind of thing about which it makes sense to distinguish between numerical and qualitative identity, as it would have to in order for what you and I believe to be two instances of the same kind, or two tokens of a type.

It is true that *your believing* that the Earth is round and *my believing* it are quite different, but this is because we are now dealing with 'believings'—if believing is rightly characterized as a state, with two states of believing: yours and mine; and at any rate with facts: the fact that you believe something and the fact that I believe something, and the same thing as you. And each of these facts might be used to explain different things. For instance, the fact that you believe that the Earth is round will presumably explain your actions (at least it could, in principle), while the fact that I believe it will explain *my* actions, etc. But none of this implies that there must be two 'qualitatively identical but numerically distinct' items of a kind that we each have, viz. a belief, as there would have to be if, without being conjoined twins, we were said to have the same nose. In this respect, to believe that p is analogous to loving N. If both Bill and Mike love Maureen, the fact that Bill loves Maureen is different from the fact that Mike does, and Bill's love for Maureen is different from Mike's. But the object of their love is one and the same, namely Maureen, and they do not love two different tokens of the 'Maureen-type'. The same goes for beliefs in the sense of 'what is believed'.

But, it may be objected, our beliefs cannot be the same because mine may be tentative while yours may be certain. But to say that my belief is tentative and yours is certain is to say something about *how* we believe what we believe, not about what we believe: 'tentatively' or 'with certainty' are ways of believing. Thus, we may both believe that p but I believe it with conviction while you believe it with hesitation: we both believe the same thing but in different ways. However, if my belief that p is false and you believe the same as I, then your belief is false too, for here we are dealing with what is believed.[27]

But if two people can believe the same thing, this suggests that what is believed, unlike one's believing it, is not a mental entity unlike, say, a mental state of John's, or an after-image he has, might be thought to be (each of which may be said to be a mental entity, albeit of rather different kinds). As we saw, what someone believes, a proposition, may be referred to as 'John's belief' only if John does indeed believe that thing, or as 'Mary's suspicion' only if Mary suspects that thing. But the possibility of referring to a proposition in these various ways does not mean that what is believed changes ontological category according to the term we use to refer to it, or that it becomes a mental entity when before it was a proposition.

Perhaps the thought that what is believed must be a mental entity is motivated by the following line of reasoning. In order to believe that p you need to have a mental representation of what you believe. For instance, in order to believe that it is raining you need to have a mental representation of its being raining. So surely, the thought goes, what you have when you believe that p *is* something mental: it is a mental representation of what you believe; more precisely, it is a token of a type of a mental representation of what you believe.

---

[27] The sentence 'I truly believe that p' seems ambiguous in that it could be used to express the claim that I do indeed believe that p, or the claim that I believe something that is true, namely, that p; while the sentence 'I falsely believe that p' does not seem ambiguous in this way: it says that I believe something that is false.

I think the concept of mental representation is less clear than its free use in contemporary philosophy of mind might suggest, but this is not the place to discuss that issue. What matters here is that, even if having a belief requires having a mental representation of what is believed, and even if what you then have is a token of a type of a mental representation, it does not follow that *what* you believe is a mental representation, let alone a token of a type of a mental representation: what you believe is what the purported mental representation you allegedly have represents, for instance, that it is raining, or that money alone does not bring happiness. And that, what you believe, is not itself a mental representation, or a token of one.

Consider an analogy. A portrait of Henry VIII is a visual representation of Henry VIII. So, if you have a portrait of Henry VIII, you have a visual representation of Henry VIII. But what your portrait represents, what the portrait is a portrait of, is not a visual representation of Henry VIII. What it represents is, rather, a man, namely Henry VIII. A portrait of Henry VIII is not a portrait of a visual representation of Henry VIII. Likewise having the belief that p might involve having a mental representation of 'the propositional content that p', but what you believe is not 'a mental representation of the content that p'; what you believe is, rather, that p—which the alleged mental representation represents.[28]

But if what is believed are not mental representations, or mental entities of some other kind, what are they?

5.4.1. *What is believed, propositions, and facts*

In the discussion so far, I have made several claims about what motivating reasons are. On the one hand, in Chapter 1, I said that all reasons are facts, which implies that motivating reasons are facts. In this chapter I have also said that a motivating reason is something that

---

[28] According to some versions of the representational theory of mind, to believe that JFK has been shot is to be 'appropriately related to' a mental representation whose propositional content is that JFK has been shot. But it is not clear why to believe that JFK has been shot should not rather be thought of as being appropriately related to *the propositional content* (or to the proposition, or state of affairs, or . . .) that JFK has been shot. Perhaps one cannot be appropriately related to a propositional content unless one has a mental representation of that content. But that does not mean that, therefore, what one is 'appropriately related to' when one believes that p is a *mental representation* of p—whatever that is.

is believed and that is the case, and have called that 'a proposition', 'a belief', 'a suspicion', 'something known', etc. But someone might think that these various ways of characterizing motivating reasons betoken confusion because facts, propositions, beliefs, suspicions, etc. are very different things, and so a reason cannot be all of these things.

That facts, propositions, beliefs, etc. are different things becomes evident if one considers that beliefs, suspicions, etc., as well as propositions, can be true or false but facts cannot be.[29] Thus, if John believes that Andrew has eloped, and he has, then what John believes is true, and what he believes, namely that Andrew has eloped, is a true proposition. So surely a reason, what is believed, cannot be a belief, a proposition, *and* a fact.

On the other hand, it is not plausible that what is believed becomes something different depending on whether we think of it as something that can be true or false (a proposition, a belief, a suspicion, etc.), or as something that is the case (a fact).

The way out of this puzzlement seems to be this. The same thing is being talked about when we talk about 'the proposition that p', 'John's belief that p', and 'the fact that p'. So the same thing is true, is a belief, and is a fact, and that is something that is specified with a 'that'-clause, for example, 'that Andrew has eloped'. However, this does not imply that a proposition is the same thing as a belief, or that either is the same as a fact: it only implies that the *same thing* can be all of these. As Strawson says:

It would indeed be wrong [. . .] to identify 'fact' and 'true statement'; for these expressions have different roles in our language, as can be seen by the experiment of trying to interchange them in context. Nevertheless, their roles—or those of related expressions—overlap. There is no nuance, except of style, between 'That's true' and 'That's a fact'; nor between 'Is it true that . . . ?' and 'Is it a fact that . . . ?'   (1950: 196)

The terms 'proposition', 'belief', 'fact', etc., have, as Strawson says, different roles in our language, they express different concepts. Nonetheless, the same thing can be labelled 'a proposition', 'a statement', 'a belief', and 'a fact'. And which label is appropriate depends on the context. For example, we tend to use 'belief' or 'supposition' when we're

---

[29] What is known can only be true but that does not affect the point above.

concerned with (possible or actual) things that people may believe; 'statement' is used typically when the concern is (possible or actual) assertions or utterances; 'proposition' is particularly appropriate in logic where issues such as truth and implication are at the fore, in abstraction from what anyone might believe or assert; and 'fact' is typically used in ordinary talk when the focus is the assessment of truths concerning situations, people, etc. But all of this is compatible with the idea that in talking about the fact that Andrew has eloped, the belief that Andrew has eloped, and the proposition that Andrew has eloped, the same thing is being talked about in every case: namely, that Andrew has eloped.

One may still demur: surely it cannot be the same thing that is being said to be all of these things. For there are things that can be predicated of a belief, and a proposition, such as that it is true or false, that cannot be predicated of a fact. And a fact and a belief can be said to be shocking or reassuring but propositions cannot be. And so on.

But this point is also accommodated by Strawson's observation that 'belief', 'proposition', 'statement', or 'fact' cannot be interchanged in all contexts because they are different concepts that play different roles. For I can assert what I believe by asserting the proposition that p, and what I thus assert may be a reassuring fact. And it is also true that, if it is a fact that p and I believe that p, then what I believe is true. Consider an analogy. A particular object, for instance, a particular bicycle, may be given as a present. Now, presents, but not bicycles, can be generous. But if Amy's bicycle was a generous present, the fact that bicycles cannot be generous does not show that Amy's bicycle was not a present, or that bicycles cannot, after all, be presents.

So the fact that there are things that it makes sense to say of what is believed, for example, that it is true or false, only considered as a belief or as a proposition but not, say, as a fact, and vice versa, does not show that when we talk about 'the (true) belief that p' and 'the fact that p', what we talk about is not the same thing. And so, the claim that what Antonio believes is a proposition is not the claim that 'belief' and 'proposition' are to be identified. It is simply the claim that what Antonio believes is something specified by a 'that'-clause, and that what that 'that'-clause specifies is also a proposition. The same goes for facts: 'the fact that p' specifies a fact; and what is so specified is the same as what is specified by 'the proposition that p', and 'the (true) belief that p', namely, that p.

There are, of course, many other issues about propositions, beliefs, facts, and related concepts, such as how best to characterize them onto-logically, what to say about negative facts and false propositions, how 'fine-grained' the individuation of each ought to be, etc., that I have not even mentioned, never mind discussed here. But it is not necessary to resolve those issues in order to achieve my purpose, which is to show that it is possible to conceive of motivating reasons as beliefs in the sense of what is believed, without commitment to the view that motivating reasons are psychological entities. For whether we think of motivating reasons as what is believed, as facts, as propositions, etc., it is clear that what we are thus thinking about are not psychological entities.

So we have seen that the view that what motivates is what is believed does not amount to a psychological conception of motivating reasons because what is believed is not a psychological entity. Nonetheless, one could be worried by the thought that what is believed is sometimes true and sometimes false; sometimes what is the case, and sometimes what is not the case. I have argued that only when what is believed is true, that is, when what is believed is the case and hence a fact, is it or can it be a motivating *reason*. But I need to say more about false beliefs, and about how, in general, what is believed motivates us to act. The last two sections of this chapter engage with those issues.

5.5. True Beliefs, False Beliefs, and Motivating Reasons

We have seen that a reason that motivates someone to act is a fact. This fact is something he is aware of, for example something he believes to be the case. Because it is something that he believes, it can be referred to as 'his belief that p'; and since, if it is a reason, what he believes is something that is the case, it can be referred to as 'his *true* belief that p'.

In order to motivate someone, what the agent believes (or knows, etc.) must seem to him to make his acting right or appropriate in some respect. For instance, in order to motivate Tim to take his umbrella, Tim's belief that it is raining must seem to him to make it appropriate to take his umbrella.

Sometimes, what the agent believes and is motivated by is something that is not the case. If so, what motivates the agent is a false belief which, because it is false, is not a motivating *reason* but only an *apparent* motivating reason. However, since it motivates, it is a motivating belief. A false belief, like a true belief, is something that the agent believes, that is, takes to be true. The fact that the agent takes it to be true shows how a false belief can motivate him to act: for as he takes it to be true, the belief can appear to him to make his acting in some way or another right, to favour so acting. For example, if Tim falsely believes that it is raining, his false belief that it is raining can make it seem to him that taking his umbrella is the right thing to do.[30]

It is true that a belief that motivates someone to act can only *justify* her so acting if the belief is true—that is, if the agent is motivated by a reason.[31] And it is true that, therefore, false motivating beliefs cannot justify an action, although the fact that someone had a false belief can make it intelligible that she acted as she did. But this does not mean that false beliefs cannot motivate an agent to act.

The thought that we are motivated by both true and false beliefs and that the former are facts while the latter are not might give rise to the following kind of objection. If I am motivated to act by a true belief, then I am motivated to act by something that is the case, that is, by a fact. And it seems plausible that one can be motivated to act by facts, as they are 'concrete' or 'out there in the world'.[32] However,

---

[30] And because of that, the fact that an agent believes something that is false can be cited to explain why he acted as he did. As we shall explore in more detail in the following chapter, in such cases what motivates, that is, the false belief that p, is not what explains: what explains is the fact that the agent had that belief.

[31] This is a necessary but not a sufficient condition for *a motivating belief* to be what justifies the action it motivates—though it is not necessary for the action to be justified. For it should be noted that, although a false belief cannot justify an agent's action, something else might, even when he acts motivated by a false belief. Thus, what motivates me to take my umbrella might be my false belief that it is raining. This false belief does not justify my taking the umbrella. But if someone had played a practical joke on me and made it look as though it was raining, then, since I was justified in believing that it was raining, I might also be justified in taking my umbrella—though not by my false belief, but by the fact that someone made it look as though it was raining (see also Stout 1996).

[32] Some authors say that facts *exist*, while possible but non-actual states of affairs do not. However, I cannot see that claiming that the fact that John is taller than James exists can amount to anything other than the claim that it is the case that John is taller than James; and, likewise, that claiming that the fact that James is taller than John does not exist amounts to anything other than that it is not the case that James is taller than John.

if I am motivated to act by a false belief, then I am motivated to act by something that is not the case, something that is not 'concrete', not 'out there in the world'. And if that is right, how can a false belief motivate?

The force of this objection, such as it is, depends on the idea that facts, unlike say, non-actual states of affairs, are 'out there in the world' or are 'concrete'. But it is unclear that the suggestion is cogent, and hence that it lends any force to the objection. If the idea amounts to the thought that facts have spatial location, then the objection is lame, because it is not clear that they do: where is one to locate the facts that many people admire Amy, or that John is taller than James, or that women are more risk-averse than men, or that the dollar has fallen for the third consecutive quarter this year? And suppose that, in fact, women aren't more risk-averse than men, where 'in the world' is that fact located? As Strawson says:

Situations and states of affairs so talked about are (like facts so talked about), abstractions that a logician, if not a grammarian, should be able to see through. Being alarmed by a fact is not like being alarmed by a shadow. It is being alarmed because . . . (1950: 197) (A way of completing Strawson's sentence might be: 'the housing market has collapsed'.)

And

Events can be dated and things can be located. But the facts which statements (when true) state can neither be dated nor located. (Nor can the statements, though the making of them can be). Are they included in the world?   (1950: 199)

So to the extent that the objection depends on this doubtful conception of facts as having spatial or temporal location in the world, the objection can be put aside. Facts are no more concrete or 'out there' than statements (what is stated), or than what is believed, or propositions, whether these be true or false.

The thought that facts are concrete, while propositions are not, has led some to reject the view that what we are motivated by are propositions, whether true or false. For example, although Dancy holds and has persuasively defended the view that motivating reasons are what is believed, he rejects the view that what is believed and motivates can be thought of as a proposition precisely on the grounds that what is believed and motivates must be 'part of the world'. He says: 'It is her being ill that gives me reason to send for the doctor, and this is a state of affairs, something that is part of the world, not a proposition' (2000: 114). And

Reasons for action are things like his self-satisfaction, her distress, yesterday's bad weather, and the current state of the dollar. They cannot be abstract objects of the sort that propositions are generally supposed to be.   (2000: 115)

But this seems wrong. And, in fact, Dancy's remarks elsewhere in the same book suggest that he himself is committed to the view that reasons are not quite as 'concrete' as he here says they must be. For he thinks that reasons are 'what can be the case' and what can be the case is not 'her distress', or 'his self-satisfaction', but *that she is distressed*, or *that he is self-satisfied*. And, as we have seen, the idea that the fact that she is distressed, etc., is 'part of the world' and not abstract is doubtful. Dancy seems here to make a mistake that Strawson diagnoses in the quotes above, the mistake of thinking that facts (or states of affairs) are 'part of world'.[33] But, to quote Strawson again:

if we read 'world' (a sadly corrupted word) as 'heavens and earth', talk of facts, situations, and states of affairs, as 'included in' or 'parts of' the world is, obviously, metaphorical. The world is the totality of things, not of facts. (1950: 198)

Thus, Dancy is right that what gives me reason to send for the doctor is that she is ill, or her being ill. But if my reason for sending for the doctor is that she is ill, even though *she*, and her illness, are 'part of the world', the fact that she is ill (or her being ill) is not, so by his own account my reason is not 'part of the world'.

[33] Strawson argues that the mistake of thinking that facts are things in the world has led some philosophers, e.g. J. L. Austin, to implausible claims: 'Because he [Austin] thinks of a statement as something in the world (a speech-episode) and a fact as something else in the world (what the statement either "corresponds to" or "is about"), he conceives the distinction as of overriding importance in philosophy, though (surprisingly) sometimes negligible for ordinary purposes. But I can conceive of no occasion on which I could possibly be held to be "neglecting or taking as irrelevant" the distinction between, say, my wife's bearing me twins (at midnight) and my saying (ten minutes later) that my wife had borne me twins. On Mr Austin's thesis, however, my announcing "The fact is that my wife has borne me twins" would be just such an occasion' (1950: 152).

So there seem to be no grounds for thinking that reasons cannot be propositions since there is no reason to think that a proposition is any more abstract than a fact, or than what is the case, or what is believed and is true.

But perhaps the claim that 'facts are out there' or that they are 'concrete' and 'real' is meant to convey the idea that facts are mind-independent, whereas what is believed but is not the case is not. But this thought is also unclear. If John is at home, his being at home is a fact independently of whether anybody believes or knows this. But equally, if he is not at home, then 'John is at home' describes a possible but non-actual way for the world to be which is also independent of what anyone thinks about it.

Thus we have found no argument against the view that false beliefs can motivate and hence against the view that true beliefs that motivate are reasons, while false beliefs that motivate are merely apparent reasons.

My discussion in Chapters 4 and 5 has focused on the questions whether desires or beliefs are motivating reasons. My conclusions are that what is desired motivates us as a goal; and that a belief, that is, what is believed, when it motivates and is true, is a motivating reason. But I have not examined an objection to my conception of motivating reasons that is often defended by philosophers of a Humean bent, namely that beliefs cannot motivate, or at any rate that beliefs *alone* cannot motivate. The final section of this chapter is devoted to examining that view.

5.6. Beliefs and Motivation

I have argued that what we believe, whether true or false, motivates us to act by making the proposed action seem right or good to us—in the broad sense of 'good' outlined in Chapter 1. According to my account, what is believed can motivate me to act by making my action seem good to me, either because it makes the action seem good in itself, e.g. what motivates me is a belief to the effect that ϕ-ing is fun, an act of friendship, an act of vengeance, entertaining, a fulfilment of a duty, aesthetically fitting, etc.; or because it is (or seems) a means to an end that I regard as good in itself.

What is believed often plays this motivating role by appearing as a premise in an agent's implicit or explicit practical reasoning. I say 'often' because not every action done for a reason is an action that results from practical deliberation, whether explicit or not. Things done for their own sake are typically done for a reason—the reason is that the action is (or seems to the agent to be) one of the forms that the good takes for that agent. But this reason need not have been a premise in any piece of reasoning. For instance, I may decide to watch a movie that is now showing on TV because I enjoy watching movies. My reason for watching it is that I enjoy movies but there needn't have been any deliberation, even implicit, about generally what to do, or more specifically about whether to watch the movie or not. If asked why I watched the movie, my answer: 'Because I like movies', would suggest that there was no reasoning (implicit or explicit) behind the decision and hence that my reason was not a premise in such deliberation.

When there is deliberation, however, the propositions that play the role of premises in that deliberation, that is, in practical reasoning, are, if true, also the reasons for which the agent performs the action that is the issue of deliberation. (If the premises are false, then the propositions that play the role of premises in practical reasoning are, as I have put it, merely apparent reasons). The deliberation that leads up to an action may be explicit, or implicit, or perhaps more commonly, a mixture of the two. For example, if asked, I might say that my reason for taking the train to work is that it is the most environmentally friendly means of making the journey. My decision to take the train may have been the result of more or less explicit calculations about the relative merits of different means of transport, and each of the premises in those calculations can be thought of as a reason for which I acted. As I said in Section 5.1 above, which one is given prominence and presented as my reason for acting is largely a matter of what a particular context calls for.

This conception of motivating reasons as things that are believed, which can be premises in practical reasoning, clearly involves a commitment to the idea that beliefs *can* motivate. Moreover, although in Chapter 4 I said that we are also motivated by our goals, that is, things we desire, I also said that among them, there are many things we desire for *reasons*, that is, things we are motivated to desire on the grounds of beliefs we have about their goodness or value. This implies not only that beliefs *can* motivate action but that, since beliefs can motivate desires, beliefs can be the fundamental motivators in action.

The idea that beliefs can motivate actions, either alone or in combination with desires, has been much disputed in the recent literature. Some philosophers reject the view that beliefs alone can motivate and, indeed, think that this is the strongest argument in favour of the Humean view of motivating reasons—the view that motivating reasons are combinations of states of believing and desiring, where states of desiring are the prime motivators.

If these philosophers were right, then the conception of motivating reasons that I have defended in this chapter would clearly be undermined. But we saw in the previous chapter that Humean arguments that we are motivated to act by states of desiring something are unpersuasive. Before finishing, I shall examine a Humean argument that says explicitly that beliefs cannot motivate, as presented by James Lenman.

Lenman claims that 'no purely cognitive state could, in combination with appropriate other beliefs, but *with nothing else*, originate a process of rational motivation' (1996: 291). But his arguments to support this claim are unpersuasive. For, first, even if his arguments proved the claim that beliefs *alone* cannot motivate, they would not prove that beliefs cannot motivate. And, in any case, his arguments do not show that beliefs alone cannot motivate.

It is worth noting that throughout his paper, Lenman fluctuates between the act/object uses of the terms 'belief' and 'desire', without signalling that he is aware that he is doing this and of the implications this has for his conclusions. He often talks about beliefs and desires as having direction of fit (see quotation below) and yet, towards the end of the paper, he says that 'a belief is a representation of the way we think the world is, a desire a representation of how we would have it be' (1996: 300). But a representation (the 'content' of a mental state of believing) and a mental state with direction of fit are quite different things. This equivocation on the use of the terms 'belief' and 'desire' vitiates Lenman's arguments, for one is never sure whether he wants to argue that *states* of believing alone cannot motivate, or whether his claim is that what is believed—the 'content' or 'representation', as he might put it—alone cannot motivate.

Consider the following passage:

Thoughts of the latter kind—*desires*—contrast with those whose direction of fit is word-world:[34] with *beliefs* whereby the thought content is supposed to match the world. The two are quite distinct: it is one thing to have beliefs about how things are in the world, another to care how they are. There is no belief to which we might not, in principle, be indifferent.   (1996: 292)

It is clear that the terms 'desires' and 'beliefs' in the first sentence are used to refer to *states*, for it is states that are said to have contents and 'direction of fit'. But it is also clear that, in the final sentence, the term 'belief' is used to refer to what is believed (the representation), for it is *that* that we may or may not be indifferent to. Given this equivocation, it is difficult to know what Lenman means when he says that 'a purely cognitive understanding of the reasons that motivate us to action appears fatally incomplete' (1996: 292): is the understanding that 'appears fatally incomplete' the idea that motivating reasons are states of believing, or is it rather the idea that motivating reasons are what is believed?

But putting this difficulty aside, and keeping the term 'belief' fixed to refer to 'what is believed', Lenman's arguments do not prove that the Humean view of motivation is right. First, his claim that 'there is no belief to which we might not, in principle, be indifferent' needs unpacking before one can decide what its force is. For it is true that I might be indifferent to *the* belief that my ϕ-ing would be good (in the broad sense of 'good') if, for instance, it is my cousin's belief. But this shows nothing about whether one's beliefs can motivate one to act. On the other hand, it is not clear that I can be equally indifferent to *my* belief that my ϕ-ing would be good. The reason why this is so is that there is a conceptual connection between its being true that 'my ϕ-ing would be good' is *my* belief, and my *not* being indifferent to that belief, so that the latter is one of the criteria of what it is for me to believe that: that is, one of the criteria of whether 'my ϕ-ing would be good' really is *my* belief. The connection between the two is not so tight as to exclude the possibility of *akrasia*, etc., but neither is it as loose as Lenman's remark suggests.

---

[34] 'Word-world' is Lenman's term for 'mind-to-world'.

It is true that it is possible for me to believe, say, that going to a Faculty meeting is my duty, and that I should nonetheless not be remotely motivated to go to the meeting because, as we might put it, I do not much care about doing my duty. But this does not show that my belief that something is good does not motivate me to do it; rather it shows that I can fail to believe that doing my duty is good or worthwhile.

And I can, it is true, be in a state of total listlessness or depression, where my beliefs about what is good have no motivating force. But it is significant that such states are pathological states, and that the pathology consists precisely in being *wholly* unmotivated by one's beliefs about what it would be good for one to do, whether one regards the actions being considered as one's duty, morally right, prudent, healthy, noble, or as something I find pleasant, fun, interesting, enjoyable, etc. We think of it as a pathology precisely because there seem to be conflicting criteria here: what I sincerely say suggests that I have the relevant beliefs, and yet those beliefs have no motivational force for me, which they would typically do.

So, if the remark is construed to make it relevant to the argument, the claim that 'there is no belief to which we might not, in principle, be indifferent' is far from obviously true.[35] But even if Lenman were right that 'there is no belief to which we might not, in principle, be indifferent', this would not show that beliefs cannot motivate us to act—if anything it suggests that they do, since if we *can* be indifferent to beliefs this is because we can also *not* be indifferent to them: for instance, we can be motivated to act by them. So even if in principle any of our beliefs could leave us cold, in practice many don't: they motivate us to want things and to act. So nothing in the claim that *sometimes* we are left indifferent by things we believe shows that, when we are not left indifferent but are instead motivated to act by them, it is not really what we believe but a state of desire, or even something we desire, that motivates us to act. So Lenman has not shown that beliefs cannot motivate.

Moreover, even if we accept a modified version of the Humean claim that desires (what is desired) are required for motivation, that

---

[35] And the fact that it must be *I*, and not someone else, that believes that ϕ-ing is good in order for that belief not to leave me indifferent should not lead us to the mistaken conclusion that it is *my believing it* that does not leave me indifferent.

would not undermine the view defended here that what is believed can motivate and even be the fundamental motivator. For, as we saw in previous chapters, many of our desires are rationally motivated by things we believe, that is, by beliefs to the effect that the things wanted are good, in some respect. In other words, many of the desires we have, we have because of the things we believe: these desires are based on beliefs about the worth of things.

What is believed, then, motivates us to want things, and to act in pursuit of the things we want. The things we want we often make our goals in acting. Thus, we might say that beliefs motivate actions via desires, in the sense that what we believe motivates us to desire precisely to do those things we believe to be good, and hence to make those things our goals in acting: and to try to attain what we desire according to our beliefs about how to do so. But the fact that we act in pursuit of goals does not mean that when we act so, we are not, or cannot be, motivated by our beliefs.

So, neither objections concerning the ontology of what is believed, nor those concerning the motivating capacity of what is believed, have presented any insuperable difficulty to the claim that what is believed can motivate, and hence to the non-psychological conception of motivating reasons that I have presented and defended here.

Conclusion

This chapter started with a question: 'What are *our reasons for* acting?'—which, according to the terminology introduced in Chapter 1, I glossed as the question: 'What are the reasons that motivate us to act?' The answer provided here has been that motivating reasons are true beliefs, that is, the things that we believe that are true—and since, if the belief that p is true, it follows that it is the case that p and therefore that it is a fact that p, we can also conclude that the reasons that motivate us to act are truths or facts. We can also be motivated to act by false beliefs. And, although false beliefs are not reasons, agents often mistake them for reasons and, on account of this, these false beliefs can motivate and, I suggested, they can be thought of as 'apparent reasons'.

In the next and final chapter I turn to the explanation of action, in particular to the explanation of intentional actions, which are generally taken to be actions performed for a reason. In that chapter we shall see how reasons play the role of explaining actions in general, and shall also explore the relation between motivating and explanatory reasons in contexts of action.

6

The Explanation of Action

Introduction

This chapter will focus on the explanation of intentional actions with particular focus on the explanation of intentional actions that are done for reasons, whether genuine or apparent.[1]

As we shall see, explanations of actions take many different forms. It is noteworthy, however, that since the publication of Davidson's 1963 paper 'Actions, Reasons, and Causes', most discussions concerning the explanation of action have focused on so-called 'Humean explanations', that is, explanations of the form 'He ϕ-ed because he *wanted* to ψ and *believed* that p', for example, 'He bought a new car because he wanted to impress her and believed that a new car would do the trick'.[2] This focus on Humean explanations has resulted, I think, in an unhelpfully narrow view of the explanation of intentional actions. Part of the aim of this chapter is to provide a broader and richer picture of the explanation of actions, and to locate Humean explanations within that broader picture.

The chapter is devoted, therefore, to exploring the various kinds of action explanation, and the relations between them. In Section 6.1, I draw a distinction between different kinds of action explanation by reference to the explanantia of each kind. Sections 6.2 to 6.5 are devoted to exploring these kinds of explanation, as well as the relations between them, in some detail.

---

[1] Everything done for a reason is done intentionally, although the reverse does not seem to hold. See Alvarez (2009).

[2] I use the term 'Humean' here to refer to a view about the explanation of action. The term is used also for views in other debates, e.g. about normative reasons; for this use see e.g. Schroeder (2007).

6.1. The Variety of Action Explanations

An action explanation may be an explanation of why someone habitually acts, is now acting, has acted, will act, etc., in a certain way. For instance, we explain why Peter joined the Party, why Anne goes to the theatre, why Sally is waving her arms, why you are going to leave your job, and so on. For the sake of simplicity, in what follows I shall examine primarily explanations why someone *acted*—in the past—but what I say applies also to the variety of cases just mentioned.

In an explanation of why someone acted, the explanans is 'the reason why' he acted. So in the explanation: 'Peter joined the Party because his girlfriend had joined', the explanans, 'His girlfriend had joined', is the reason why Peter joined the Party. But, as already noted in Chapter 1, it is somewhat misleading to talk about *the* reason why, because a 'Why?'-question can have many answers, and *which* answer (that is, which reason) is given as the reason why depends, among other things, on the context in which the question is asked. I shall have more to say about this below but will continue to talk about 'the reason why' with this qualification in mind.

Some explanations that give the reason why someone did something have a distinctive feature, which arises from the fact that there are reasons for acting and that we can, and often do, act for reasons.[3] Because of this, the reason why someone acted is sometimes also *her reason for acting*, whereas the reason why an event occurs, or the reason why things are this or that way, is never the event's reason for occurring, or the thing's reason for being this or that way. If a radiator explodes because there was an increase in pressure, the fact that there was an increase in pressure is the reason why the radiator exploded—but it was not the radiator's reason for exploding. And if the reason why there is no life on Mars is that Mars has no atmosphere this is not Mars' reason for not having any life on it.

The reason why A ϕ-ed can be also A's reason for ϕ-ing only if A is a creature that can ϕ for reasons. However, the reason why A ϕ-ed need not be A's reason for ϕ-ing, even when A ϕ-ed for a reason. For

---

[3] For the sake of simplicity I shall talk about persons when talking about ϕ-ing, putting aside the question whether any beings other than humans can act for reasons.

instance, the reason why Tom sat at the back of the class is that he is shy but that is not *his* reason for sitting there—his reason is, say, that he's more likely to avoid being noticed there.

Because of this, when ϕ-ing is something that can be done for reasons, the answer to the question why someone ϕ-ed may vary in kind, that is, different kinds of explanation can be given. Consider the following examples:

(a) Fred bought cream because he needed it for the cake he was baking.
(b) Alison went to the police because she thought her car had been stolen.
(c) Tom sits at the back of the class because he is shy.
(d) I exercise in order to keep fit.

What are the differences and similarities between these explanations?

The first three explanations are all 'because'-statements, and the reason why the agent acted is given after the 'because'. The fourth explanation, by contrast, names a goal or purpose for the sake of which I act.

But even though the first three have the same form, there are nonetheless important differences between them. In (a), 'Fred bought cream because he needed it for the cake he was baking', the explanans—viz. that Fred needed cream for the cake he was baking—is also Fred's reason for buying cream. By contrast, in (b), 'Alison went to the police because she thought her car had been stolen', the explanans—viz. that Alison thought her car had been stolen—is not Alison's reason for going to the police. As we saw in Chapter 5, Alison's (real or apparent) reason was that her car had been stolen, which is not itself the explanans but is contained in it: the explanans is a fact about Alison's thinking something, whereas her reason is not.[4] As for (c), 'Tom sits at the back of the class because he is shy', I already said above that the explanans in this case is not

[4] As noted above, all these explanations could be supplemented with other reasons, for example that there was no cream at home, or that her insurance company won't pay unless the theft has been reported to the police. And, as I have already noted, whether we offer one rather than the other of these reasons as the agent's reason for acting, or as the explanation of the action, is a matter of context and background assumptions. I say more about this in Section 6.3.

Tom's reason for sitting at the back; and unlike in (b), Tom's reason is not contained in the explanans. However, the explanans does give an indication of what his reason was.[5]

So, if we attend to the differences between their explanantia, these explanations can be seen to fall into two groups:

(i) The first group comprises explanations whose explanantia are the agent's reasons for acting. I shall call explanations of this kind, '*reason explanations*' (or, on grounds that will become clear, 'reason explanations *proper*').

(ii) The second group is constituted by explanations whose explanantia are not the agent's (real or apparent) reason, though some may mention it. A subgroup of (ii) comprises explanations whose explanantia are psychological facts about the agent: facts about his mental states, character traits, etc., which, to repeat, are not the agent's reason for acting. This kind I shall call '*psychological explanations*'.

These psychological explanations are themselves varied. Among them, of special interest to us are so-called '*Humean explanations*', where the answer to a 'Why?'-question provides a reason why that is some fact to the effect that the agent believed (knew, thought, etc.) and wanted certain things. An example of this kind would be: 'The manager changed the rota because he wanted to increase productivity and believed that changing the rota would achieve that end'. These explanations mention the (real or apparent) reason that motivated the agent to act in a 'that'-clause following a psychological verb: 'because he believed that p': the agent's (real or apparent) reason is that p: in our example, that changing the rota would increase productivity; but (part of) the explanans, that is, (part of) the reason that explains his

---

[5] What I have said about reasons for acting applies to reasons for believing, wanting, feeling emotions, as well as to reasons for failing to act. If Martin wanted to miss the party because he dislikes parties then the reason why he wanted to miss the party was also *his reason for* wanting to miss it, and this is an explanation similar to (a) above. And if Jane believed that Martin would be at the party because she thought Martin had said he would, then this is an explanation of type (b) where the reason why Jane believes what she does (that she thought that . . .) is not her real or apparent reason for believing it, although it contains it ; moreover, (b) suggests that the alleged reason, namely that Martin (allegedly) said he would, was only an apparent reason.

action is, in our example, that *the agent believed that* changing the rota would increase productivity.

Other psychological explanations do not mention the agent's reason, but like (c) above they mention some character trait, motive, emotion, etc., of the agent. Often, explanations of this kind imply that the agent acted for a reason, and perhaps provide a clue about what that reason might have been.

There are some psychological explanations which, unlike the two kinds just described, imply or suggest that the agent did not ϕ intentionally. For example, 'He messed up the accounts because he was distracted by the loud music'. Explanations of this kind are often given for omissions. Sometimes one omits to do something for a reason: for example, you may omit to greet someone because she has slighted you in the past. But many omissions are unintentional, and explanations of such omissions are often of this psychological kind. For example, if Jess missed a meeting because she forgot about it, the reason why she missed the meeting was not her reason for missing the meeting, and her failure to attend the meeting was not intentional.

Sometimes agents do things unwittingly in (or by) doing something else deliberately. For example, I may deliberately burn some old papers without realizing that I am thereby burning a title deed that shows that I am the owner of some property. So, I burn the old papers, but not the title deed, intentionally and for a reason. Here, the answer to the question: 'Why did you burn the title deed?' is, for example, 'I didn't realize it was a title deed'. Anscombe says this is a way of refusing application to a question 'Why?' that asks for your reason for doing that thing (1957: 11). Similarly, there are cases where one intends to do one thing but does another—as when, for example, one puts the banana peel in the laundry basket and one's socks in the bin. The answer to 'Why?' here would be something like 'I was distracted' or 'I didn't notice what I was doing'. Again, the particular actions were done unawares and not for a reason. Sometimes one can do something purely accidentally. For instance, one can fall against a vase, and thus knock and break it. Here the answer to 'Why did you break the vase?' might be 'I broke it accidentally'.

The explanations considered in the last two paragraphs are psychological explanations, but they are not explanations of actions or omissions done for reasons, and in some cases they are not explanations of intentional actions or omissions, so I shall not say anything more about them.

In addition to action explanations that are 'because'-statements, there is an important kind of explanation, exemplified in (d) above, which is peculiar to actions or omissions (as opposed to beliefs or wants). These are *purposive explanations*, which are a kind of teleological explanation. These explanations explain by reference to the agent's goal or purpose: 'He ϕ-ed *in order to* ψ', where the agent's goal or purpose was 'to ψ'. They are characterized by the use of 'in order to' or equivalent expressions ('so as to', 'with a view to', etc.).

These explanations give the agent's goal or purpose, for instance, to have children, which, as we saw in Chapter 4, is also the agent's intention in acting. However, they do not *state* the fact that the agent had such a goal. And, when they are explanations of things done for reasons, they do not state the reason the agent had for doing what he did, though they often suggest what that reason was.

In the following sections, I examine each of these kinds of action explanation in some detail.

6.2. Reason Explanations of Action

A reason explanation, in the sense in which I am using this phrase, is an explanation whose explanans is the agent's reason for acting. It is true that any explanation that cites a reason why could be called a 'reason explanation'. But the phrase 'reason explanation' is a term of art in contemporary philosophy, which is generally used as I have said I shall use it: to refer to an explanation whose explanans is the agent's reason for acting.

I shall therefore be using the term 'reason explanation' as contemporary philosophers generally *intend* to use it. But note that this is not how the label is *actually* used in the recent literature, because the majority of philosophers actually apply the label 'reason explanations' to Humean explanations. But in doing so they are not applying the term according to its intended meaning because the *explanans* of a Humean explanation is '[A acted because] he wanted to ψ and believed that p'. But, as I have argued, the fact that A wanted to ψ, or the fact that A believed that p are not, typically, A's reasons for acting. Hence the explanans of a Humean explanation is not the agent's reason for acting, even though it often mentions it.

The defender of the Humean model of explanation is likely to reply that this is a trivial point since what I call 'reason explanations proper' are actually *elliptical* and, when fully spelled out, they conform to the Humean model. The Humean may admit that, as a matter of fact, few of the action explanations we give to each other in real life fit the Humean pattern. But he will argue that this has to do with the pragmatics, rather than the logic, of explanation. That is, explanations are given in specific contexts where a number of assumptions on which the explanation depends are taken for granted and therefore need not be made explicit. But when those assumptions are made explicit, the Humean will claim, all reason explanations conform to the Humean model.[6]

It is important to understand what this Humean claim amounts to. The claim is not merely that it is possible to formulate a Humean explanation for every action done for a reason (real or apparent). That may be true but the Humean claim is stronger. It is that a reason explanation is explanatory *to the extent* that it conforms to the Humean model, and precisely because of that.[7]

The Humean may advance three arguments in defence of this claim (they mirror the arguments in favour of the psychological conception of motivating reasons examined in Chapter 5).

First, an explanation that mentions something the agent believed is explanatory *only* on the assumption that there was something that the agent desired (his goal on acting). So a reason explanation must, when fully spelled out, mention a *desire*.

---

[6] It must be noted here that if this view about explanatory reasons is right, and if what I have called 'reason explanations proper' are elliptical for Humean explanations, we should have to conclude that, strictly speaking, there are no *reason* explanations. The conclusion would follow from the fact that an explanation whose explanans *is* the reason for which the agent acted would be in fact elliptical for an explanation whose explanans is *not* such a reason, although it includes that reason—in the 'that'-clause that follows 'because he believed'.

[7] Smith says that the 'philosophy of action begins with the claim that it is always possible to construct a Humean, belief/desire, explanation of action' and, he adds, 'all other explanations supplement this basic Humean story' (1998: 17–18). For a contrasting view, see Thompson (2008).

Second, a fact can only explain an agent's action if the agent is aware of that fact; and a goal can only explain an agent's action if the agent has that goal. So what really explains the action is *that the agent was aware* of the fact and *that the agent had* that goal—or as the Humean would say, *that the agent believed and desired* the relevant things.

Note that these two arguments are different. The first argument says that the explanation cannot work if its explanans cites only *what* the agent believed: it must also cite *what* the agent desired. The second argument says that the explanation cannot work if its explanans includes only *what* the agent believed and *what* he desired: it must also include the fact that *he believed and desired* those things.

The third argument concerns the kind of error cases discussed in Section 5.3. When an agent is motivated by a *false* belief, the explanans of a reason explanation cannot be what he believed, because what he believed is false and a true explanation cannot have a false explanans. In these cases, the explanans must be the fact that he believed it. However, the argument continues, 'the difference between false and true beliefs on the agent's part cannot alter the *form* of the explanation which will be appropriate to his action' (Williams 1981: 102). So the explanation must have that form *also* in veridical cases.

These three arguments are thought to show that an explanation of action that cites the agent's (real or apparent) reason, when spelled out, will always conform to the Humean model. I shall address them in turn, in Sections 6.2.1, 6.2.2, and 6.2.3.

6.2.1. *Reason explanations and the agent's desires*

The objection about desires is that an explanation whose explanans is something the agent believed explains only in so far as it contains an implicit reference to what the agent desired. Thus, for instance, 'She bought some milk because she had run out' explains why she bought milk only because it contains an implicit reference to something she desired, for instance, to have milk at home. Likewise, 'He ran because it was the only way to get there on time' explains why he ran only because it contains an implicit reference to a goal, a want of the agent's: to get there on time. And 'John visited his friend because she was ill' explains why John visited her only, it is claimed, if we assume the presence of some desire in John that was suitably related to his visiting her: that is, a desire that would be served by visiting her, perhaps the desire to be kind to her.

I agree that any explanation of an action performed for a reason involves explicit or implicit reference to the goal or purpose in pursuit of which the agent acted because the goal shows the connection, in the agent's eyes, between that reason (what the agent believed) and the action. In the case of things done for the sake of something else, this is because the things that an agent believes appear to him as reasons because of certain goals he has. For instance, the fact that one has run out of milk will seem a reason to buy milk only for someone who wants to have milk at home. In the case of actions done for their own sake, knowing the reason *is* often knowing the goal. For example, if someone's reason for listening to music is that they enjoy it, then knowing that that is their reason is also knowing their goal, because their goal is the enjoyment of music. This does not mean, as we saw in Chapter 4, that such a person listens to music as a means to a further end, namely, enjoying himself—rather the goal is 'enjoying listening to music'.

Does this, however, imply that reason explanations must, when fully spelled out, conform to the Humean model—at least concerning goals or desires? That is, does it follow that part of its explanans will be 'He wanted to ψ'?

Well, first we should remember that, as just mentioned, some things that are done for a reason are done for their own sake and not (also) for the sake of some other thing. So if I go to see someone in hospital because she's my friend, this is something I do for a reason—namely, that she's my friend—but not for the sake of something else: I visit her out of friendship, or for the sake of friendship. In such a case, there isn't, or there needn't be, any desire for the sake of furthering which I visit her, no desire that would explain why the fact that she's my friend is a reason for me to visit her. I have a goal: to visit her, but this is not a goal that is different from my action—rather my goal is, precisely, to do that thing—which I do for its own sake, because she's my friend.

Moreover, when one does something instrumentally, for the sake of something else, it is possible to make the agent's further goal explicit by introducing 'in order to' expressions, or similar, as in: 'He ran *in order to* make the meeting, since he was late'; or 'She bought some milk so as to have some at home since they had run out'. In other words, we could make the agent's goal explicit by supplementing the reason explanation with a purposive explanation (which I'll discuss below, in Section 6.5). So it does not seem true that when fully spelled out an explanation must mention the fact that the agent *wanted* that thing (to make the meeting, to have milk at home).

The Humean may think that to concede this is to concede the point, at least for instrumental actions (those things done for the sake of something else), because, if an agent acts *in order to* ϕ, it follows that the agent *wanted* to ϕ (at least in the thin sense we have already encountered), and that he believed that . . . In other words, to concede this is to concede that what explains an (instrumental) action is the fact that the agent *wanted and believed* certain things. This is, in essence, the second argument in support of the Humean model mentioned above, which I address in the next section.

6.2.2. *Reason explanations, believing, and wanting*

This objection focuses on the idea that it is not your reason (what you believe) and your goal (what you want) that explain what you do but rather *your believing* and *your wanting* those things. So, although the explanation in context may mention only your reason, or your goal, or both, when we spell out the explanation fully, the explanans will be that you have such-and-such a goal (that you wanted to ϕ) and that you believe that p, as that is what really explains your action.

But what grounds are there for saying that what *really* explains your action is your believing and wanting those things, *rather than* what you believe and the goal you have?

One such ground might be that, since unless you believe that p, that p cannot explain your action, then it follows that what explains your action is that you believe that p. But in fact this reasoning shows only that your believing that p (or your knowing it, etc.) is a *necessary condition* for the fact that p to explain your action.[8] If what explains

---

[8] Dancy claims that we should think of the agent's believing the relevant things not as the explanans but as the 'enabling conditions' for the explanation—in his words: 'The suggestion is therefore that the believing, conceived traditionally as a psychological state, is an enabling condition for an explanation which explains the action in terms of the reasons for (that is, in favour of—the good reasons for) doing it (. . .) But the believing does not

why I failed a student is that he cheated, it is true that unless I am aware that he cheated, the fact that he cheated cannot explain my action; but if I am aware that he cheated, then it can explain it, and we need an independent argument to conclude now that something else, for example, my being aware that he had cheated, rather than his having cheated, is what explains my action. Thus, the necessity of my being aware of a reason in order for the reason to explain my action does not support the conclusion that what explains my action is my being aware of that reason, that is, my believing that thing.

After all, it is obvious why my being aware of the reason is necessary for *the reason* to explain my action. As we saw in Chapter 1, unless I am aware of the fact that p, the fact that p cannot be the reason that motivates me to act. And unless the fact that p is the reason that motivates me to fail him, the fact that p cannot be a 'reason why' which is *also* a 'reason for which' I acted. Hence, in order for the fact that p to be the explanans of a reason explanation, I must have been aware of the fact that p. But this does not compel us to conclude that what really explains my action is my being aware of the fact that p.

The Humean might insist that it is implausible to suggest that the fact that p alone can explain my action, for the fact was there, so to speak, before I was motivated to act. And the fact that p is there both for you and for me but, if the fact that p was *my* reason for acting, then it is *my* being aware of it, rather than *your* being aware of it, that explains my action. So, he might conclude, it is my being aware of the fact, rather than the fact itself, that explains my action. Perhaps something like this thought can be found in this argument of Williams's:

But nothing can explain an agent's (intentional) actions except something that motivates him so to act. So something else is needed besides the truth of the external reason statement to explain action, some psychological link; and that psychological link would seem to be belief. *A*'s believing an external

contribute directly to the explanation' (2000: 127). I argue in Section 6.2.3 that Dancy's suggestion can be right only for veridical cases; in error cases it must be the agent's believing what he believed that explains his action, since what he believed, being false, cannot be what explains the action. In any case, the believing that 'contributes' to the explanation is a fact, and not a psychological state, even though it is a fact concerning a psychological state.

reason statement about himself may help to explain his action.   (Williams
1981: 107)[9]

But first, if it shows anything,[10] what Williams's argument shows is
that in order for a reason to explain an action, the agent must take
what he believes to be a reason for him to act. To use his example, if
there is a reason for Owen Wingrave to join the Army, in order for
that reason to explain his action of joining, Owen must believe that
that is a reason for him to join the Army. But we have seen that it
would be a non sequitur to conclude from this that what explains his
joining the Army is *his believing* that there was such a reason.

Second, it is true that someone's *believing* that the fact that p is a
reason for him to φ *may* help to explain his action (as the last sentence
of the quote above asserts). But this does not show, as it might appear
to, that *only* such a thing can explain his action, or, as the Humean
claims, that someone's believing something *must* be part of a full and
explicit explanation of his action.

So this argument does not show that, when fully spelled out, all
explanations that cite the agent's reason must conform to the Humean
model.

As far as I can see, the Humean objector has one more move open
to him, which is to accept this but to argue that, in the kind of error
cases mentioned, what the agent believed, since it is false, *cannot be*

---

[9] It is striking that his example of 'an external reason statement' is something like 'There
is a reason for Owen Wingrave to join the Army' because, although that is a statement that
there is a reason, it is not a statement *of the reason* that there is for Owen Wingrave to do so.
(Such a reason would be rather something like 'There is a long tradition of Army careers
in my family'; or 'The Army is a noble career to pursue'.) One is very rarely motivated
by the belief 'that there is a reason for one to φ'. It is more common to be motivated by
something one believes which one takes to be a reason for one to φ. So to show that an
'external reason statement' so conceived does not explain the agent's action would not be
to show that what is believed cannot explain the agent's action alone, and that it must be
his believing it that does.

[10] I say 'if anything' because the first premise, viz. that only what motivates an agent to
act can explain his intentional action, is, as stated, false. Moreover, it is a claim that Williams
himself contradicts elsewhere in the same paper, when he says that 'If there are reasons for
action, it must be that people sometimes act for those reasons, and if they do, their reasons
must figure in some correct explanation of their action (*it does not follow that they must figure
in all correct explanations of their action*)' (1981: 102, my italics). This implies that things other
than the reasons for which people act can also explain their intentional actions. What is true
is that nothing can be a *reason* explanation of action that does not have as its explanans the
reason for which the agent acted—but clearly that doesn't favour the Humean position.

what explains his action. So, in *those* cases at least, what explains his action must be the fact *that he believed* what he believed, as the Humean model for explanation of actions says. Moreover, if the other claim of Williams's quoted earlier (in Section 6.2) about the form of action explanations is right, then all reason explanations must, when spelled out, conform to the Humean model. The next section examines this argument.

6.2.3. *Reason explanations and error cases*

In order to decide the question about the form of explanations, we need first to establish whether the Humean is right that, at least in the error cases under consideration, the belief that motivated the agent cannot be the explanans of a reason explanation.

We must put aside one reason to reject this Humean claim. This is the thought that if we accept that the explanans of an action explanation is of the form 'that he believed that p', then we are committed to saying that this was the reason that motivated the agent to act. We must put it aside because we have seen that the reason that explains why someone ϕ-ed need not be her reason for ϕ-ing.

As far as I can see, one can accept the unappealing view that in these error cases the explanans of an action explanation is what the agent believes only if one is prepared to accept that an explanation may have a false statement as its explanans; for only thus can one accept that an explanation such as 'He ran because he was being chased (although he wasn't being chased)' is a legitimate action explanation.

Few philosophers seem tempted by this position.[11] Indeed, the thought that this position on the nature of reason explanations is

---

[11] But some have been tempted, for example, Dancy. He says that a statement like 'Her reason for failing him was that he had cheated, although he hadn't' is more like 'She believed that he had cheated, although he hadn't', than like 'She knew that he had cheated, although he hadn't' (2000: 131–7). This last statement is implicitly contradictory because the verb 'to know', unlike the verb 'to believe', creates factive contexts: the truth of the statement implies the truth of the proposition expressed by the 'that'-clause. Dancy thinks that expressions such as 'Her reason for failing him was that, as he supposed, he had cheated, (although he hadn't)' are not strictly speaking contradictory, and he thinks that this suggests that this form of words provides an explanation of her action that is not factive (2000: 134). I think Dancy is right in saying that such statements allow us to explain the relevant action but wrong in saying that such explanations are not factive. For the explanans here is 'she supposed that he had cheated (although he hadn't)'.

the inevitable corollary of the conception of motivating reasons I defended in Chapter 5 has led some philosophers, I think, to reject that conception. But the thought that these two views must go hand in hand is, as we have seen, simply wrong: it is possible to embrace a non-psychological conception of motivating reasons and yet to reject the view that a true explanation can ever have a false explanans.

I do not see any reason to accept the view that a true action explanation may sometimes have a false explanans. For, if I say that the reason that explains why I did something was that p and then discover that p is false, I will withdraw that explanation and substitute some other one with a true explanans. For instance, if I say that the reason that explains why I waved at that person is that he is my boss and then realize that he isn't, I'll replace that explanation with something like: 'The reason that explains why I waved is that *I thought that* he was my boss'; that is, I substitute a true explanans ('I thought that he was my boss') for the false one ('He was my boss'). And what reason could there be for me to do this except the principle that a true explanation cannot have a false explanans?

So I agree that in cases of false beliefs, explanations conform to the Humean model, at any rate to the cognitive part of it. But does this conclusion about error cases show that all reason explanations are elliptical and that, when spelled out, they all conform to the Humean model? It is not clear that it does because it is not clear that, in general, we should generalize from any conclusion about error cases to all cases.

Some philosophers, however, think that the argument from error does hold here and that action explanations cannot take a different form in veridical and error cases respectively. As I noted above, Williams, for example, says that 'the difference between false and true

---

Dancy uses examples about reasons for believing to support his claims about the possibility of non-factive explanations. He says, and I agree, that if I say that I believe that p because I believe that q, then *my grounds* for believing that p (that is, the belief that leads me to believe that p) is (the consideration) that q. And this is so whether or not it is true that q. However, this does not show that if q is false, and if we explain why I believe that p, then we may provide a non-factive explanation. For, if it is false that q, then the explanation of why I believe that p is not that q; it is rather *that I believe* that q. And this explanation is, again, factive. But here, as in the case of actions, we must be careful not to let this fact about explanation lead us to the mistaken conclusion that in these cases, my grounds for believing that p is, after all, *that I believe* that q.

beliefs on the agent's part cannot alter the *form* of the explanation which will be appropriate to his action' (1981: 102).

But Williams does not say why this should be so, nor does he explain whether, and if so why, a change from 'He did it because p' to 'He did because he believed that p' counts as a change in form. After all, we may say that both have the form 'r because z'.[12] So his remark falls short of a persuasive argument.

In fact, one may think that there is a good reason why a difference of this kind between explanations in veridical and error cases is legitimate. For, as we saw in the previous chapter, in veridical cases what motivated the agent is a motivating reason, and that reason can also be the reason that explains his action. However, in error cases what motivates the agent is a false belief and thus it is not a *reason* (it is only an apparent reason). Because of this, in error cases it is not possible to construct a *reason* explanation, and so, in those cases, we must resort to a Humean explanation: one whose explanans is a statement to the effect that the agent believed that p; for example: 'She left her job because she believed that she had a fatal disease'.[13]

Perhaps the view that the form of the explanation has changed is motivated by the view that, if the explanans is 'that p', then the explanans is a fact, whereas if it is 'I believed that p', then the explanans is a mental state. But this suggestion is confused. For, as we saw in Chapter 2, even if to believe that p is to be in a mental state, and even if 'my believing that p' may sometimes be used to denote a mental state, the statement 'I believe that p' does not denote a mental state—rather, it is a statement of fact, a fact that concerns me and my mental states. And, if the explanation is 'I ϕ-ed because I believed that p', since 'I believe that p' is a statement of fact, the difference between the explanans 'p' and the explanans 'I believe that p' is not that between a fact and a mental state but that between two facts, where the second concerns my believing something.

---

[12] I say that both these explanations have the form 'r because z' because 'I believed that p' and 'p' are both statements of fact. So it seems that, here, what has changed is not so much *the form* as *the content* of the explanation.

[13] Note that this point is not about the pragmatics of explanation, that is, about the idea that this is explanatory against a background assumption of other things known about the situation, including some other psychological facts about the agent. (I discuss this other point below.) The point under discussion here is about what can be the explanans of an explanation, whether it has been made explicit or not.

It may be that the basic Humean idea here is that, while it is not always possible or appropriate to provide a reason explanation, for instance, when we do not know whether what motivated the agent is true, it is always possible and appropriate to provide a Humean explanation of action. Consider this remark of Davidson's:

Your stepping on my toes neither explains nor justifies my stepping on your toes unless I believe you stepped on my toes, but *the belief alone, true or false,* explains my action.   (Davidson 1980: 8, my italics)

Davidson's wording is somewhat careless, for it is false that the *belief* alone, true or false, can explain, never mind justify, his action. If the belief (viz. that you had stepped on Davidson's toes) is false, that belief can neither explain nor justify Davidson's action. What Davidson clearly means is, rather, that *his believing* that you had stepped on his toes can explain his action—regardless of whether what he believes is true or false, although it can only explain it if it *is* true that he believes that you had stepped on his toes. And this shows that, once we know the belief that motivated an agent (the belief that p), it is always possible to construct a true Humean explanation of his action (whose explanans *is* that he believed that p), independently of whether the belief in question was true or false; whereas we can only construct a true reason explanation proper, one whose explanans is the belief, if we know that the belief is true.

However, it is important to notice that Davidson's argument here only shows that Humean explanations are always possible: it does not show that proper reason explanations are never genuine explanations or are elliptical for Humean explanations—on the contrary, for he says 'your stepping on my toes neither explains nor justifies my stepping on your toes *unless* I believe you stepped on my toes' (my italics). And this suggests that, provided he believes you did, the fact that you stepped on his toes can explain his action.

But, the Humean could respond as follows. It is true that, in veridical cases, it is possible to provide both a reason explanation *and* a Humean explanation. However, anyone who rejects the view that the former is elliptical for the latter needs to explain how these two explanations are related—in such a way that we are not left with some form of over-determination, or rather of over-explanation of the action: one in terms of the fact that motivated you, and one in terms of your being aware of that fact.

In the next section, I provide an account of the relation between explanations of the two kinds that is not committed to the ellipsis view, and which addresses the objections mentioned in the last few paragraphs.

6.3. The Relation between Reason and Humean Explanations of Action

As we have seen, although Humeans exaggerate the frequency of use and importance of explanations of the believing-desiring model, it is undeniable that we often use explanations of this kind: we have seen that we *have to* use them in error cases in order to convey the belief that motivated the agent, and that we may also use them in veridical cases. This notwithstanding, it is possible to provide an account of the use we make of explanations of both kinds which does not commit us to the view that reason explanations proper are ellipses for Humean explanations, or that either kind of explanation is more basic than the other.

I want to suggest that the relationship between Humean and reason explanations should be understood, not in terms of ellipses, or of one being more basic or fundamental than the other, but rather in terms of the *pragmatics* of explanation. Reason explanations and Humean explanations have different uses and hence they are appropriate in different contexts.

Humean explanations have a threefold use: they serve (i) to identify the belief that motivated the agent, whether true or not; (ii) to convey, directly or indirectly, the speaker's own view about the truth or otherwise of what motivated the agent; and (iii) to specify whether what motivated the agent was something that the agent believed, or something he knew, or suspected, etc. (Humean explanations also serve to provide further details about the desire that motivated the agent but here I shall focus on beliefs for the sake of simplicity of exposition.)

The first aspect of the use of Humean explanations we have already seen: an explanation such as 'She lent him the money because she believed he was in need' identifies the motivating belief. This is something that a reason explanation can also do but, as we have seen, when the belief is false, we need to resort to some kind of psychological locution because a reason explanation is not possible in these cases.[14]

Moreover, and relatedly, these Humean explanations can be used by the speaker providing the explanation to control the strict implications and the conversational implicatures of the explanation, and doing so allows the speaker to do what is noted under (ii): convey her own views about the truth-status of what motivated the agent. Let me explain what this means.

The reason explanation 'She took a taxi because there was a public transport strike', for instance, explains why she took a taxi *and* implies that there was indeed a strike. On the other hand, 'She took a taxi because she thought that there was a public transport strike' explains why she took a taxi by stating what motivated her to take a taxi, without implying that things were as she believed, that is, without implying that there was a strike—indeed it has the conversational implicature that there was no strike. Thus, the psychological locution 'he believed that' and similar locutions can be used when the speaker wants, for whatever reason, to distance himself from the truth of what the agent believed and was motivated by. This may be because the speaker *knows* that what the agent believed is false, or wishes to suggest that it is, or wants to leave it open whether it is; which in turn may be because what the agent believes is something whose truth is uncertain, for example, 'He gave up because he thought his boss would have never agreed to it'; or because it is something that is recognized to be controversial, for instance, 'She voted against the motion because she believes that private education is inequitable'.

It must be noted, however, that some psychological locutions, far from suggesting that what motivated the speaker may be false, *imply* that it is true. 'She left because she knew the concert had finished' implies that the concert had finished, and it states that the agent knew

---

[14] Resort to the psychological form won't work, at least not in a straightforward way, with first-person present-tense forms. 'I'm giving him the money because I believe he's in need, although he isn't' is still paradoxical. The explanation of why these statements won't do is, simply, that these explanations are instances of Moore's paradox about belief. I discussed the relation between reasons and Moore's paradox in Chapter 5.

it and that the fact that it had finished was her reason for leaving. But this does not show that the corresponding reason explanation, 'She left because the concert had finished' is elliptical for 'She left because she knew that the concert had finished' because, while the agent may have known that the concert had finished, the speaker may not want to commit himself to the claim that the agent *knew* that it had.

Whether a psychological explanation implies the truth of what motivated the agent, then, depends on whether the psychological verb used is factive, that is, whether 'A V*s* that p' (knows, believes, suspects, perceives, etc.), implies that p.

And this brings out the third feature that these Humean explanations have, which is that they allow the speaker to specify further whether the agent knew, or believed, or feared, etc. that p. A reason explanation such as 'She left because the concert had finished' implies that the agent was, in one way or another, aware that the concert had finished, although it does not specify whether the agent knew it or merely believed it. A psychological locution of the Humean kind, however, permits the speaker to specify this more precisely: 'She left because she knew/believed/thought/deduced/conjectured/etc. . . ., that the concert had finished'. And this is true for desires also, for the corresponding Humean explanation can specify whether the agent felt like, was desperate, strongly desired, had a mild inclination to ϕ.

Moreover a Humean explanation can disambiguate cases where it is not clear whether we are dealing with an action performed for a reason, whether real or apparent, or not. For instance, 'He sneezed because she opened the window' could be a reason explanation if he sneezed *for the reason* that she had opened the window (perhaps it was a prearranged signal), as opposed to the more natural interpretation, say, that a cold draught made him sneeze. For it to be a reason explanation, we saw, it is necessary that the agent should be aware that someone had opened the window and that this should have been his reason for sneezing. So if one wants to make it explicit that the agent was motivated to sneeze by a reason, rather than caused to do so by a draught, one could turn this into a Humean explanation such as 'He sneezed because he noticed that she had opened the window'.

We have seen, then, the uses that Humean explanations can be put to, and how they are related to reason explanations when both are possible: they are often used to supplement the information that the latter provide.

The question of *when* we use explanations of either kind has been implicitly answered: this is a matter of the pragmatics of explanation, of what is appropriate in the context, given the logical implications and the conversational implicatures that explanations of each kind have. Thus, depending on whether the speaker wishes to (or can, epistemically speaking) endorse or not the truth of the statement that captures the motivating belief,[15] and depending on how much detail is appropriate or necessary, he'll use a reason explanation or a Humean explanation.

My discussion has shown that there is no reason to accept the view that Humean explanations provide *the* basic model for the explanation of intentional actions that mention the agent's reason and, hence, that it is wrong to insist, as some authors do, that 'all the other explanations we give simply supplement this basic Humean story' (Smith 1998: 18).[16] Humean explanations are closely related to reason explanations: although the explanans of a Humean explanation is *not* the agent's reason for acting, if the agent acted for a reason, then a Humean explanation mentions that reason. This is why, although Humean explanations can only be called 'reason explanations' in a derivative sense—namely, because of their connection with reason explanations proper—it is misleading to insist that they are the basic reason explanations since their explanatia are not the agent's reason for acting. And, as we have seen, it is partly the facts of the matter, partly the pragmatics of explanation, and partly stylistic preference, that determines whether in a particular context it is appropriate to use a reason explanation, a Humean explanation, or some combination of the two.

---

[15] Note that to endorse the truth of a reason statement is not to endorse the reason as a good reason for that agent to do what he did, that is, to judge that the agent did what he did for a good reason.

[16] See Collins (1997) and Thompson (2008) for further arguments against this view. In Section 3.2.1, I discussed things done simply because one wants. Many Humeans think that these actions are done for a reason and are also explained by Humean explanations. But this seems wrong: these actions are explained by psychological explanations of the form 'Because he wanted to' or 'Because he felt like it' but I cannot see any reason, except an a priori attachment to the Humean model of action explanation, to accept that if Ann sang just because she wanted to, this explanation is enthymematic for something that fits the Humean model, e.g. 'Ann sang because she wanted to sing and believed that her action (under the description 'singing') would result in her/constitute an act of/singing'. See Section 4.2.1.

Humean explanations are an important subset of psychological explanations of action but they are by no means the only explanations within that type of explanation. In the following section, I shall explore some of those non-Humean psychological explanations and attempt to provide an overview of how those psychological explanations relate to reason and Humean explanations of action.

6.4. Non-Humean Psychological Explanations of Action

Non-Humean psychological explanations have as their explanantia statements concerning the agent's emotions, feelings, character traits, habits, etc. (these are not mutually exclusive categories). The following are examples of such psychological explanations: 'She left because she was angry'; 'You protect her because you love her'; 'He turned down the job because he is rather ambitious', 'He got there so early because he's very punctual', 'She gave him the money because she was feeling generous', 'I get up at 6 a.m. because I am in the habit of doing so'. Psychological explanations of this kind are quite varied, and their classification is not straightforward. Here I shall simply outline some of the more distinctive kinds among them.

Psychological explanations can cite emotions and feelings, such as hatred, ambition, pride, generosity, and these often constitute an agent's motive for acting.[17] Among these motives, some have cognate terms referring to a character trait—for instance, generosity/generous; pride/proud—while others do not—for example, anger, pity, admiration; for someone who is often motivated by generosity is a generous person, but someone who is often motivated by pity is not a pitiful or piteous person.

But not all character traits that can be motives relate to corresponding feelings or emotions. For instance, punctuality, reliability, or tidiness are character traits and they can be motives for action but they do not involve any particular emotion or feeling.

---

[17] For discussions of the concept of emotion that are particularly illuminating in this context, see Kenny (1989: ch. 4) and Hacker (2004).

Finally, there are habits that may be cited to explain someone's action, such as the habit of smoking, or the habit of brushing one's teeth before going to bed. Such habits are not motives for action, nor do they concern emotions or feelings, and they explain actions in ways that are different from the way those other psychological features do.

Psychological explanations of these various types, however, are formally characterised by their susceptibility to paraphrase into expressions of the form 'A ϕ-ed out of X'. For example, 'He lied because he is a coward', 'She kept quiet because she felt pity for him', 'She left at three because that is her habit', can all be paraphrased as 'He lied out of cowardice', 'She kept quiet out of pity', 'She left at that time out of habit', etc.

But it is worth noting that although some of those 'out of X' paraphrases explain by citing an emotion or feeling that explains the action, they leave it open whether that was a one-off emotion for the agent, or whether it is a character trait. By contrast, a psychological explanation of the form 'He ϕ-ed because p' allows us to specify which it is. Thus, if we know that a person did something out of shyness, we still do not know whether she did it because she *is* shy or because she was, on that occasion, *feeling* shy.

To explain an action by citing a motive is not to explain it by citing the reason, real or apparent, for which the agent acted. But, just as motives are closely connected to reasons and purposes, as we saw in Chapter 3, psychological explanations that cite motives are also closely connected to reason explanations and to purposive explanations. For an explanation that cites or imputes a motive typically suggests that the agent acted for a reason, and for the sake of something (his goal or purpose), and it also gives an indication of what those might be or, at any rate, it demarcates a range within which the agent's reason and purpose are likely to fall. For example, the explanation 'Bill turned down the job because he is very ambitious' does not tell us Bill's reason for turning down the job, nor his purpose in doing so, as the fact that he is ambitious is a reason why that is not also *his* reason for turning down the job. However, that explanation suggests that his reason is concerned with some perceived negative aspect of the job relative to Bill's career, for instance, that the job was not sufficiently senior, or not a good stepping stone, or something similar. In addition, we know that Bill's purpose in turning down the job was, somehow, to further his career. Similarly, in knowing that he denounced her because he hates her we know that he must have believed or known that denouncing her was a way of causing her harm. And so on.

In Chapter 3, I agreed with Alan White that motives typically indicate a desire for the sake of which an action is performed. Thus, sometimes a motive explains an action because it helps to see how the action is (or appears to the agent to be) a means to the desired end. In the example just discussed, knowing that the agent's motive in denouncing someone is hatred tells us that his goal in denouncing her was to harm her. And if, for instance, my motive in reading her diary is curiosity about her love life, then it follows that I regard reading her diary as a way of finding out about her love life. Here, my goal in reading her diary is to find out about her love life, my reason is that her diary is likely to contain that information, and my motive is curiosity.

But sometimes the motive for an action is not some further goal to which the action is a means; rather, the action is performed for its own sake, and the motive explains in what way the action constitutes a satisfaction of that motive. In such cases, as Anscombe suggests, giving the motive is just saying 'see the action in this light': see this action as an instance of this kind of act. And, hence, in such cases, giving the motive is not giving some ulterior goal for the sake of which the action was done. For example, 'I killed him out of revenge' is such a case, as the motive indicates that the action, killing him, was, in the circumstances, an act of revenge, which was the action's goal or purpose. Likewise, the motive in helping someone may be, say, friendship, so that the action of helping is something done out of friendship. If so, friendship is not a further goal for the sake of which one helps. Rather, saying that friendship was the motive is a way of saying that helping him was an act of friendship—as Anscombe puts it, to give this kind of motive is often 'descriptive of the spirit' in which someone did something (1957: 18).

So emotions and feelings, whether they are character traits or not, can be motives for action, and when they are, the action is typically done for a reason and with a purpose. But not every action that is explained by reference to an emotion or a feeling is an action performed for a reason. For instance, one can do something out of anger and do it for a reason and with a purpose: consider a man who cuts his son out of his will as a punishment because he is angry at his son's behaviour: he acts so out of anger, which is his motive, and his reason may be that his son has misbehaved, and that cutting him out of his will is a way of punishing him—which is his purpose in acting. But a man may also act out of anger, or in anger, but not for a reason, or for any purpose. For example, an explanation such as 'He shouted because he was angry' may be a psychological explanation of someone's shouting where it would be implausible to say that the agent acted for a reason and in pursuit of a goal.[18] An action that is explained by an emotion in this way should, I think, be regarded as merely *expressive* of the relevant emotion: that person, we say, shouts *in* anger. In such a case, the fact that he was feeling that emotion is the reason *why* he acted and that is why citing that fact explains the action. So in our example, his shouting was *expressive* of his anger, and the fact that he was angry was the reason why he shouted. Nonetheless, our agent did not shout for any reason, nor was there any purpose he pursued in acting so. (To be sure, a person who is angry may shout for a reason or with a purpose, for example, to show how important the object of his anger is.[19] My point is simply that a person who shouts because he is angry may not shout for a reason or a purpose.)[20]

The same seems true of actions that are merely expressive of joy or cheerfulness, and also of certain things that are done out of fear, etc. Consider someone who dances on hearing some good news: dancing is an expression of her joy but this does not mean that she dances for a reason, or with any purpose, although the fact that she feels joyful is a reason that explains her dancing.

As I noted above, many motives are feelings or emotions but not all are. For instance, to say that a person left home so early because he is very punctual is to explain his action by reference to a character trait that is not an emotion or a feeling. Nonetheless, these explanations also impute a motive because punctuality motive is a for action. And,

---

[18] The fact that you are angry may seem to you a reason *not* to shout, lest you should lose control and say things you didn't mean to. And if you have enough self-control, you may manage not to shout precisely for the reason that you are angry.

[19] This, I think, is what Raz means when he says that 'the fact that an action has expressive meaning is a reason to perform it when such expression is appropriate' (1998: 55 n. 15).

[20] For an excellent discussion of these issues see Hursthouse (1991). I discuss this further in Alvarez (2009).

as is the case with many character traits, it is not only someone who has the character trait that can act for motives of this kind: someone who is not generally punctual or dutiful may act, as we say, out of a *sense* of duty, or of punctuality, etc. And like motives that are feelings or emotions, these motives also indicate the agent's reason and goal. So the person who leaves early because he's punctual, or out of punctuality, has as his goal to arrive on time, and his reason for leaving early is the fact that leaving early is a way to ensure that he does arrive punctually.

Finally, there are psychological explanations that do not refer to motives, emotions, feelings, or character traits at all but that explain by citing the fact that a person has a certain *habit*. A habit is not a character trait, though character traits often give rise to habits. A habit is rather a disposition to a pattern of behaviour acquired through the regular repetition of actions of the same type, so that, if one has a habit, one is disposed to perform the corresponding action. Smoking, brushing one's teeth at a certain time, using certain turns of phrase, etc., are all habits. And an example of an action explained by reference to a habit would be: 'He called her that night because he is in the habit of doing so'.

Thomas Reid says that a habit is a 'facility of doing a thing frequently, acquired by having done it frequently' which differs 'from instinct not in its nature, but in its origin; the latter being natural, the former acquired' (1969: 114). He adds, 'both operate without will or intention, without thought, and therefore may be called *mechanical principles*' (ibid.). Kenny gives a slightly different characterization; he says that although not all dispositions are habits, all habits are dispositions, and he adds:

> The difference between [dispositions and habits] may be brought out crudely thus. If one has a disposition to do X then it is easier to do X than if one has not: examples are being generous and speaking French. If one has a habit of doing X then it is harder not to do X than if one has not: examples are smoking and saying 'I say' before each sentence.   (1989: 85)

Kenny's claim seems true only if having a habit is distinguished from being in the habit of doing something, because someone may be in the habit of getting up at 6 a.m. without its being true that it is harder for him not to get up at 6 a.m. than to do so.

Reid attributes such importance to habits that, he says: 'without habit, man would remain an infant through life' (1969: 116) for it is habits that enable us to do a myriad number of things without thought, will, or attention (use language, get dressed, play sports, operate all sorts of machines, etc.); things that are necessary to achieve our more important, explicit, and deliberate ends. Bill Pollard (2006) has rightly drawn attention both to the importance of habit explanations and to the fact that they do not fit the Davidsonian-Humean conception of action explanations.[21]

The fact that one has a habit of doing something is the reason why one does the corresponding action but it is not (normally) *one's reason* for doing that thing, even when the habit was taken up for a reason. So on the one hand, there are habits, like brushing one's teeth after every meal, calling one's mother every day, or making one's bed in such-and-such a way, that one develops for a reason: that it is part of good dental hygiene, a way of keeping in touch, or an efficient way of doing something respectively. Once the habit is established, your doing the thing in question is explained by reference to your having the habit, even though your reason for doing the action may be said to be whatever reason you had for taking up the habit.

On the other hand, there are habits that one develops for no reason. In those cases the fact that one has the habit explains why one does the thing in question, even though one does not do that thing for a reason—Kenny's example of saying 'I say' before each sentence would seem such a case. Indeed, often, such habits are things one is not aware one is in the habit of doing, and so the corresponding explanations will show that the action in question is not intentional and a fortiori not something done for a reason.

---

[21] Pollard provides a detailed and interesting explanation of what he takes habits to be and of how they explain actions. In particular, he argues, rightly I think, against the prevalent view that 'since habits, being patterns of behaviour, are not amongst states of this sort [psychological entities] they cannot themselves provide explanations of actions, or at least not of those which can be regarded as "intentional" ' (2006: 2). Note that his claim that habits are patterns of behaviour is compatible with my claim that explanations that cite habits explain by citing a psychological fact about an agent, since the fact that someone has a habit of behaviour is a psychological fact, though the habit is not a 'psychological entity' and even less a psychological state.

6.5. Purposive Explanations

We have now examined a variety of explanations of action that take the form 'A ϕ-ed because q', where 'q' is (i) the reason for which the agent acted; or (ii) a reason why A ϕ-ed which is a fact concerning A's beliefs and desires, knowledge, emotions, feelings, motives, character traits, habits, etc. But when I introduced the variety of action explanations, I noted that there is a kind of explanation which is characteristic of actions: namely purposive explanations. I now turn to examine them, as well as their relation to reason explanations.

Purposive explanations are distinctive because they explain by reference to an end towards which the action is directed. As we saw in Chapter 4, Aristotle emphasized the importance of explanations which give the end or *telos* towards which an action or activity tends, which are called 'teleological explanations'.[22] Teleological explanations can be given of a range of phenomena, including the activity of plants and animals, and they are also prominent in biological explanations of the functions of organs and micro-organisms—although some philosophers would argue that these explanations are not genuinely teleological and are best understood as functional explanations.[23] Be that as it may, teleological explanations of human and animal actions are distinctive because their *telos* is a *purpose* or *goal* of the creature. So these teleological explanations are *purposive* or *goal* explanations.

Purposive explanations explain by citing a purpose or goal that the agent pursued in his action, and they are formally characterized by the use of 'in order to', 'with the purpose of', 'for the sake of', or equivalent expressions. Here are some examples: 'Mrs Bartlett poisoned her husband in order to inherit his money', 'K. went to the Castle to talk to the authorities', 'Road pricing is being introduced

---

[22] The notion of teleological explanation is associated with Aristotle and his distinction between four causes. He thought of 'the *telos*' of a change as one of the four 'kinds of cause', namely, the final cause, the end towards which a change tends (see *Physics* 198a, 18 ff., and *Nicomachean Ethics* 1139a32 ff.). Aristotle did not think that teleological explanations were restricted to human actions but he was the first philosopher to emphasize that the explanation of human action by reference to the agent's goals is teleological.

[23] For a very helpful discussion of this issue and its relation to human purposive actions, see Schueler (2003).

with the purpose of discouraging car use', 'He compromised for the sake of a quiet evening'.

Purposive explanations are sometimes referred to as reason explanations, although that is somewhat misleading because purposive explanations explain by citing the agent's purpose or goal and, as we saw in Chapter 4, although purposes and goals are often called 'reasons', this is only by extension of the term.

When humans act with a purpose they often act also for a reason but this need not be so: there are things we do for a purpose but not for a reason. We do this typically when our actions are instinctive, mechanical, reactive, habitual, etc., or when, as we might put it, our animal natures are in the driving seat. (These are not mutually exclusive possibilities.) Many of the actions of human babies are instinctive, and are closer in character to the purposive actions of non-human animals than to those of rational creatures in that they are done for a purpose but not for a reason; an example of such instinctive actions is suckling.

Actions that are done for a purpose but not for a reason can be explained with purposive explanations. For instance, we can say a baby suckles in order to satisfy its hunger. In these cases, the agent acts for a purpose, and there is a reason why the agent does what he does: the reason why a baby suckles is that suckling is a way of satisfying its hunger. However, this is a reason why that is not also the *baby's reason* for suckling because the baby is not yet capable of reasoning.

It may be perhaps more controversial to say that human adults who are capable of reasoning also sometimes perform actions for a purpose but not for a reason. However, this seems the right way to characterize some of our actions. For example, as we saw in Chapter 4, it is plausible to argue that sometimes the actions involved in satisfying one's bodily desires are of this kind: we sometimes drink in order to satisfy thirst and yet do not drink for a reason.

And there are many other actions that fit this pattern: many reactions to pain, danger, etc., seem to belong here too. Consider, for example, a driver who instinctively swerves his car in order to avoid a collision, or a person who moves her hand away from a fire: these are things that these agents do for a purpose (to avoid danger or pain) but not for a reason. In these cases, we can explain why the agent acted by citing the goals for the sake of which she did what she did but these are not things done for a reason. This is not because no reasoning is explicitly engaged in, prior to or during the action, but because the action, although directed by the agent, is merely reactive and requires no thought, choice, decision, etc., and such actions can be explained without the need to attribute to the agent any explicit or implicit calculation or reasoning.

It is also here that we should include the variety of bodily movements performed in the exercise of skills that involve moving one's body (riding a bike, skiing, dancing, driving, etc.). Those bodily movements are actions one does for a purpose (for instance, keeping one's balance, going faster) but not for a reason—although, again, there is a reason why one performs those actions. An important feature of these skilled actions is that, because once the skill has been acquired the feedback mechanism involved in controlling one's movements operates at a non-explicit level of consciousness, what explains why the agent makes those movements are not factors that the agent is aware of at the level that would allow her to cite them as *her* reasons for making those movements. Nonetheless, the agent is in control of those movements and directs them towards her overall purpose, which is the successful performance of the activity she is engaged in.

Purposive explanations are common to the activity of humans and non-human animals, since both have the capacity to direct their actions towards ends, which are their purposes. And as we've just seen, this shows that a purposive explanation of an action need not be an explanation of something that can also be explained with a reason explanation. However, since humans, as rational beings, have the capacity to conceptualize their purposes as purposes, and to reason both about the value of those purposes and the means of achieving them, many purposive actions are also done for reasons, and indeed, actions performed for a reason (including for an apparent reason) are done for a purpose. Because of this, whenever we can give a reason explanation of an action, it is always also possible to provide a purposive explanation of that action. For instance, suppose that my reason for giving my daughter antibiotics is that she has pneumonia, and that antibiotics will combat her pneumonia. Then it follows that I gave her antibiotics *in order to* combat her pneumonia. And vice versa: whenever we give a purposive explanation of something done for a reason, we can construct a reason explanation. So, if Mrs Bartlett killed her husband in order to inherit his money, her purpose in killing him was to inherit his money. From this explanation we can deduce that her reason for killing her husband was that killing him was a way of inheriting his money.

I say that this is *Mrs Bartlett's* reason for acting and not merely the reason why she did it because Mrs Bartlett can kill her husband in order to inherit his money only if she is capable of reasoning that killing him is a means to inheriting his money. In other words, reasoning—implicit or explicit—is what links the action of killing her husband with her purpose: inheriting his money. The same is not true of the purposive actions of non-human animals: if a dog digs in order to get a bone, the reason why he digs is that digging is the means of getting the bone. But this is not the dog's reason for digging because, in order to explain the dog's behaviour by reference to its goal, we don't need to attribute to the dog the capacity to reason, that is, to think that digging is the means to get the bone. All we need to attribute to the dog, in order to explain its behaviour, is the desire to get the bone, together with some awareness of the bone resulting from its capacity to smell the bone, or to remember where the bone is.

When a purposive explanation is supplemented by a reason explanation, the reason will sometimes be a fact that guided the agent in his pursuit of the goal mentioned in the explanation: the goal or purpose is the end towards which the action is directed; the reason is the fact in the light of which the agent directs his action towards that end. The reason, as we have seen, is a fact concerning the action that, in the agent's eyes, makes that action good, either in itself, or as a means to an end. And as we have seen, this reason is sometimes a premise in the agent's implicit or explicit practical reasoning, in which he engages for the sake of an end that will be his goal in acting. For example, in the explanation 'He took a taxi to get to the meeting on time because his bike had been stolen', the purpose of taking a taxi is to get to the meeting on time, and his reason for doing so is that his bike had been stolen, and that taking a taxi was a means to getting to the meeting on time. (And, *mutatis mutandis*, something similar is true when I act for an apparent reason).[24]

When, by contrast, the agent does something for its own sake, the reason will be a fact that makes the action itself valuable in the agent's eyes, and hence something he regards as worth doing intrinsically. For instance, if my goal in visiting someone is friendship, the reason for visiting her is that she is my friend, and the fact that she's my friend is what makes it good in my eyes to visit her.

We also saw in Chapter 4 that the concepts of purpose and intention are closely linked to each other since our purposes in acting are the intentions with which we act. Thus, since a purposive explanation provides the agent's purpose in acting, it also provides the *intention with which* the agent acts. For example, if I work out in order to get fitter, my purpose in working out is to get fitter, which is also the intention with which I work out. And if Mrs Bartlett killed her husband in order to inherit his money, inheriting his money is the intention with which she killed her husband. In these cases, the agent's purpose or intention is an end, and her action is the means she takes towards that end. Because of this, explanations that mention the intention with which something is done are also purposive explanations: for example in 'I lent him my notes with the intention of helping him', my purpose is my intention, namely, to help him.[25] And these explanations also allow us to work out the agent's reason: in the examples just discussed, that killing her husband is a way of inheriting his money, and that lending him my notes is a way of helping him.

---

[24] In cases where an agent acts for an apparent reason (that is, is motivated by a false belief), the purposive explanation cannot be supplemented by a reason explanation but it can be supplemented by a *Humean* explanation. For example, 'She sold her house very quickly in order to maximize her profits because she believed that the housing market was about to collapse' can explain her action, especially against a context where it is known that she was wrong in believing that the housing market was about to collapse.

[25] As has been noted by others, the expression 'A ϕ-ed with the intention of ψ-ing' is not always used to give the purpose for the sake of which A ϕ-ed. If I leave my house today with the intention of coming back tomorrow, this does not mean that coming back tomorrow is the purpose for the sake of which I leave my house. Rather, in this example I do something, presumably for a purpose and with an intention, e.g. to visit my sister, *and* in addition have the intention of coming back tomorrow.

Kenny says the following about the relation between explanations that refer to reasons, motives, and intentions:

> Roughly speaking, when a reason for action concerns something prior to, or contemporaneous with, the action, it is a motive; when it refers to some future state of affairs to be brought about by the action, then it expresses an intention. 'Why did he kill him? Because he had killed his father'—there we have a motive, revenge. 'Why did he flatter the Prime Minister? In order to become a bishop'—there we have an intention. As these examples illustrate, the distinction between motive and intention is hardly a sharp one.   (1989: 62)

Although I agree with the spirit of these remarks, as I think they capture the close connection between the three concepts, it seems to me that the letter of them needs refining.

First, contrary to what Kenny says, in both examples the agent's reason for acting (or at least part of it) 'concerns something prior to, or contemporaneous with, the action'; in the first case it is that the victim killed his father; in the second it is, for instance, that the prime minister, who chooses bishops, is likely to choose the agent if the agent flatters the prime minister. That the victim killed the agent's father and that the prime minister chooses bishops we might say, are facts that concern how things stand prior to, or contemporaneously with, each of the actions in question.

Second, both agents have an intention in acting—which would be given in a purposive explanation of their actions. The intention of the first agent is to avenge his father's death; and the intention of the second is to become a bishop. The difference between these is that the first intention is realized *in* the action of killing his father's killer; while in the second, the intention will be realized (the agent hopes) by means of the action of flattering the prime minister. The first is an action performed for its own sake, for killing is a form of revenge. In the second case, flattering is a means to the appointment (or so the agent hopes). And this is the only reason to regard one example as more forward-looking than the other—but it is not the agent's reasons or motives but his *actions* that are either present-looking ('this action is revenge') or forward-looking ('this action will bring me a bishopric').

Finally, both agents act for a motive. In the first case, the motive is revenge; in the second the motive is, most likely, ambition.

Conclusion

We have seen that actions performed for a reason can be explained in a variety of ways. First, it is possible to explain them by giving reasons 'why'—reasons why the agent did what he did. A reason why in this context may be a fact that the agent took as a reason for acting, or a psychological fact about the agent, such as the fact that he believed and wanted certain things, or the fact that he had certain motives, character traits, emotions, habits, etc. When the reason why an agent acted is *also* a reason for which the agent acted, the explanation is what I have called a '*reason* explanation proper'. When an agent acts for an apparent reason, the explanation that cites this apparent reason is a Humean explanation: he ϕ-ed because he believed that p.

In addition, actions performed for a reason can be explained with purposive or intentional explanations. Purposive explanations of actions done for a reason identify the agent's purpose, which is also his intention in acting. These explanations can be supplemented by a reason explanation. When they are so supplemented, the reason that explains the action is a fact which in the agent's eyes makes the action good and in the light of which he acted, in pursuit of his goal.

What has been said about reason and purposive explanations offers a picture of the way in which reasons explain actions. When someone acts for a reason, he is motivated by something he wants to do or achieve (his purpose in acting) which he regards as either intrinsically or instrumentally good; and also by reasons, that is, by facts that, in his eyes, make his action good. These reasons are facts that concern the goodness of what he wants to do or achieve (his purpose), or the goodness of his action as a means of achieving that purpose. These reasons can be premises in the agent's implicit or explicit practical reasoning.

These explanatory factors, that is, the agent's purpose and reasons, may be given in a variety of ways: explicitly in reason, Humean, or purposive explanations, or implicitly in the variety of psychological explanations that we have examined, which cite motives, emotions, character traits, etc. Thus, we typically explain actions by citing either the agent's purpose (or intention) in acting, or his (real or apparent) reason for acting, or both. And we do so in one of the many forms we have explored in this chapter, depending on what the relevant context requires or recommends.[26]

[26] And the same is true *mutatis mutandis* of Humean explanations.

Conclusion

There is, to be sure, more to be said about the relation between reasons and action. My purpose throughout this book has been to explore the concept of a reason and to provide a clear account of how we use this concept when we are concerned with human actions, and in particular, with actions performed for reasons. In the process of doing so, I have challenged a number of received positions—among others, the view that our reasons for acting are states of believing and desiring, and the tendency to equate the reasons that explain our actions with our reasons for acting. This challenge has led, I hope, to a more refined and nuanced account of what our reasons for acting are and of the varieties of reason that motivate and explain our actions.

Among the questions I have not explored are two mentioned in Chapter 1, which dominated action theory for decades after the publication of Davidson's paper 'Actions, Reasons, and Causes', namely, whether our reasons for acting cause our actions and the related question whether reason explanations are causal explanations. Following Davidson, most philosophers working in the theory of action today maintain that the answers to at least one of these questions, if not both, is 'yes', although there is a minority of dissenters.[1]

The questions are certainly interesting ones. But if the argument of this book is on the right lines, they have been debated in terms which are frankly muddled, since reasons have been mistakenly equated with mental states, the reasons that motivate and the reasons that explain our actions have been systematically run together when it is sometimes necessary to separate them, the variety of explanations of intentional action has been underestimated, and explanations of different kinds

---

[1] See Section 1.4.1 for a list including some of them.

have been conflated or confused. It would be interesting to reassess the questions Davidson put on the table with a clearer grasp of what reasons for acting and action explanations are, and a clearer picture of the variety of forms they take. Perhaps it would be possible to draw more robust conclusions, which philosophers influenced by Davidson on the one hand and (say) Anscombe on the other, would feel equally able to accept. But perhaps that is too optimistic. In any event, this is a task for another occasion, maybe another book. The principal aim of this one has been to distinguish and examine kinds of reasons. If, as I have tried to show, we can make some progress with that task without even broaching the contentious questions about causation, that is an interesting fact all by itself, and maybe one we should be grateful for.

References

Alvarez, M. (2007). 'The Causalism/Anti-Causalism Debate in the Theory of Action: What It Is and Why It Matters', in A. Leist (ed.), *Action in Context* (Berlin and New York: de Gruyter), 103–23.

—— (2009). 'Acting Intentionally and Acting for a Reason', *Inquiry*, 52/3: 293–305.

Anscombe, G. E. M. (1957). *Intention* (Oxford: Blackwell).

—— (1958). 'Modern Moral Philosophy', *Philosophy*, 33: 1–19.

—— (1974). 'Comment on Chisholm's "Practical Reason and the Logic of Requirement"' in Körner (ed.) (1974: 19–28).

—— (1989). 'Von Wright on Practical Inference', in P. A. Schlipp and L. E. Hahn (eds.) (1989), *The Philosophy of Georg Henrik Von Wright* (La Salle, Ill.: Open Court), 377–404.

Aquinas, St T. (1960–73). *Summa Theologiae*, ed. T. Gilby (London: Blackfriars).

Aristotle (1984). *The Complete Works of Aristotle: The Revised Oxford Translation*, ed. J. Barnes (Princeton: Princeton University Press).

Audi, R. (1993). *Action, Intention, and Reason* (Ithaca, NY: Cornell University Press).

—— (2001). *The Architecture of Reason* (Oxford: Oxford University Press).

Augustine, St (1943). *Confessions*, trans. J. F. Sheed (London: Sheed & Ward).

Austin, J. L. (1956). 'Ifs and Cans', repr. in Austin (1961), *Philosophical Papers* (Oxford: Clarendon).

Bacon, F. (1909–14). *Essays, Civil and Moral* (Harvard Classics (New York: P. F. Collier & Son)).

Ben-Yami, H. (1997). 'Against Characterizing Mental States as Propositional Attitudes', *Philosophical Quarterly*, 47: 84–9.

Bittner, R. (2001). *Doing Things for Reasons* (Oxford: Oxford University Press).

Broome, J. (2004). 'Reasons', in Wallace et al. (eds.) (2004: 28–55).

Chang, R. (2004). 'Can Desires Provide Reasons for Action?', in Wallace et al. (eds.) (2004: 56–90).

Collins, A. (1987). *The Nature of Mental Things* (Notre Dame, Ind.: University of Notre Dame Press).

—— (1997). 'On the Psychological Reality of Reasons', *Ratio*, 10/2: 108–23.

Crane, T, and Mellor, D. (1990). 'There Is No Question of Physicalism', *Mind*, 99: 185–206.

Cullity, C., and Gaut, B. (eds.) (1997). *Ethics and Practical Reason* (Oxford: Oxford University Press).

Dancy, J. (2000). *Practical Reality* (Oxford: Oxford University Press).

Davidson, D. (1963). 'Actions, Reasons, and Causes', repr. in Davidson (1980: 3–19).

—— (1976). 'Hempel on Explaining Action', repr. in Davidson (1980: 261–76).

—— (1980). *Essays on Actions and Events* (Oxford: Oxford University Press).

Frankfurt, H, (1988). *The Importance of What We Care About* (Cambridge: Cambridge University Press).

Geach, P. (1976). *Reason and Argument* (Oxford: Blackwell).

Ginet, C. (1993). *Actions* (Oxford: Oxford University Press).

Hacker, P. M. S. (1990). *Wittgenstein: Meaning and Mind: An Analytical Commentary on the* Philosophical Investigations, vol. 3 (Oxford: Blackwell).

—— (2004). 'The Conceptual Framework for the Investigation of Emotions', *International Review of Psychiatry*, 16/3: 199–208.

Haldane, J. (1994). 'Some Metaphysical Presuppositions of Agency', *Heythrop Journal*, 35: 296–303.

Harcourt, E. (2004). 'Instrumental Desires, Instrumental Rationality', *Proceedings of the Aristotelian Society*, 78: 111–29.

Hempel, C. G. (1962). 'Explanations in Science and History', in R. G. Colodny (1962), *Frontiers of Science and Philosophy* (Pittsburgh: University of Pittsburgh Press), repr. in P. H Nidditch (1968), *The Philosophy of Science* (Oxford: Oxford University Press).

Hempel, C. G., and Oppenheim, P. (1948). 'Studies in the Logic of Explanation', *Philosophy of Science*, 15: 135–75.

Heuer, U. (2004). 'Reasons for Actions and Desires', *Philosophical Studies*, 121: 43–63.

Hooker, B., and Streumer, B. (2004) 'Procedural and Substantive Practical Rationality', in Mele and Rawling (eds.) (2004: 55–74).

Hursthouse, R. (1991). 'Arational Actions', *Journal of Philosophy*, 88/2: 57–68.

Hutto, D. (1999). 'A Cause for Concern: Reasons, Causes and Explanations', *Philosophy and Phenomenological Research*, 59: 381–401.

Hyman, J. (1999). 'How Knowledge Works', *Philosophical Quarterly*, 49: 433–51.

Jackson, F., Pettit, P., and Smith, M. (2004). *Mind, Morality and Explanation* (Oxford: Oxford University Press).

Kant, I. [1785] (1991). *Moral Law: Groundwork of the Metaphysics of Morals*, ed. and trans. H. J. Paton (London: Routledge).

Kenny, A. J. P. (1963). *Action, Emotion and Will* (London: Routledge).

—— (1989). *The Metaphysics of Mind* (Oxford: Oxford University Press).

Körner, S. (ed.) (1974). *Practical Reason* (Oxford: Blackwell).

Korsgaard, C. (1996). *The Sources of Normativity* (Cambridge: Cambridge University Press).

—— (1997). 'The Normativity of Instrumental Reason', in Cullity and Gaut (eds.) (1997: 215–54).

Lenman, J. (1996). 'Belief, Desire and Motivation: An Essay in Quasi-Hydraulics', *American Philosophical Quarterly*, 33: 291–301.

Lewis, D. (1988). 'Desire as Belief', *Mind*, 97: 323–32.

Lowe, J. (2000). *The Possibility of Metaphysics* (Oxford: Oxford University Press).

McDowell, J. (1978). 'Are Moral Requirements Hypothetical Imperatives?', *Aristotelian Society Supplementary Volume*, 52: 13–29.

—— (1982). 'Reasons and Actions', *Philosophical Investigations*, 5: 301–5.

Mele, A. R. (2003). *Motivation and Agency* (Oxford: Oxford University Press).

Mele, A. R., and Rawling, P. (eds.) (2004). *The Oxford Handbook of Rationality* (Oxford: Oxford University Press).

Nagel, T. (1970). *The Possibility of Altruism* (Princeton: Princeton University Press).

O'Shaughnessy, B. (1980). *The Will: A Dual-Aspect Theory* (Cambridge: Cambridge University Press).

Peters, R. S. (1958). *The Concept of Motivation* (London: Routledge & Kegan Paul).

Pettit, P., and Smith, M. (1990). 'Backgrounding Desire', *Philosophical Review*, 99: 565–92.

Platts, M. (1979). *Ways of Meaning* (London: Routledge & Kegan Paul).

Pollard, B. (2006). 'Explaining Actions with Habits', *American Philosophical Quarterly*, 43: 57–68.

Price, H. H. (1969). 'Self-Verifying Beliefs', in Price (1969), *Belief* (London and New York: Allen & Unwin), 349–75.

Quinn, W. (1993). 'Putting Rationality in its Place', in Quinn (1993), *Morality and Action* (Cambridge: Cambridge University Press), 228–55.

Raz, J. (1975). *Practical Reason and Norms* (Oxford: Oxford University Press).

—— (1997). 'When We Are Ourselves: The Active and the Passive', reprinted in Raz (1999a: 5–21).

—— (1998). 'Inconmensurability and Agency', reprinted in Raz (1999a: 46–66).

—— (1999a). *Engaging Reason* (Oxford: Oxford University Press).

—— (1999b). 'Agency, Reason and the Good', in Raz (1999a: 22–45).

Reid, T. [1788] (1969). *Essays on the Active Powers of the Human Mind* (Cambridge, Mass.: MIT Press).

Rundle, B. (1997). *Mind in Action* (Oxford: Oxford University Press).

Russell, B. (1919) 'On Propositions: What They Are and How They Mean', repr. in Russell (1956), *Logic and Knowledge: Essays 1901–1950*, ed. R. C. Marsh (London: George Allen & Unwin), 283–320.

Ryle, G. (1949). *The Concept of Mind* (London: Hutchinson).

Scanlon, T. M. (1998). *What We Owe to Each Other* (Cambridge, Mass.: Harvard University Press).

Schroeder, M. (2007). *Slaves of the Passions* (Oxford: Oxford University Press).

Schueler, G. F. (1991). 'Pro-Attitudes and Direction of Fit', *Mind*, 100: 277–82.

—— (1995). *Desire: Its Role in Practical Reason and the Explanation of Action* (Cambridge, Mass.: MIT Press).

—— (2003). *Reasons and Purposes: Human Rationality and the Teleological Explanation of Action* (Oxford: Oxford University Press).

Sehon, S. (1994). 'Teleology and the Nature of Mental States', *American Philosophical Quarterly*, 31: 63–72.

—— (1997). 'Deviant Causal Chains and the Irreducibility of Teleological Explanation', *Pacific Philosophical Quarterly*, 78: 195–213.

—— (2000). 'An Argument against the Causal Theory of Action', *Philosophy and Phenomenological Research*, 60: 67–85.

Smith, M. (1987). 'The Humean Theory of Motivation', *Mind*, 96: 36–61.

—— (1994). *The Moral Problem* (Oxford: Blackwell).

—— (1998). 'The Possibility of Philosophy of Action', in D. Bransen and S. Cuypers (eds.) (1998), *Human Action, Deliberation and Causation* (Dordrecht: Kluwer Academic Publishers), 17–41.

—— (2004). 'Instrumental Desires, Instrumental Rationality', *Proceedings of the Aristotelian Society*, 78: 93–109.

Steward, H. (1997). *The Ontology of Mind: Events, Processes, and States* (Oxford: Oxford University Press).

Stocker, M. (1979). 'Desiring the Bad: An Essay on Moral Psychology', *Journal of Philosophy*, 76: 738–53.

—— (2004). 'Raz on the Intelligibility of Bad Acts', in Wallace et al. (eds.) (2004: 303–32).

Stout, R. (1996). *Things that Happen Because They Should: A Teleological Approach to Action* (Oxford: Oxford University Press).

Stoutland, F. (1998), 'Intentionalists and Davidson on Rational Explanation', in G. Meggle (ed.) (1998), *Actions, Norms, Values: Discussions with Georg Henrik von Wright* (Berlin and New York: de Gruyter), 191–208.

—— (2001). 'Responsive Action and the Belief-Desire Model', *Grazer Philosophische Studien*, 61: 83–106.

Strawson, P. F. (1950). 'Truth', repr. in Strawson (1971), *Logico-Linguistic Papers* (London: Methuen), 147–64.

—— (1987). 'Causation and Explanation', repr. in Strawson (1992), *Analysis and Metaphysics* (Oxford: Oxford University Press), 109–31.

Tanney, J. (1995). 'Why Reasons May Not Be Causes', *Mind and Language*, 10: 103–26.

Thompson, M. (2008). *Life and Action. Elementary Structures of Practice and Practical Thought* (Cambridge, Mass.: Harvard University Press).

Velleman, D. (1992). 'The Guise of the Good', repr. in Velleman (2000), *The Possibility of Practical Reason* (Oxford: Oxford University Press), 99–122.

von Wright, G. H. (1963). *The Varieties of Goodness* (London: Routledge & Kegan Paul).

Wallace, R. J., Smith, M., Scheffler, S., and Pettit, P. (eds.) (2004). *Reason and Value: Themes from the Moral Philosophy of Joseph Raz* (Oxford: Oxford University Press).

Watson, G. (1975). 'Free Agency', *Journal of Philosophy*, 72: 205–20.

White, A. (ed.) (1968). *The Philosophy of Action* (Oxford: Oxford University Press).

Wilkins, B. T. (1963). 'He Boasted from Vanity', *Analysis*, 23/5: 110–12.

Williams, B. (1981). 'Internal and External Reasons', in Williams (1981), *Moral Luck* (Cambridge: Cambridge University Press), 101–13.

—— (1995). 'Internal Reasons and the Obscurity of Blame', in Williams (1995), *Making Sense of Humanity* (Cambridge: Cambridge University Press), 35–45.

Williamson, T. (2000). *Knowledge and Its Limits* (Oxford: Oxford University Press).

Wilson, G. (1989). *The Intentionality of Human Action* (Stanford: Stanford University Press).

Wittgenstein, L. (1953). *Philosophical Investigations* (Oxford: Blackwell).

Zangwill, N. (1998). 'Direction of Fit and Normative Functionalism', *Philosophical Studies*, 91/2: 173–203.

Index